Opening the Books of Moses

BibleWorld

Series Editors: Philip R. Davies and James G. Crossley, University of Sheffield

BibleWorld shares the fruits of modern (and postmodern) biblical scholarship not only among practitioners and students, but also with anyone interested in what academic study of the Bible means in the twenty-first century. It explores our ever-increasing knowledge and understanding of the social world that produced the biblical texts, but also analyses aspects of the Bible's role in the history of our civilization and the many perspectives—not just religious and theological, but also cultural, political and aesthetic—which drive modern biblical scholarship.

Opening the Books of Moses

Diana V. Edelman, Philip R. Davies,
Christophe Nihan and Thomas Römer

Published by Equinox Publishing Ltd.
UK: Unit S3, Kelham House, 3, Lancaster Street, Sheffield S3 8AF
USA: ISD, 70 Enterprise Drive, Bristol, CT 06010

www.equinoxpub.com

First published 2012

British Library Cataloguing-in-Publication Data

A catalogue record for this book is available from the British Library.

ISBN-13   978-1-84553-684-8 (hardback)
           978-1-84553-685-5 (paperback)

Library of Congress Cataloging-in-Publication Data

Opening the books of Moses / Diana Edelman ... [et al.].
    p. cm.—(BibleWorld) (The books of Moses ; v. 1)
Includes bibliographical references and index.
ISBN 978-1-84553-684-8 (hb)—ISBN 978-1-84553-685-5 (pb) 1. Bible.
O.T. Pentateuch—Criticism, interpretation, etc. I. Edelman, Diana Vikander, 1954-
BS1225.52.O64 2012
222'.106—dc22
                                        2011011032

Typeset by S.J.I. Services, New Delhi
Printed and bound in the UK by MPG Books Group

CONTENTS

Illustrations   vii

Preface   viii

1. The Present State of Pentateuchal Research and
   the Task of This Volume   1

2. The Shape, Dating and Audience of the Pentateuch   11

3. Yehud in the Persian Period   51

4. Key Themes in the Pentateuch   93

   Glossary   181

   Index of Ancient Citations   189

   Index of Authors   199

ILLUSTRATIONS

1. Map of places named in movements in the Pentateuch   12
2. Map of places in Genesis   15
3. Map of the boundaries of Yehud   52
4. Map for Mozah jars   57
5. Map of Persian empire   60
6. Map of grain storage facilities in coastal plain   62
7. Map of administrative facilities and new settlements   66
8. Yehud coin   71
9. Map of Egypt   76
10. Map of Borsippa and environs   83
11. Map of Israelite deportee relocations   86
12. Map of the 'Promised Land'   124

Preface

The present volume is meant to be an introduction to a forthcoming new study of the Pentateuch that will look at each of the five books in turn through a Persian lens. It will focus primarily on the final form of each book and then also on editorial links that have joined the individual books into its present sequence to create an introduction about the forefathers followed by a biography of Moses. The concern will be to see how the themes of torah, ethnicity, geography, Yahweh and other deities, cult, treaty, loyalty oath and royal grant, and Moses are developed across the books as central, unifying concerns and are likely to have addressed concerns in the socio-political setting of the Persian period. This is when the books are likely to have come together to form a written core proclaiming the nature of the relationship between Yahweh and his people, Israel, in emerging forms of Judaism.

It is anticipated the entire series will be used by undergraduates and interested non-specialists, although it may be of interest to graduate students and colleagues as well. The decision has been taken to transliterate Hebrew and Aramaic terms in a way that would approximate pronunciation rather than reflect linguistic exactitude to make the books user-friendly for those without any knowledge of biblical Hebrew. The glossary and maps have also been included for the benefit of the less initiated; I am indebted to Dr Russell Hobson for generating from scratch all but one of the maps. Footnotes and citations of secondary literature have been kept to a minimum to facilitate readability but allow students to pursue topics of particular interest.

The astute reader will note that the four authors hold differing views on a number of controversial topics. We feel this enhances our cooperative venture and the volumes we will produce. We will benefit from the input of our colleagues and present a more balanced final product.

Diana Edelman, project coordinator

Chapter 1

The Present State of Pentateuchal Research and the Task of This Volume

The Pentateuch, or Torah, has been a distinct component of the Jewish Scriptures since at least the second century BCE. Until the advent of critical scholarship it was traditionally accepted by both Jews and Christians as written by Moses. Problems with Mosaic authorship were noted already in the Middle Ages, when Isaac ben Jesus and Ibn Ezra compiled a list of 'post Mosaica' verses that Moses could never have written, though they dared not openly challenge entrenched belief in the Mosaic authorship of most of the text. In the seventeenth century we find a more systematic questioning of this notion, especially by Spinoza (1632–77) and Hobbes (1588–1679), but only with the advent of source-criticism was the integrity of the 'Five Books of Moses' as a literary corpus challenged.

By the beginning of the nineteenth century, the 'Documentary Hypothesis' as elaborated by A. Kuenen and J. Wellhausen became the standard model to explain the formation of the Pentateuch, or even more, the Hexateuch (Genesis–Joshua). The book of Joshua was considered to be the original conclusion to the books of the Pentateuch since it narrated the near-fulfillment of the land-promise, a major pentateuchal theme. The 'Documentary Hypothesis' postulates that there are four major 'sources' or 'documents', the Yahwistic source, the Elohistic source, the book of Deuteronomy, and the Priestly document, which, except for Deuteronomy, narrate a coherent story running from the Patriarchs at least to the conquest of the land. Each document was written in a specific period in Israel's history, from the beginning of the monarchy to the Persian period.

This model, strongly influenced by an evolutionary framework, was dominant until the 1970s. It was thought that the earliest documents showed a free, independent and prophetic religion whereas the ritualistic and legalistic Priestly document was late and evidenced religious 'sclerosis'. The model had been modified in the first half of the twentieth century to emphasize the importance of oral traditions deriving from the pre-monarchic period that were collected and recorded for the first time by the Yahwist or the Elohist. There was great confidence in the ability to reconstruct the very beginnings of the pentateuchal traditions in the second half of the second millennium BCE and it is interesting to read Martin Noth's *The History of Israel* (1958 [1954]), where the pre-monarchic period occupies as much space as the time from David to the Persian period.

Since the 1970s, such a view has been criticized on several levels. Ethnological studies of 'oral traditions' have shown they are not at all stable and it is almost impossible to claim an unaltered, verbatim oral transmission of legends and epics. Literary analyses of the 'old sources' J and E have underlined their closeness in outlook to the 'Deuteronomistic' texts in the Former Prophets, which stem from the seventh century BCE and later. It has become questionable whether or not the formation of the Pentateuch can be explained by the fusion of parallel, originally independent, documents. The stories about the patriarchs in Genesis reveal a different style and ideology from what is found in the traditions of Moses and the Exodus; it seems that they were juxtaposed at quite a late stage.

In evaluating recent developments in pentateuchal research, it must be conceded that the only point of consensus in the current debate is that the Pentateuch came into existence during the Persian era. It also seems evident that the development of a complex literary culture in Judah, such as might have produced the tradition-history of the Pentateuch, can no longer be imagined during the period proposed by the classic documentary analyses. The pentateuchal 'Israel' is not likely, then, to have originated in the imagination, let alone the memory of any social or national group before the end of the northern kingdom in 721 BCE—the crucial event that permitted the possibility of Judah absorbing Israelite identity. The reign of King Hezekiah (ca. 715–687 BCE) or of King Josiah (ca. 640–609 BCE), the so-called exilic (Neo-Babylonian) period (586–538 BCE) or the Persian period (538–333 BCE) now appear to most scholars as more plausible moments for such literary creativity. Given the degree of fictionality of the pentateuchal narrative, an increased emphasis has now come to be laid on the ideology of this narrative and its social, religious and political function, implying a quite different kind of relationship between literary *text* and historical *context*. How, why and when did the pentateuchal 'Israel' come to be created, and to what kind of real society does it correspond? The increased awareness in biblical scholarship of socio-historical issues also requires us to consider the social, economic, political and material conditions that necessitated the Pentateuch and shaped it.

These challenges have prompted the present venture: a new analysis of the origin and growth of the Pentateuch that reflects the huge changes in scholarship since Noth's work and pays more attention both to the overall shape of the entire structure as a complex of ideological statements and also to the social and religious history of the communities that created these statements, fashioned the completed narrative occupying this sequence of five scrolls, and transformed it into what Judaism inherited (or framed) as 'torah', 'teaching'.

The unity of the Pentateuch consists not in its supposed Mosaic authorship, which is not overtly claimed in the texts themselves or in any canonical status. Rather, it is inherent in the structure: a narrative interspersed with law that defines a society. Israel's emergence from humanity as a whole, as a distinct *family* chosen by the creator god, is narrated in Genesis; and a land is also promised to the various descendants of Abraham. In Exodus, the family—now restricted to the descendants of Jacob—becomes immediately a *people* who escape from Egyptian captivity into the wilderness, in the direction of its promised land. It receives from its deity a law that is effectively a national constitution or even a culture, which defines its identity in terms beyond those merely of genealogical descent, as in the book of Genesis.

In Leviticus, Numbers and Deuteronomy the nature of that 'Israel' becomes even more closely defined through cultic and social laws and through narrative accounts of its travels towards the land it is to occupy. The occupation east of the river Jordan is attained, but Moses dies before entering the land beyond the river. Thus, while land occupation remains an essential component of 'Israelite' identity, indicated by the many laws that imply a settled life in Canaan, the pentateuchal narrative ends with this yet to be acquired. That the Pentateuch closes on the eve of territorial (re-)occupation may provide a significant clue to its ideology and its social function rather than posing a problem. In a similar way, the next canonical division of 'Former Prophets' is demarcated by the occupation of the land and its loss, both accomplished by means of warfare and at the instigation of the divine will. It too, therefore, ends with a landless nation.

This account of the formation and structure of Israel has no counterpart in Iron Age history (ca. 975–586 BCE): we now know that the populations of Israel and Judah were in fact indigenous or from neighbouring territory and that their religious culture was not, during the Iron Age, monolatrous or monotheistic. Since de Wette's work on the origin of the Book of Deuteronomy (1805), it has been deduced that much of the 'Mosaic' legislation, especially that pertaining to the cult, is not apparent in the narratives of Israel's history up to the end of the monarchy. The meaning of such a portrait cannot, therefore, be linked to historical events as a simple recording of folk memory (even with elaboration).

The creation of such a narrative and its embedded laws presupposes the need for an account of the origins and nature of an idealized 'Israel', one that consisted of twelve tribes, was governed by a notion of divine law, and bonded into an exclusive relationship with a deity who is defined as both the god of Israel and also of the whole world. This 'Israel' displays a degree of animosity towards neighbouring and indigenous populations, but the story also tells of periods of peaceful cohabitation. Extraneous origin, however, is favoured above indigenous: twice, 'Israel' enters Canaan, once in the person of the ancestor Abraham and later again from Egypt; the land is each time promised to these 'outsiders'— both to the ancestors and again in the wilderness. The historical context in which this literary complex was assembled into its canonized form must provide an explanation for these features and it is the purpose of this project to provide and to illuminate that context.

In this introductory volume we shall explain the framework within which each of the subsequent commentaries will work—the overall conception that we develop of the origins and growth of the Pentateuch as a whole. Rather than the traditional agenda dealing with literary sources, redactional layers, textual variants and chapter-by-chapter (or verse-by-verse) exegesis, these commentaries will focus on how each of the pentateuchal books, individually, contributes to the definition and illustration of essential aspects of the monotheistic cult of Yahweh Elohim, which served as the basis for the Judaism (or Judaisms, and also Samaritanism) that began to emerge in the second half of the Persian period (ca. 400 BCE onwards). Of central importance is the notion of a divinely chosen nation and its culture, which more than any other in the ancient Near East, is defined exclusively in terms of its religion.

The fundamental premise of this account of the Pentateuch, then, is that the 'Israel' it creates presupposes a set of specific historical and cultural conditions and requirements. These have generated, for compelling reasons, a unique literary enterprise that can only partially be compared with the cultural achievements of the dominant civilizations of the time. Its major components can be now be enumerated: these will serve as the major topics each of the commentaries will address.

1. Torah

While 'Torah' is one of the terms by which the Pentateuch is known and its translation as 'law' is long established, its meaning has evolved. In the Bible, such instruction—regarded as of divine origin—can be priestly, prophetic or scribal ('wisdom'). The Pentateuch uses it in a number of ways, from a specific 'instruction' to a codified set of laws. In Leviticus and Numbers it predominantly means specific priestly *torot*, (laws or teachings), most often relating to the cult. It is rare in Genesis, while in Deuteronomy (like the Former Prophets), it is a singular noun (*torah*) and denotes divine revelation mediated through Moses. But, as in most other biblical passages, such Mosaic instruction refers only to the book of Deuteronomy. It is from here that the term seems to have spread to cover all of what Moses was said to have uttered on Sinai, and then to all the five scrolls. This wider usage appears in Ezra and Nehemiah—or at least, a combination of Deuteronomy with the so-called 'Priestly' material in Exodus–Numbers.

How this process occurred and how the Mosaic teaching came to be embedded in a narrative framework is unclear, but both 'law' and narrative function together as ethnic definitions of 'Israel'. The process was probably substantially complete by the time of the Chronicler (probably in the fourth century BCE); it involved the combination of differing traditions and the elimination of some rival ones. It has long been held that the creation of the Pentateuch was stimulated by a Persian imperial initiative. However, the evidence supporting such an assumption is problematic. More recently, scholars have tended to emphasize the importance of native processes in the creation of the Pentateuch, even though external influences remain likely. It also seems to reflect more than one Yahwistic community (Judean, Samarian, Transjordanian, diasporic), though Jerusalem may have been the dominant matrix. Finally, the composition of the Torah reflects a struggle for authority over the interpretation of the Mosaic revelation, a struggle that continued after the scrolls achieved a canonical status.

2. Geography

A clearly demarcated space for 'Israel' is imposed through boundaries that define the extent of the land given to Israel and even the tribal territories within it. However, the pre-eminence of Judah and Jerusalem, evident elsewhere in the Hebrew Bible, is curiously muted in the Pentateuch, which stresses the unity of Judah and Samerina (a province named after Samaria, the capital of the former kingdom of Israel) within a single 'Israel' and embeds this 'Israel' within a wider family of Abrahamic nations such as Ammon, Moab, Edom and Aram. The last region is from where Abraham's own family migrated and the patriarchs took their wives. The area settled by these nations corresponds to the geo-political region known from the later Neo-Assyrian period (eighth–seventh century BCE) onwards as 'Across the River' (Heb; *abar ha-nahar*). The earliest attestation so far is in a text dating to the reign of Esarhaddon (681–669 BCE; Tuell 1991). The Mesopotamian and especially Egyptian links with the origins of the ancestors suggest an even wider geographical spread, which would embrace Jewish communities living in these regions.

3. Ethnicity

Fundamental to this issue is the definition of 'Israel'. As we have seen, the *qehal yisra'el* ('congregation of Israel') is furnished with a common origin and history that binds ethnic and cultural characteristics and integrates the populations of the former kingdoms of Israel and Judah into a single people. Significantly, the Pentateuch is shared by the successors of both populations: Jews (Judeans) and Samaritans (Samarians). The books of Joshua and Judges maintain this unity in depicting the conquests under Joshua and the distribution of land but hints of Judean hegemony appear already in Judges, while the books of Samuel and Kings introduce and maintain a division into the 'houses' of Israel and Judah as separate political and social entities—without explaining how this division came about.

The centrality of Jerusalem is also a dominant theme in Kings. In the Pentateuch, by contrast, the shadow of the historical division between Israel and Judah is quite absent. Judah is not prioritized and Jerusalem is not mentioned. It can be argued that Deuteronomy and possibly the 'Priestly' material (e.g. Leviticus) presuppose a single cult centre, but nowhere is such a place named. Each of the two 'Israelite' communities has, in fact, nominated its own exclusive temple: the Jews have chosen

Jerusalem and the Samaritans Mt Gerizim near Shechem, where today they retain something of the biblical sacrificial cult.

The sense in the Pentateuch of a single community that includes the 'twelve tribes' whose descendants populated the twin kingdoms of Israel and Judah obliges the historian to reconsider the portrait offered in the books of Ezra and Nehemiah of a deep animosity between Jerusalem and Samaria. Indeed, the almost identical Samaritan Pentateuch provides the most eloquent evidence of a community of religion between the two territories and their populations at the time these books describe. The Judah-centred portrait of the books of Kings, which seeks to condemn the apostate kingdom Israel to permanent exclusion—while appropriating its name—does not fit the Pentateuch and must be regarded as reflecting a different historical context, or at least a different ideological definition of 'Israel'.

Ethnicity is also defined by shared cultural habits. Existing customs such as the observance of sabbath, circumcision and diet are transformed through the Pentateuch into ethnic markers, while specifically religious practices and objects such as *tefillin* (phylacteries) and *mezuzot* (attached to doorposts) are introduced (Deut. 6:8–9; 11:20). Ethnic solidarity is further promoted through the discouragement of mixed marriages and the condemnation of cultural habits practised by neighbours. The exclusive ritual cult the Pentateuch prescribes includes national festivals and severely limits local religious celebrations for the purpose of ensuring orthopraxis and uniformity to the cult of the 'god of Israel'.

In short, the Pentateuch defines 'Israel' in terms of both 'nation' and 'religion'—a duality that persists in modern Jewish identity.

4. Religion and Cult

The Pentateuch retrojects onto Israel's beginnings a religion of exclusive worship of a god usually named as either Yahweh or Elohim (or both).[1] This god has no female consort and is not to be represented by any images. Such a religious system does not correspond to the religions of either Israel or Judah in their monarchic periods but seems to have developed in the Persian era. We have allusions to the introduction of such a system in other biblical books (such as Ezra and Nehemiah), but Samaria must also have shared this cult. The characteristics of this god derive largely from the El and Baal deities of the region, but in the monotheistic context other deities can be transformed into 'messengers' (or 'angels'). However, as a universal 'high' god, Yahweh assumes all of the functions assigned to deities in the ancient Near East. This role is to a degree in tension with the older profile of a national god, leaving Israel in a privileged position among the nations of the earth. The Yahweh of the Pentateuch (indeed, of the Bible) is something of a mixture of the local national deity and an imperial high god such as the Persian Ahura-Mazda.

In a monarchy, the king served as representative of the god and mediator, the chief cultic performer and issuer of laws as guardian of divine order. The Pentateuch rather envisages Yahweh as facing the people either directly or via a mediator (Moses) whose profile is variable, but certainly has a strong prophetic element, especially in Deuteronomy.

Cultic activity is rather vaguely described until the detailed laws on Sinai: in Genesis, there is very little sacrificial activity, but several altars are erected by the ancestors. Exodus–Numbers offer extensive and detailed cultic prescriptions for a portable tent-sanctuary that is clearly a prototype for later temples. The prominence of the priesthood in these books varies: in Leviticus it is paramount, whereas in Deuteronomy it is less apparent. Deuteronomy is actually more concerned than Exodus–Numbers with the concentration of cultic activity in designated sanctuaries, or perhaps a single sanctuary, in which the 'name' or 'reputation' of Yahweh 'dwells'.

The conceptual and terminological differences within the Pentateuch can be explained to a large degree by positing two major ideologies, or even 'schools', 'Priestly' and 'Deuteronomic'. The integration or combination of these two ideologies into a single account and their embedding into a single historical narrative represents the process of the development of 'Judaism' into a single religious system, though one not completely harmonized, which subsequently diverged into two separate cults of Yahweh in Jerusalem and Gerizim.

5. *Treaty, Loyalty Oath and Royal Grant*

The covenant between Yahweh and Israel is the modification of a political regime in which a patron/suzerain 'protects' a client/vassal in return for service. The client may be a bodyguard or the ruler of a less powerful kingdom. The arrangement was well known in the ancient Near East and is exemplified especially well in Hittite and Neo-Assyrian texts. Legally sworn loyalty oaths are part of this relationship, which is typically characterized as a 'favour' on the part of the patron/suzerain. In the covenant ideology of Deuteronomy, Yahweh acts as the patron deity and the whole people are collectively and individually the clients. Hence, disobedience on the part of even one individual can incur punishment on the whole people. The primary aim of such transactions was to prevent a switching of allegiance to other rulers, or in this case, to other deities.

Conversely, a royal grant is a reward for services rendered; on occasions these rewards may be inherited, and they sometimes take the form of land. While in legal theory such 'covenants' or 'treaties' were made in bilateral agreement, in practice they were usually imposed by the more powerful party. Unlike the conception of Deuteronomy, the Priestly 'covenant' is granted or imposed by Yahweh unilaterally (as with, for example, Noah or Abraham). Whether or not the relationship between Yahweh and Israel is conditional remains unresolved; while a breach of the conditions may be punished (e.g. by loss of land), there is a strong implication that Israel is essentially always bound to this god and vice-versa.

6. Moses

The Pentateuch is above all a monument to Moses. Here, too, we face an intriguing challenge. The figure of Moses is attested outside the Pentateuch, but the pattern of occurrences is instructive. In Joshua, his name is mentioned 59 times, in Judges five times, in Samuel–Kings 12 times, in Chronicles 21 times, in Ezra–Nehemiah ten. His name occurs in only five Psalms, and only five times in the Latter Prophets (twice in Isaiah 63, once in Jeremiah, Micah and Malachi), plus once in Daniel. On the other hand, Moses is very popular in Greek texts stemming from diaspora Jews and also non-Jewish authors. In the Pentateuch the role with which he is most associated is that of law mediator. However, Moses is given many other roles as well, such as prophet, warrior, intercessor, or thaumaturge. The bringing together of these different roles is intimately related to the creation of the Pentateuch as the most authoritative document for the emergent Judaism in the Persian period.

7. Concluding Comments

One final but important observation needs to be made about the project of clarifying the social, political and historical context of the Pentateuch. In comparison with the Iron Age (ca. tenth–sixth centuries BCE), we have less information about the history and archaeology of the Levant under the Persians and the Ptolemies (fifth–third centuries BCE). The task of modern pentateuchal historical-critical scholarship thus faces an additional obstacle, but at the same time a challenge: not only to understand the literature against what little we know of the background, but also, by careful induction, to discover more about the processes that must have occurred to compel its creation and so to expand our knowledge of the inner history of ancient Judah and its religion. Such a process of induction can easily become circular, as have so many reconstructions of ancient Israelite and Judean history developed from the biblical narratives. On the other hand, biblical criticism has also proved that it can correctly interpret historical contexts and developments even without the aid (and sometimes despite the opposition) of archaeology. The historicity of the patriarchs, Exodus and conquest of Canaan were, for example, either thrown into doubt or disproved through literary critical analysis before archaeological confirmation was forthcoming. Now that pre-monarchic contexts for the Pentateuch are no longer valid, and given the relatively poor achievements of archaeology in the Persian and early Hellenistic era, the real context of the Pentateuch will need to be investigated through careful attention to what the texts themselves say—and what they do not!

Notes

1. Many passages in the Pentateuch require the exclusive worship of Yahweh but do not deny the existence of other deities. This form of religion is not monotheistic in the strict sense but can be described as 'monolatry'. Other passages, however, presuppose that Yahweh is the only existing deity and are, therefore, monotheistic.

Works Cited and Suggested Further Reading

Blenkinsopp, Joseph. 1992. *The Pentateuch: An Introduction to the First Five Books of the Bible.* Anchor Bible Reference Library; New York: Doubleday.

Nicholson, E. 1998. *The Pentateuch in the Twentieth Century: The Legacy of Julius Wellhausen.* Oxford: Clarendon. (Contains all bibliographical indications for the authors not mentioned here.)

Noth, Martin. 1958. *The History of Israel.* New York: Harper and Brothers (German original, 1954).

— 1972. *A History of Pentateuchal Traditions.* Englewood Cliffs, NJ: Prentice-Hall; repr. 1981. Atlanta, GA: Scholars Press (German original, 1948).

Tuell, Stephen. 1991. 'The Southern and Eastern Borders of Abar-Nahara.' *Bulletin of the American Schools of Oriental Research* 234: 51–57.

Chapter 2

THE SHAPE, DATING AND AUDIENCE OF THE PENTATEUCH

1. Introduction to the Contents and Shape of the Pentateuch

The Pentateuch comprises a long narrative beginning with the creation of the world and humanity and ending with Moses' death at Mount Nebo facing the Promised Land. In that narrative it is possible to identify several distinct episodes: the origins of humanity, the ancestors of Israel, Israel's sojourn in Egypt and the exodus, and so on. All these episodes are arranged in a chronological framework, and the impression that they form a linear history is reinforced by the giving of the age of the characters in addition to other various chronological notes. Moses is said to have died at the age of 120 (Deut. 34:8), and the exodus is supposed to have happened after the Israelites had sojourned in Egypt for 430 years (Exod. 12:40–41; Gen. 15:13 predicts there will be 400 years of oppression in Egypt). This chronological system is not restricted to the Pentateuch: it can be traced further in the Former Prophets (the books from Joshua to Kings). In 1 Kgs 6:1 Solomon's construction of the temple takes place 480 years after the exodus. This is an indication that the Pentateuch was also considered to be the first part of an ongoing story in the Former Prophets; this 'primary history' running from the Book of Genesis to the end of Kings is frequently referred to as an 'Enneateuch', that is, a collection of *eleven* books, just like the 'Penta-teuch' is a collection of five books.

The pentateuchal narrative is also characterized by changes in geography: it narrates a move from the Garden of Eden to the land of Moab. Genesis 1–11 ends with humanity's dispersion all over the world, whereas the narratives about the patriarchs—Israel's ancestors—in Genesis 12–36 are consistently located in the land of Canaan, after Abraham's family left the city of Ur in Mesopotamia. The story of Joseph explains how the Israelites, who are already in their land, arrive in Egypt, where the first part of the Book of Exodus (1–15) is located. Having left Egypt, Moses leads the people to the mountain of Sinai, where Yahweh reveals his Law. The whole manifestation of Yahweh's will, which runs from the second half of Exodus to the first part of Numbers (Exodus 20–Numbers 10), is located at Sinai. After the departure from Sinai, the people sojourn at different places in the wilderness (Numbers 11–21) until they arrive in the land of Moab, where Moses' final speech takes place. Because he dies immediately thereafter (Deuteronomy 34), the speech comprises a testament of sorts (Deuteronomy 1–30), concluding with a blessing (Deuteronomy 33).

The Pentateuch can also be understood as a biography of Moses, with the Book of Genesis serving as a 'prologue'. The Book of Exodus begins with the story of his birth and the last chapter of the Pentateuch, Deuteronomy 34, narrates his death, highlighting Moses' status as the most important non-divine character in the pentateuchal narrative. Describing the Pentateuch as a biography of Moses implies a major division exists between the Book of Genesis and the ensuing four books, Exodus–Deuteronomy. Several other features reinforce this impression; one, for instance, is the prominence in Genesis of genealogical lists, which are almost entirely absent from the remaining books. The distinction between Genesis on one hand, and Exodus on the other, can be variously assessed, but it points to a major difference between Moses and earlier figures such as Abraham or Jacob: contrary to Israel's patriarchs, Moses is not an ancestor. There is some hesitation in the narratives about the

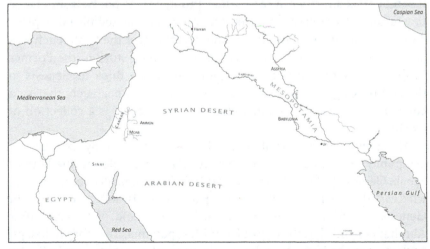

Figure 1. Map of places named in movements in the Pentateuch (created by R. Hobson)

number of his sons; notwithstanding, they do not play a role during Moses' life or after his death.

i. Genesis

The Pentateuch opens with accounts of the origins of the world and of the first human couple. In the first account (Gen. 1:1–2:3), God (*elohim*) creates the world in six days and rests during the seventh. Thus, the weekly organization of time with the Sabbath as the seventh day is portrayed to be as old as the creation of the universe. In the first account, humanity is created male and female from the very beginning, whereas in the second account, Yahweh-Elohim creates the wife much later as a 'help' for the primitive man, Adam. After the first couple is expelled from paradise, the first murder occurs (Genesis 4), prompted by Yahweh's failure to accept Cain's offering. The spreading of human violence is the reason given to explain why Yahweh decides to exterminate humanity (as well as the animals) through the Flood. Only Noah, his family, and selected specimen of animals survive (Genesis 6–9). After the Flood, Noah's three sons and their wives represent the new humanity that spreads all over the world (Genesis 10). In the ensuing story, all humans are supposed to live a nomadic lifestyle. Their decision to build a city with a tower, which may reach to the sky and, therefore, to Yahweh's dwelling place, leads Yahweh to intervene and to create different languages, making communication between the humans impossible (Genesis 11). The story ends with a pejorative wordplay on the name of Babel ('confusion').

The ensuing story of Abraham begins with his genealogy, which informs the reader that his family is located in Babylonia, in 'Ur of the Chaldeans' (11:28). Abraham, whose original name is Abram, receives a divine call after his family has moved to Harran. The story of Abram's call (Genesis 12) is constructed to serve as a contrast to the story of the 'tower of Babel'. In 11:4, the humans wanted to make for themselves a 'great name', an attempt that led to dispersion; in 12:2–3 Yahweh assures Abraham that he will make his name a great one and that all the families of the earth (or of the land) will be blessed in Abram. After having moved from Harran to Palestine, where Yahweh tells him he will give this land to the patriarch's offspring, Abram heads immediately to Egypt because of a famine. Thus, the story of the patriarchs opens with a crossing of the entire 'fertile crescent', from southern Mesopotamia via Syria and Palestine to Egypt. In Egypt, Abram allows his wife to be married to Pharaoh, pretending she is his sister (Gen. 12:10–20). But Pharaoh, alerted by Yahweh's plagues, sends Abram out of Egypt back to his land. This looks like an (ironic) allusion to the exodus narrative. Back in the land, Abram separates from Lot (Genesis 13), who is going to dwell in the paradise-like region of Sodom and Gomorrah, but before the story turns to the wickedness of the Sodomites, Lot is first caught in a sort of world war in which four kings from all over Mesopotamia fight. Abram rescues Lot and is then blessed by a mysterious king of Salem, Melchizedek (Genesis 14). The reader has already been informed at the beginning of the story that Abram and his wife Sarah (first called Sarai) are quite old and in addition, Sarai is sterile (11:30). Nevertheless, when Yahweh announces Abram will have descendants as numerous as the stars, he believes the promise and Yahweh concludes a 'covenant' with him, telling him of the future Egyptian oppression and exodus (Genesis 15). In the next story, Sarai (Genesis 17) seems less faithful; she suggests that Abram sleep with her maidservant, Hagar, so she can have a son with Abram through her. Abram complies and becomes the father of Ishmael, the ancestor of the Bedouin tribes in the Arabian desert. After Ishmael has grown up, Yahweh, presenting himself as El Shaddai, reiterates that Abram will have offspring with Sarai, and a (second) covenant is concluded. Abram and Sarai have their names changed to Abraham and Sarah and circumcision becomes the sign of this second covenant. Interestingly, Ishmael is also circumcised, thereby participating in the divine covenant made between God and Abraham. Abraham's exemplary hospitality to three unknown visitors who reveal themselves to be divine manifestations engenders a new announcement of a son for Sarah, who is incredulous when she hears the promise.

Yahweh then has a theological discussion with Abraham about whether or not he, Yahweh, has the right to destroy the city of Sodom if righteous people can be found in it. Yahweh agrees not to destroy the city if at least ten righteous people are found, but the ensuing story shows that number does not exist (Genesis 19). The city is destroyed by fire and earthquake; only Lot and his two daughters are able to escape. Fearing the inability to find husbands, the daughters have incestuous relations with their drunken father and become the ancestresses of the Ammonites and the Moabites. Genesis 20 is a remake of Gen. 12:10–20; again, Abraham presents his wife to a foreign king as his sister. This time, however, the king is informed about the situation by Elohim in a dream and does not consummate the union. Abraham is rehabilitated and is presented as a prophet. Finally, the promised son, Isaac, is born. Hagar and her son Ishmael are driven out of Abraham's household on Sarah's initiative (Genesis 21).

After Isaac is born, God (*ha-elohim*) asks Abraham to sacrifice his son. Apparently, Abraham is willing to do so but is stopped in the nick of time by Yahweh's angel. The story contains an intriguing element. Before the sacrifice, Abraham tells his servants that he and his son will return to them (22:5), but after the aborted sacrifice he returns alone (22:19).

After Sarah's death and the purchase of a burial place for her and himself at Hebron (Genesis 23), Abraham sends his servant to seek a wife for Isaac in Mesopotamia, because he shall not marry a woman from 'the people of the land'. This wife is Rebecca, the daughter of Abraham's niece (Genesis 24). Before he dies, Abraham marries a woman named Qeturah ('Incense'), who gives birth to the ancestors of people all along the incense road. Then Abraham is buried by Isaac and Ishmael (Genesis 25).

The story of Abraham's son Isaac is limited to one chapter (Genesis 26). While sojourning in the land of the Philistines, he repeats some of

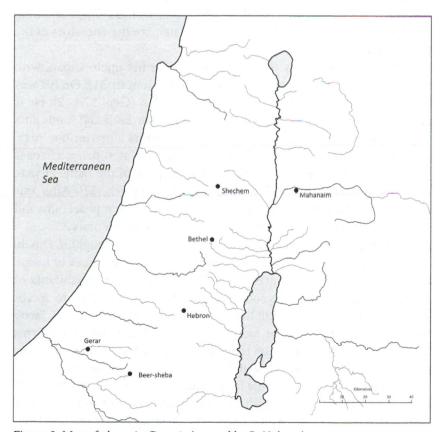

Figure 2. Map of places in Genesis (created by R. Hobson)

the adventures of his father, presenting his wife Rebecca as his sister. Like Sarah, Rebecca is also barren, but Yahweh finally makes her the mother of twins: Esau and Jacob, who are in conflict already inside the womb (Gen. 25:19–28). Jacob is a trickster. He deceives his brother twice and steals his right of the first-born son (Gen. 25:29–34; 27). He has to leave his family in order to escape the anger of Esau, who seeks to kill him, but also because, like Abraham, his mother Rebecca wants him to take a wife from his Mesopotamian family (Gen. 27:41–28:9). En route to Haran, Yahweh presents himself to Jacob in a dream and in response the latter founds the sanctuary of Bethel (Gen. 28:10–21).

During his sojourn in Aram, Jacob the trickster is deceived by his uncle, Laban. Jacob wants to marry the beautiful Rachel, but Laban puts his less attractive, older daughter Leah in the wedding tent. Eventually, Jacob marries both. The rivalry between Leah and Rachel provokes a 'birth competition' in which their maidservants also participate. Jacob becomes the father of eleven children from four women. These children, together with Benjamin, who will be born later, are the ancestors of the twelve tribes of Israel (Genesis 29–30).

Before Jacob becomes Israel he has to leave his uncle Laban, with whom he concludes a pact of non-aggression (Genesis 31). On his way home, Jacob arrives at Mahanaim in Transjordan (Gen. 32:1–2). He is afraid of an anticipated encounter with his brother Esau and sends gifts to pacify him. That same evening, Jacob encounters a mysterious 'man' who struggles with him and, before leaving him at sunrise, changes Jacob's name to Israel, explaining that the purpose of the name change is to commemorate his having struggled with God (ch. 32). After this struggle, the dreaded encounter with Esau takes place peacefully and Jacob enters Cisjordan and settles down in Shechem (Genesis 33).

The reader/listener now learns that Jacob also has a daughter, Dinah, who is apparently raped by a man called Shechem. He agrees to marry her and even to be circumcised, as will all other male inhabitants of the town. But two of Jacob's sons, Levi and Simeon, unwilling to accept such 'interracial' contacts, kill the entire population (Genesis 34). Jacob then receives a divine order to travel again to Bethel, which confirms his change of name from Jacob to Israel (Genesis 35). On the way home, Rachel dies while giving birth to Benjamin, the last of Jacob's 12 sons, who will play an important role in the story of Joseph and his brethren. After listing Esau's offspring (ch. 36), the narrative turns to the story of Joseph (Genesis 37–50), which marks the geographical transition from Canaan to Egypt.

Joseph's story relates how he was sold into slavery by his brothers and taken to Egypt, where he becomes the personal servant of a high official (Genesis 37). His wife tries unsuccessfully to seduce Joseph but then falsely accuses him of having tried to seduce her, which leads to his imprisonment (ch. 39). The two accounts are separated by another account of a love affair, this time between Judah—Joseph's elder brother—and a prostitute named Tamar (ch. 38).

While in prison, Joseph's ability to interpret dreams causes him to be brought to the royal court, where he becomes a chamberlain of sorts for Pharaoh, as well as the son-in-law of a high priest (Genesis 40–41). The famine predicted by Joseph occurs and causes his brothers to go to Egypt to buy food. Joseph does not reveal his identity to his brothers and forces them to come back with Benjamin, the youngest brother, who had remained with Jacob, their father. It is only after all the brothers have been reunited that Joseph discloses his identity (Genesis 42–45). At Joseph's invitation backed by Pharaoh's hospitality, Jacob also arrives eventually in Egypt (Genesis 46). Joseph's further economic and political successes are recounted in ch. 47, as is the death of the patriarch, Jacob. In Genesis 48–49, Jacob's blessing of his 12 sons is recounted, which has a counterpart at the end of the Pentateuch in Moses' blessing in Deuteronomy 33. The funerals of Jacob and Joseph are narrated in ch. 50; whereas Jacob is taken back to Canaan to be buried, Joseph is buried in Egypt. However, in his last words Joseph already predicts the exodus, asking that on this occasion his bones be taken back to Canaan. The fulfilment of this request is related in the final chapter of the Book of Joshua.

ii. Exodus
The Book of Exodus recounts four major events: Israel's dwelling in Egypt, the exodus itself, that is, Israel's departure from Egypt, the temporary stay in the wilderness and, lastly, the arrival at Sinai, the 'mountain of God', where Yahweh reveals to Israel a series of instructions. Overall, the transition from Genesis to Exodus corresponds to the beginning of Israel's 'national' history. This is signalled in the opening verses of Exodus by the notice recounting how the sons of Jacob (= Israel) had multiplied themselves to the point that 'the land was full of them' (Exod. 1:7).

Even so, at the beginning of the book, 'Israel' is still a clan: it has no land, no king, and no patron deity, all of which were essential features for defining a nation/kingdom in antiquity. In the early chapters, the Israelites are often designated 'Hebrews' (*ibrim*)—an apparently ethnic term, though this is disputed. The central theme of the Israelites' enslavement by Pharaoh drives home the point that they have no political autonomy: they are in a foreign land under the rule of a foreign king. They are slaves to Pharaoh, and their very existence as an ethnic group is threatened. By the end of the book, however, Israel has found both a patron deity—Yahweh—as well as a human representative of that deity—Moses—who takes up the role traditionally played by the king. The land comes up much later in the biblical narrative, but this is deliberate: the 'Israel' defined in the Pentateuch is no longer centrally defined by the possession of a land, a fact which, from a historical perspective, should be tied to the situation of Judaism at the time of the composition of the Pentateuch. More important are a sense of kinship ties and of shared customs, shared rites and a national cult. Kinship ties have already been provided in the Genesis genealogies; this theme is built up further in Exodus. The concepts of shared customs, shared rites and a national cult are developed in Exodus and in the ensuing three books (Leviticus, Numbers and Deuteronomy).

The first part of the Book of Exodus (1:1–15:21) takes place entirely in Egypt. It introduces the main characters of the exodus narrative according to a deliberate pattern: first, Israel and Pharaoh (Exodus 1), then Moses (Exodus 2), later Yahweh (Exodus 3) and lastly, Aaron, Moses' brother (Exodus 4). Chapter 1 recounts how the sons of Jacob prosper and multiply in Egypt until they become a threat to Pharaoh. Pharaoh then decides to enslave them and devises a policy to annihilate them by requiring the midwives to kill all newborn males. There is significant plot development from the final chapters of Genesis. On one hand, the setting is the same as in the Joseph story (Genesis 37–50). On the other hand, the general perspective is clearly distinct: Pharaoh, once the protector of Joseph, has become the enemy of Israel. This radical change reflects the central theme of Exodus, that is, the transformation of 'Israel' from a clan into a 'nation' (Heb. *am* or *goy*) distinguishable from other nations.

Chapter 2 introduces the figure of Moses, recounting how he was saved from death by being adopted by Pharaoh's daughter. Later, he kills an Egyptian who was smiting a Hebrew. Like the trickster of international folklore, Moses is from the onset a truly ambivalent figure: he belongs neither to the Egyptians, although he was adopted by them, nor to the Hebrews, who do not accept him even though he is kin. At the same time, Moses already appears as a *mediator* between two worlds or two cultures, Egypt and Israel, a function he will retain in the course of the first half of the book.

After the murder, Moses is forced to flee Egypt for fear of being denounced to Pharaoh and finds asylum with Jethro, a priest of Midian (an Arabic tribe living in the wilderness south of Palestine) who gives him one of his own daughters as a bride. Chapter 2 ends with the sudden appearance of Yahweh, who is said to 'remember' his former covenant with the patriarchs Abraham, Jacob and Israel and decides to intervene for his people (2:23–25). This brief notice prepares the reader for the ensuing scene, in ch. 3, which relates the encounter between Yahweh and Moses at Mount Horeb (already referred to as 'the mountain of God'), where Moses was tending the flock of Jethro, his father-in-law. Moses receives the instruction to lead Israel out of Egypt to the very same mountain where they shall 'serve' Yahweh (3:12, see also 3:18). Yahweh also discloses his proper name to Moses—according to several passages in Genesis, even Israel's ancestors worshipped God as *el shaddai* ('a mighty god'), but not yet as Yahweh—and he also foretells the conflicts that will oppose Moses to Pharaoh.

Moses' hesitation to accept that mission leads to the introduction of Aaron, the last major character of the exodus plot, whose task is to convey to the people the commands of Moses (Exodus 4). The role conferred on Aaron may surprise the reader at first, but the view that Levitical priests are the teachers *par excellence* of the Torah—Moses' words—is a common notion both in the canonical and extra-canonical literature.

After Moses' return to Egypt at the end of ch. 4 (Exod. 4:18–31), a first plea to Pharaoh fails, resulting in a worsening of the Hebrews' situation in Egypt (Exodus 5). This leads to a new divine revelation (Exodus 6) where Yahweh basically restates his former commands to Moses. A new encounter takes place between Moses, Aaron and Pharaoh. This time, however, Moses and Aaron receive the command to confront Pharaoh until he allows the Hebrews to leave Egypt (Exod. 7:1–7). This leads to the recounting in Exodus of a series of 'wonders', magical acts performed by Moses and Aaron consisting primarily of various plagues affecting the Egyptians and their land (frogs, vermin, hail, locusts, darkness; Exodus 7–11). These plagues follow a pattern of growing severity and culminate in the announcement of the death of all Egyptian first-borns in ch. 11; its fulfilment is then recounted in ch. 12, after which instructions are given to Israel for the celebration of the Passover.

That ultimate plague, which counterbalances the theme of the death of the Israelite first-borns at the beginning of the exodus narrative, marks a turning point. Pharaoh lets Israel leave Egypt, thus marking the end of its enslavement. The importance of that moment is highlighted by the first celebration of Passover, one of the central ritual customs of emergent Judaism in the Second Temple period.

Soon after their departure, however, Pharaoh changes his mind and pursues the Israelites. His army overtakes them at the Sea of Reeds (Exodus 13–14). Israel is eventually delivered from Pharaoh's army by a further wonder of Moses, who opens a path into the sea for the Israelites, before the waters close again on Pharaoh's army. This wonder is celebrated at the end of ch. 14 in the statement, the people 'believed in Yahweh and in Moses, his servant' (Exod. 14:31). Then Moses sings a victory song to celebrate the defeat of Pharaoh (Exod. 15:1–18). As in other biblical books, this canticle plays a major structuring role, marking the transition between the first and second halves of the exodus narrative; the Song not only recalls the mighty acts of Yahweh, who delivered his own people, but also alludes to future events, especially Israel's arrival at Yahweh's holy mountain (Exod. 15:17).

The second half of the book focuses on Israel's sojourn in the wilderness, telling the people's encounter with God at Mount Sinai and the proclamation of various instructions (Exodus 19–40). Before that, Exodus 16–18 (more exactly, 15:22–18:27) acts as a transition in recounting the journey from the Sea of Reeds to Sinai. The episodes during that journey anticipate the same kind of events that will be narrated later in the Book of Numbers. Two brief accounts about the people's complaint regarding the lack of water (Exod. 15:22–27 and 17:1–7) frame a longer account about the lack of food in Exodus 16. The latter narrative, in particular, anticipates several key motifs in Numbers, such as the people expressing regret over leaving Egypt. The major difference, however, is that in Exodus 16–18 the people are not yet punished by Yahweh for complaining: it is only after God's laws have been revealed at Sinai that such punishment will take place.

The battle against Amalek (Exod. 17:8–16) prepares the reader/listener for the stories in Numbers about Israel's hostile encounters with other nations on its way to the Promised Land (see especially Numbers 20–25), while Moses' encounter with Jethro in Exodus 18, just before the arrival at Sinai in Exodus 19, explores the possibility of Israel's positive relationship with foreigners.

The account of Israel's stay at Sinai in Exodus 19–40 is complex; nonetheless, it is easy to identify major units. Exodus 19 recounts how Yahweh appears to Moses at Sinai and announces to him the conclusion of a covenant (*berit*) with the people (Exod. 19:3–8). He then manifests himself to the people as a whole (19:16–19, 20) and communicates his laws and instructions to them: first, the Decalogue (the Ten Commandments), Exod. 20:2–17, and secondly, another series of various commands pertaining to civil and religious law (Exod. 20:22–26; 21–23). In-between, however, a major development takes place. After the proclamation of the Decalogue, the people announce to Moses that they cannot stand in the presence of Yahweh; as a result, the ensuing commands in Exod. 20:22–26 and chs 21–23 are disclosed to Moses exclusively (see Exod. 20:18–21). He then writes these commands in a book and reads that book to the people in the context of a ceremony celebrating the covenant between Yahweh and Israel (Exod. 24:1–8).

That covenant ceremony is followed by a further ceremony in which Aaron and his two elder sons, accompanied by 70 elders, are allowed to 'eat and drink' in the presence of Yahweh at the top of the mountain (24:9–11). After that climax, Moses once again climbs God's mountain, this time with Joshua, his servant (24:12–14); after residing six days on the summit of the mountain, he then receives a series of detailed instructions (Exodus 25–31) for the construction of a portable sanctuary for Yahweh on the seventh day. They entail the construction of various cultic objects—the ark, the golden table, the menorah or light stand (25:10–40)—the sanctuary itself, consisting of a portative tent called the 'Tent of Meeting' (Exodus 26), the outer altar and the temple court, made of curtains (ch. 27). Then, Yahweh's instructions shift to the production of priestly vestments (Exodus 28) and the anointing of the priests themselves (Exodus 29). This may seem surprising to modern readers, but in the context of ancient cultures, the priests and their belongings were an integral part of the temple.

Lastly, chs 30–31 give instructions for the incense altar, the temple tax, the basin and the temple's artisans. The instructions in chs 25–31 end with a prescription regarding the observance of Sabbath (Exod. 31:12–17); here again, this may seem surprising at first, but the parallel between temple and Sabbath occurs in several places in biblical literature (compare, e.g., Lev. 19:30 and 26:2). Lastly, Moses is given two 'tablets of stone' written by God himself before he descends the mountain (Exod. 34:18). According to Exod. 24:12, the two tablets contained 'the Law (*torah*) and the commands (*mitsvot*)'. It is not entirely clear to what these terms refer (see further the discussion in the section on 'Torah' in Chapter 4), but they probably included the Decalogue at least, as in Deut. 4:13; 10:3–5.

The next chapter, Exodus 32, recounts what the people who had remained at the foot of the mountain during that time had been doing. Left under the supervision of Aaron, Moses' brother and the future high priest, they ask him to fabricate for them a golden statue representing a calf, which they begin worshipping (Exod. 32:1–6). This is an explicit transgression of the command against the worship of 'images' or 'statues' of Yahweh in the Decalogue (compare Exod. 20:4).

While he is staying on the mountain, Moses learns of these events directly from Yahweh and then returns to the Israelites' camp. Angry at what he encounters, he breaks the divine tablets he has just received, destroys the calf and, with the help of the Levites, puts the culprits to death. There follows a lengthy discussion between Moses and Yahweh, where Moses pleads for Yahweh to remain present amidst the people despite their wrongdoing (Exodus 33). As a result of his successful plea, Moses is required by Yahweh to ascend the mountain again, where he receives two *new* stone tablets. Yahweh dictates further commands to him (Exod. 34:11–26), which are said to comprise a 'covenant' between Yahweh and Israel (see 34:10). Moses then writes these commands on the two tablets and takes them back to the people.

Chapters 35–40 give a detailed account of the construction of the sanctuary, which more or less follows the instructions already narrated in Exodus 25–31. Although the story of the golden calf and its consequences in Exodus 32–34 interrupts the command/fulfilment pattern in Exodus 25–31 and 35–40, the transition from Exodus 34 to 35 is not without logic: the renewal of the covenant between Yahweh and Israel warrants Yahweh's presence among Israel and the construction of the wilderness sanctuary establishes a place where Yahweh's 'glory'—that is, his personification on earth—may reside (compare Exod. 25:8 and 29:45–46). The successful construction of the sanctuary is immediately followed by a brief account in Exod. 40:34–35 recounting the entrance of Yahweh's 'glory' (*kavod*) into the newly built sanctuary. On the one hand, the exodus narrative ends with a glorious climax. On the other hand, however, Yahweh's entrance into the sanctuary also raises a new issue, because Moses is not (yet) allowed to approach the deity (see 40:35). It will be the role of the Book of Leviticus to resolve that dilemma by teaching Moses, the priests and the people as a whole how to approach the deity through various rites.

iii. Leviticus

The Book of Leviticus opens with Yahweh calling Moses from inside the 'tent of meeting' (Lev. 1:1) to disclose to him further instructions about sacrifices. These instructions occupy chs 1–7 and detail the main types of offerings to be brought to the deity residing inside the wilderness sanctuary: the burnt offering, the cereal offering, the 'peace' offering, as well as two special kinds of offerings for sins and sacrileges. The disclosure of these instructions then leads to the consecration of the first priests, Aaron and his sons, after which the first public sacrifices are offered (Leviticus 8–9). The two episodes are part of an eight-day ceremony (7 + 1) that culminates in the manifestation of Yahweh's 'glory' before the entire community (Lev. 9:23–24).

Leviticus 10 then narrates a cultic transgression involving Aaron's elder sons, Nadab and Abihu, who are killed by a divine fire; the chapter ends with a series of additional prescriptions for Aaron that emphasize the importance of the correct handling of rituals. In particular, the insistence on the strict division between 'clean' and 'unclean' (Lev. 10:10–11) introduces the next section of the book, chs 11–15, which involves a series of instructions about various types of uncleanness: unclean animals (ch. 11), bodily flows and secretions (chs 12 and 15), as well as various sorts of skin disease grouped under the Hebrew term *tsaraat*, which is usually translated 'leprosy'. Chapter 16 details instructions for a great purification ceremony for the sanctuary and the community—the so-called 'Day of Atonement'; it forms a fitting climax, not only for the collection dealing with physical impurities in Leviticus 11–15, but also for the entire system of offerings in Leviticus 1–16.

The significance of ch. 16 is also evident from the fact that it combines two different rituals; in particular, a rite for cleansing the temple using animal blood with a rite for eliminating impurities and transgressions by physically relocating them outside the community by transferring them to a goat. Whereas chs 1–16 focus on the sanctuary and its servants, chs 17–27 contain a series of divine speeches to the entire community addressing a great variety of topics. As in Exod. 20:24–26 and Deuteronomy 12, Leviticus 17 opens with a law concerning the bringing of offerings to the altar. Chapters 18 and 20 deal with various sexual transgressions inside and outside the family sphere; they frame ch. 19, which is a complex collection of civil and sacral laws, many of which have parallels in Exodus 20–24 as well as in Deuteronomy 12–26.

Leviticus 21–22 contains other instructions primarily concerned with the holiness of the priests and the sanctuary. Chapters 23–25 comprise another sub-section within chs 17–27, whose main topic is the observance of sacred times during the year (23; 24:1–9) and every seven years (the sabbatical years and jubilee: Leviticus 25). The narrative in 24:10–23 deals with the sanctity of the divine name. The blessings and curses in ch. 26 emphasize the importance of observing the laws revealed by Yahweh to Moses; as such, they offer a first conclusion to the Book of Leviticus and to the entire revelation at Mt Sinai that began in Exodus 19 (see Lev. 26:46). A second conclusion follows in Leviticus 27, where additional instructions are given concerning the restitution of persons, animals and objects consecrated to the temple; there is an obvious parallelism with the very beginning of Leviticus, ch. 1, which rounds off the book and underlines its thematic and structural coherence.

iv. Numbers

The Book of Numbers opens with a number of complementary legal prescriptions (chs 1–10) said, however, to have been given to Moses 'in the wilderness of Sinai' (Num. 1:1). Chapters 1–4 deal exclusively with organization of the camp, beginning with a census of the twelve tribes (ch. 1) and their disposition around the central sanctuary (ch. 2). There follows an additional census of the Levites (ch. 3) and a description of their duties with regard to the transport of the wilderness sanctuary (ch. 4). Chapters 5–10 primarily comprise additional prescriptions concerning rites already described in Exodus and Leviticus: unclean persons (5:1–4), the reparation offering (5:5–10, see Leviticus 5), the offering to be brought by a woman suspected of being an adulteress (5:11–31), the rite of the Nazirite (6:1–21), a priestly blessing (6:22–24), the description of a ceremony for the dedication of the sanctuary (Numbers 7, compare with Exodus 40), instructions for lighting the sanctuary's lamp-stands (8:1–4; compare Exod. 27:20–21), details for the consecration of the Levites (8:5–26), and alternative dates for celebrating Passover (9:1–14; compare Exodus 12). Chapter 9 ends with a description of the divine fire and pillar of cloud that accompanied Israel as it journeyed in the wilderness (see Exod. 40:36–38), serving as a transition to the next section of the book. Likewise, ch. 10 gives further instructions for the upcoming journey of the people in the wilderness, which is then related in the ensuing chapters.

In Numbers 11–20 we find a series of rebellion stories, all located in the wilderness. Seven stories can be distinguished. Numbers 11:1–3 introduces the entire cycle, employing a pattern used in the ensuing stories: the people complain, Yahweh gets angry and sends punishment,

Moses intervenes, and the punishment is attenuated. The second story (11:4–35) combines the people's complaint about manna, food sent by God to feed the people, and Moses' complaint against Yahweh, whom he accuses of having burdened him with the entire responsibility of leading the people. The people are punished and Moses is discharged.

The third narrative contains a denial of Moses' authority by Miriam and Aaron, who also criticize him because of his foreign wife; Miriam is punished and Moses' exceptional status is confirmed (ch. 12). The fourth story, in Numbers 13–14, which is the pivot of the entire cycle, narrates the people's rebellion against the proposed conquest of the land. Their desire to return to Egypt provokes Yahweh's anger, who decides to annihilate the entire people. It is only because of the intervention of Moses that the punishment is modified; the first generation has to remain in the desert and the second generation is enjoined to conquer the land. Before the fifth story of rebellion, ch. 15 deals with cultic concerns, as do chs 18–19. These three chapters frame two stories concerned with rebellions against priestly authority. The narrative in 16:1–17:5, constituting the fifth rebellion, combines rebellions by different groups (Korah and his band, Dathan and Abiram) who oppose the claim of Moses and Aaron to have the right to lead Israel by advancing the notion that the entire community has priestly prerogatives (see Exod. 19:3–8). In this story, Moses does not prevent Yahweh from executing his punishment. Korah and his followers perish in a fire from heaven and *Sheol* swallows Dathan and Abiram.

The sixth story in 17:6–27 is closely related to the fifth. The people accuse Moses and Aaron of having tolerated unjust divine punishment and criticize the Aaronite priesthood. Again, a large number of rebels meet their death via divine punishment. Numbers 16–18 establish the legitimacy and supremacy of the Aaronite priesthood above other groups.

The seventh narrative in Num. 20:1–13 builds upon the story in Exodus 17; the people complain about the lack of water. In this retelling, however, the story explains why Moses and Aaron were excluded from entering the Promised Land. Although the nature of the transgression of Moses and Aaron is not entirely clear, Yahweh accuses them of lacking faith in him, thereby profaning him. Chapter 20 announces the end of the sojourn in the wilderness, but a first attempt to reach the Promised Land fails because Edom refuses to let Israel pass (20:14–21). Only after Aaron's death and the installation of a new high priest (20:22–29) does the conquest begin, properly speaking (Num. 21:1–3).

The first victories in Transjordan (Num. 21:10–35), however, are preceded by a further rebellion account, in which the community now accuses Yahweh of putting it in its present situation (21:4–9). The stories and oracles about Balaam (Numbers 22–24), a foreign seer hired by the king of Moab to curse Israel and cause its military defeat, highlight the divine favour granted to Israel: despite all his attempts, Balaam is forced to bless Israel and cannot prevent them from pursuing their campaign towards the Promised Land. In Numbers 25 the people turn to the gods of Moab, provoking Yahweh's anger; the punishment brings about the final extermination of the first generation. The change of generation is underlined in ch. 26 by a second census that is undertaken, which parallels the opening census in Numbers 1.

The final section of the book, chs 27–36, includes narratives that take up themes initially explored in Numbers 11–15 and various laws, several of which relate to the projected occupation of the land. It opens with a story dealing with the possibility of women inheriting land. Numbers 27:12–23 recounts Moses' appointment of Joshua as his successor, thus preparing for the conquest accounts in Joshua. This account is closely related to the announcement of Moses' imminent death, although the latter is actually postponed until the end of Deuteronomy. Numbers 28:1–30:1 provides instructions for bringing offerings on sacred days, which supplement the festival calendar of Leviticus 23. Numbers 30:2–17 then gives detailed legislation on another cultic topic: a woman's vows. Chapter 31 takes up one of the themes of the account of Numbers 25—Israel's conflict with Midian—and narrates a punitive campaign against the Midianites. Chapters 32–35 focus entirely on the conquest of the land. Numbers 32 details the installation of three tribes in Transjordan, outside the Promised Land, while Numbers 33 summarizes Israel's itinerary from Egypt to Canaan (vv 1–49) and provides further instructions for the conquest (vv 50–56). Chapter 34 gives instructions for the division of the land among the tribes and ch. 35 enumerates specific cities to be set aside for Levites (35:1–8) and for murderers seeking asylum (35:9–34). Finally, Numbers 36 returns to the topic of land inheritance by women, which opened chs 27–36, rounding off the entire section.

v. Deuteronomy

The Book of Deuteronomy is set in the plains of Moab in Transjordan, where the Book of Numbers ends. It consists primarily of a farewell speech by Moses (Deut. 1:1–30:20), with a few interruptions, and concludes in chs 31–34 with an account of Moses' blessing and his death. At the centre of the book stands a collection of laws in chs 12–26, which have several parallels to Exod. 20:24–23:19.

Moses' speech begins with a recapitulation of central events from the time of Israel's sojourn in the wilderness (chs 1–3): the appointing of judges to discharge Moses from this task (Exodus 18), the people's refusal to conquer the land (Numbers 13–14), and the conquest of Transjordan (Numbers 21 and 32). In Deut. 3:23–29 an alternative explanation is given for Moses' death outside the Promised Land (compare with Num. 20:1–13). Chapters 4–5 are also concerned with recapitulating previous events, this time in connection with the giving of the Law to Moses. Deuteronomy 4 recalls the theophany at Mt Sinai—which is consistently called (Mt) Horeb in this book—and places special emphasis on the observance of the Law and the uniqueness of Israel's deity, Yahweh. Chapter 5 presents another version of the Decalogue compare with (Exodus 20) and recounts the installation of Moses as Israel's mediator. Deuteronomy 6 introduces the law collection in chs 12–26; it stresses the importance of practicing the divine commands in everyday life. Chapter 7 completes Deuteronomy 6 by underlining Israel's strict separation from the nations.

Deuteronomy 8 offers a general reflection on the wilderness wanderings; in that text, Israel's sojourn in the desert is considered a time of divine testing rather than one of rebellion, as in Numbers. Chapters 9–10 then return to a recapitulation of events from the sojourn at Mt Sinai/Horeb, recalling the episode of the fabrication of the golden calf (see Exodus 32–34). Chapters 11 and 27–28 frame the law collection in 12–26 with a series of blessings and curses, depending on the people's obedience to the Law.

As in Exod. 20:24–26, the law collection opens with a law concerning the bringing of offerings to the altar; but contrary to Exodus, Deuteronomy 12 apparently envisions a single, central sanctuary for all Israel. This notion has a counterpart in ch. 13, which insists on the exclusive worship of Yahweh as Israel's sole deity. Chapter 13 also introduces the notion of Israel as a nation entirely consecrated to Yahweh, which is illustrated in Deut. 14:1–21 by the enumeration of unclean animals not to be eaten by the people (compare with Leviticus 11). There follows in 14:22–16:17 a series of instructions concerning the calendar and cultic events: the tithe, the release of slaves every seventh year, the consecration of every first-born and the three pilgrimage festivals in the year. The next section details rules for the main offices in Israel (Deut. 16:18–18:22): town and central-sanctuary judges, king, priests and Levites, and prophet. The last office is the only one directly assigned to Moses and clearly appears to be the most significant one.

Chapters 19–25 contain diverse civil laws, some of which are particularly concerned with protecting fringe groups within the population such as widows, orphans or resident aliens. Most prominent among the laws in Deuteronomy 19–25 are instructions for cities of refuge (ch. 19; see also Numbers 35), for Israel's wars (20; 21:10–14; 23:10–15; 24:5), for deciding the social status of abused or divorced women (22:13–29 and 24:1–4), and for fair social and economic relationships (23:20–21; 23:6–7, 10–15; 25:1–3, 11–16). Chapter 26 concludes the collection by prescribing an annual offering of first fruits at the central sanctuary, accompanied by a recitation of the exodus tradition.

The recitation of blessings and curses on Mt Ebal and Mt Gerizim in Deuteronomy 27–28 is followed by a final recapitulation of past events in the context of a covenant ceremony in the plains of Moab (ch. 29). In the last part of his speech (ch. 30), Moses already predicts the people's disobedience that will lead to the exile, as well as the possibility of a change of heart and a return from exile. Deuteronomy 31 takes up the narrative of Num. 27:12–23: it retells Joshua's appointment to be Moses' successor; in addition, however, the episode expands on the theme of the writing down of the Law by Moses and its regular recitation in Israel. Moses' psalm in Deuteronomy 32 announces in several ways the forthcoming story of exile and deliverance as related in the Former and Latter Prophets. After a final blessing of the twelve tribes that parallels Jacob's blessing (Genesis 49), Deuteronomy concludes with a report of Moses' death. He views the Promised Land but is nevertheless buried outside of it by Yahweh himself (Deuteronomy 34).

2. Internal Indications for the Existence of a Pentateuch

The literature of the Second Temple documents several references to a 'book of the Torah of Moses', *sefer torat mosheh* (Josh. 8:31; 23:6; 2 Kgs 14:6//2 Chron. 25:4; Neh. 8:1; 2 Chron. 34:14) or simply to a 'Torah of Moses', *torat mosheh* (Josh. 8:32; 1 Kgs 2:3; 2 Kgs 21:8; 23:25; Mal. 3:22 [Eng. 4:4]; Dan. 9:11, 13; Ezra 3:2; 7:6; Neh. 8:14; 2 Chron. 23:18; 30:16). However, it should not merely be assumed that such expressions always refer to the Pentateuch. Initially, *sefer torat mosheh* or *torat mosheh* apparently referred only to the Book of Deuteronomy. This is clear, for instance, in 2 Kgs 14:6, where *sefer torat mosheh* introduces a quotation from Deut. 24:16; a reference to Deuteronomy is also apparently intended in Josh. 23:16 and 2 Kgs 23:25. In most instances, however, *torat mosheh* designates other books along with Deuteronomy. Thus, the 'book of the Torah of Moses' from which Nehemiah reads in Nehemiah 8 comprises an instruction for celebrating the Feast of Booths that is clearly derived from Leviticus (see Lev. 23:33–43). However, it is often difficult to tell what precisely the extent of this larger Torah was and whether it already comprised the five books as we have them. Nevertheless, there are some indications in the Hebrew Bible of the delineation of the Torah as a discrete collection of five books.

i. Deuteronomy 34, Joshua 1 and the Editorial Closure of the Pentateuch
An initial indication of the existence of an editorial division between the first five books of the Hebrew Bible and the ensuing ones can be found in the last chapter of Deuteronomy. Deuteronomy 34 recounts the death of Moses; the chapter ends with a final commentary on Moses in vv 10–12:

> 10 And never again did there arise in Israel a prophet like Moses, whom Yahweh knew face to face. 11 In all the signs and the wonders that Yahweh sent him to do in the land of Egypt to Pharaoh, and to all his servants, and to all his land, 12 and in all that mighty hand, and in all the great terror that Moses did in the sight of all Israel.

These verses form a summary of the Moses account contained in Exodus to Deuteronomy. While vv 11–12 place special emphasis on his role in the exodus, v. 10 highlights the unique function assigned to Moses as the mediator of God's will.

The statement that 'never again did there arise in Israel a prophet like Moses' has special significance at the end of Deuteronomy: it implies that, from the viewpoint of the pentateuchal editors, Moses' death ends a *specific period* in the history of Yahweh's revelation to Israel. The scribe who composed this passage does not deny there will be further prophets and further revelations in the era following Moses' death, but he clearly implies such revelations no longer have the importance and the significance of the revelation made to Moses, whose status as prophetic mediator remains unsurpassable. Such a statement demonstrates that the separation between the first five books and the ensuing ones is not arbitrary but was deliberately devised by the editors of the Pentateuch. In Deut. 34:10, Moses' death is identified with the closure of a specific body of divinely revealed instructions. This only makes sense if the books related to Moses were conceived as having extra authority inside the community in which they were transmitted. As will be shown in the section on 'Torah', there are other passages in the Pentateuch, such as Exod. 33:7–11 and Numbers 12, which develop a similar conception of Moses' exclusive authority.

This division between the Pentateuch and the following books is further acknowledged in the Book of Joshua, the first book of the Prophets. Joshua 1 opens with the following admonition by Yahweh to Joshua:

> 7 Only be strong and very courageous, being careful to act in accordance with all [the Torah—missing in the Greek] that my servant Moses commanded you; do not turn from it to the right hand or to the left, so that you may be successful wherever you go. 8 This book of the Torah shall not depart out of your mouth; you shall meditate on it day and night, so that you may be careful to act in accordance with all that is written in it. For then you shall make your way prosperous, and then you shall be successful.

In the present form of Joshua 1, the 'book of the Torah' in v. 8 refers to the entire Pentateuch. As in Deut. 34:10–12, Torah is here clearly conceived as a revelation that closed with Moses' death; therefore, Joshua and the ensuing books logically belong to a different collection. In v. 7 observance of the Torah in the Massoretic text is the very condition for the conquest and occupation of the land, which is related in the remainder of the book. Verse 8 is even more general and presents obedience to the Torah as a necessary condition for successful living. By highlighting the authority of the Torah of Moses in defining how one should live one's life, this verse operates as the introduction not only to the Book of Joshua but to the entire collection of the Prophets.

Significantly, the same phenomenon occurs in Psalm 1, which closely parallels Josh. 1:8:

> 1 Happy are those
> who do not follow the advice of the wicked...
> 2 but their delight is in the Torah of Yahweh,
> and on his Torah they meditate day and night.

As in Josh. 1:8, daily meditation on the Torah is the condition for success and happiness; like the Prophets, the Psalms (or perhaps even the Writings as a whole) are related to the Pentateuch in such a way that they cannot be read apart from the first five books. As for the Prophets, this device only makes sense if the Psalms (or the Writings) and the Torah are considered two separate collections.

ii. Internal Divisions of the Pentateuch as a Clue to Its Editorial Organization

Another indication that the Pentateuch is to be seen as a discrete collection within the Hebrew Bible can be found in the notices that open and close the first five books, which appear to reflect some form of editorial arrangement of these books (see especially Ben Zvi 1992 and Mathys 2002). For instance, the middle book of the Torah, the Book of Leviticus, is framed by two notices referring to the revelation made to Moses at Mt Sinai: Lev. 1:1 (MT): 'And he (Yahweh) called Moses from inside the tent of meeting and spoke to Moses' and Lev. 27:34: 'These are the commandments Yahweh commanded to Moses for the Israelites at Mt Sinai.' Leviticus is thus 'book-ended' by these two notices, and with Leviticus 27, the revelation made to Moses at Mt Sinai has come to an end. The revelations that take place in Numbers are no longer located at *Mount* Sinai but in the '*wilderness* of Sinai' (*bemidbar sinay*), in the opening notice of Num. 1:1: 'Yahweh spoke to Moses in the *wilderness* of Sinai, inside the tent of meeting.' Although the reference in this passage to the 'tent of meeting' as the place for divine revelations connects Numbers 1 with Leviticus, the shift in the location marks a neat contrast. The reference to the 'wilderness of Sinai' in Num. 1:1 aptly introduces the general theme of the book to be Israel's wanderings in the wilderness, but it may also suggest, simultaneously, a distinction between the divine instructions revealed in Numbers and those of Leviticus.

The Book of Numbers closes in 36:13 with a notice that parallels Lev. 27:34 but functions at the same time as a reminder of the journey accomplished in Numbers by the Israelites, from Mt Sinai to the plains of Moab. Numbers 36:13: 'These are the commandments and the statutes that Yahweh commanded by the hand of Moses to the Israelites, *in the plains of Moab by the Jordan, near Jericho.*' Moreover, the concluding notice of the Book of Numbers offers a calculated transition to the Book of Deuteronomy. The latter opens with a notice similar to the one in Num. 36:13, in which Moses' 'words' (*devarim*) have now replaced Yahweh's 'commandments' (*mitsvot*). Deuteronomy 1:1: 'These are the *words* Moses spoke to all Israel beyond the Jordan in the wilderness.' The shift from Yahweh's commandments in Num. 36:13 to Moses' words encapsulates the main distinction between Deuteronomy and the previous books, since Deuteronomy is presented as being entirely *proclaimed* by Moses in the plains of Moab (see Deut. 1:5).

Lastly, a similar device can be observed in Genesis and Exodus. Genesis concludes with the death and burial notice of Joseph (Gen. 50:26); since Joseph is the last patriarch, this notice equates the closure of Genesis with the closure of the era of Israel's ancestors. By contrast, Exod. 1:1–5 recapitulates the names of the sons of Jacob who went to Egypt, summing up the list already found in Gen. 46:8–27. This recapitulation serves to contrast the generation of the exodus with the *last* generation of Genesis, as is made clear in the verses immediately following (vv 6–7). It thereby identifies the transition from Genesis to Exodus with a shift in *generation*. In addition, the enumeration in Exod. 1:1–5 is concluded in v. 6 with a notice picking up on the previous notice of Joseph's death that ends the Book of Genesis in 50:26.

In short, the introductory and concluding verses of Leviticus, Numbers and Deuteronomy function very much like editorial superscriptions and subscriptions, emphasizing the distinctive character of each book while at the same time connecting one book to the next. In addition, the connection between the introduction of a book and the conclusion of the previous one (see Num. 1:1 and Lev. 27:34; Deut. 1:1 and Num. 36:13; or Exod. 1:1–6 and Gen. 50:26) recalls the technique of 'catch-lines' in the literature of ancient Near East, in which the *last* line of a tablet is repeated *verbatim* on the next one.

The presence of super- and sub-scripts in Genesis, Exodus, Leviticus, Numbers and Deuteronomy strongly suggests that the divisions among the first five books of the Hebrew Bible were neither arbitrary nor accidental, even though this view is still frequently held by biblical scholars (see, for example, Van Seters 1999). If the division into five scrolls had been for merely practical or technical reasons, we would not have expected the variation in scroll length that exists. Genesis is twice as long as the Book of Leviticus, for example. The division appears to reflect instead the specific understanding the pentateuchal editors had of the coherence and topical unity of each of those books, as well as their distinctive contribution to the overall logic of the Pentateuch as a whole.

iii. Summaries of the Pentateuchal Narratives in the Psalms and Other Books

Apart from the Pentateuch itself, there are various references to the pentateuchal narrative in so-called 'historical summaries' that occur in the Psalms and some other books. Some psalms mention selected episodes that have an exemplary, didactic function. While a few psalms refer to episodes found in the books of Judges (Psalm 83) or Samuel (e.g. Psalm 89), most only mention episodes narrated in the Pentateuch (see, e.g., Psalms 95, 114 or 81; compare also various poetic texts outside the Book of Psalms such as Isa. 63:11–14; Mic. 6:4–5).

Several psalms apparently seek to summarize the history of Israel's origins (Psalms 105, 106, 135, 136); in such summaries, detailed attention is paid to major episodes in the Pentateuch, whereas events such as the conquest are noted in very general terms. Note, for instance, that contrary to Moses or even Aaron, Joshua is never mentioned in the Psalms or in any historical summaries of the Hebrew Bible. In Psalm 105, the summary of the Pentateuch almost takes the entire psalm, which is framed in vv 6 and 42 with references to the patriarch Abraham; only two verses at the very end of the psalm briefly mention life in the land. The same arrangement is used in other texts, such as Ezek. 20:1–31 or Nehemiah's prayer in Nehemiah 9. In both instances, the narrative traditions of the Pentateuch take precedence over and are treated differently than other traditions in the Hebrew Bible. This clearly suggests that the Pentateuch, as Moses' Torah, was consistently perceived as a discrete collection, with a unique authoritative status.

3. External Evidence for the Dating of the Pentateuch

The dating of ancient literary documents is far from a straightforward operation. First, we must acknowledge that documents are often built upon earlier compositions and second, once the document has acquired its overall shape, it may still undergo considerable modification. The Pentateuch has almost certainly developed in this way, so that its literary history stretches over several centuries. To speak meaningfully of 'dating the Pentateuch', then, we must exclude its source material (to which we have no direct access in any event), ignore any late minor alterations, and focus on a particular stage of development: the congealing of the text into scrolls and the creation of a sequence of five forming a literary unit in the sense of offering a continuous narrative from the creation of the world to the verge of Israel's occupation of the land of Canaan. It is unwise to assume in advance how much earlier the individual scrolls existed prior to the creation of the Pentateuch as a whole; nevertheless, we shall attempt to tackle this question, primarily in terms of the evidence provided by the individual books.

It is therefore essential to distinguish between the criteria for dating individual elements or groups of elements within the Pentateuch—such as the law code of Deuteronomy (chs 12–26), the 'Book of the Covenant' in Exod. 20:22–23:33 or the 'Holiness Code' in Leviticus 17–26—and the Pentateuch itself, as a whole. In addition, it is much easier to formulate criteria for the *terminus ad quem*, the latest possible date, from the *terminus a quo*, the earliest possible date, since both the Pentateuch and its components might conceivably contain quite ancient elements. But until these individual compositions appear as part of one of the pentateuchal scrolls, their antiquity counts for very little.

A very good example of this problem is the silver amulets in the form of scrolls, discovered in 1979 just above the Hinnom valley. They contain a text very similar to the priestly blessing in Num. 6:24–26 and are dated to the seventh century (Barkay 1992). But, as Ada Yardeni, who first deciphered the text, says: 'they cannot prove that the blessing was already incorporated into the Pentateuch in the early 6th century BCE. They also cannot prove the existence of a written Pentateuch in the pre-exilic period' (1991: 181).

Likewise, to take a more extreme example, we cannot date the Genesis story of the Flood to 2,000 BCE, when we have the earliest (and quite similar) Mesopotamian accounts. It has sometimes been suggested that literary and other cultural parallels between biblical and non-biblical texts can help establish dates for the biblical sources. However, the influence of Mesopotamian law codes on the 'Book of the Covenant' does not prove the antiquity of the Book of Exodus, since such texts continued to be copied, not just in Akkadian but also in Aramaic translation, well into the Greco-Roman period (333 BCE– 476 CE).

The geopolitical worldview implied in the 'Table of Nations' in Genesis 10, the text from Deir 'Alla that mentions the seer Balaam (Hackett 1984), and the Neo-Assyrian vassal treaty formula that seems to have influenced the structure and language of Deuteronomy (McCarthy 1981) have likewise been used to establish dates for the biblical texts they have influenced. But we must remember two things: first, we cannot deduce the date of a literary text from the probable age of its individual components. Second, while external parallels may provide an earliest possible date, the latest possible date also has to be determined, or else the exercise is futile. Many defenders of the antiquity of biblical texts fail to understand this principle. It is obvious—or should be—that while a later text can use sources from an earlier period, an early text cannot use sources from a later period! Thus, it is the date of the latest rather than the earliest elements in a text that provide a more telling indication for dating the work as a whole.

This being so, it is better not to begin with the earliest possible date, but to work backwards. We can then begin with the most certain date, the time at which the Pentateuch *must* have existed, and end with the less certain: when it *might* have existed. Let us begin with the most direct material evidence. Our earliest biblical manuscripts come from Qumran and have been dated between the second century BCE and the first century CE. These constitute our *terminus ad quem*. Now, there is no surviving Hebrew manuscript among these Dead Sea Scrolls that contains the entire Pentateuch, but it is possible that some of the fragments from this site belonged to such a manuscript: four manuscripts contain, respectively, parts of Genesis and Exodus (4Q1, 4Q11), Exodus and Leviticus (4Q17), and Leviticus and Numbers (4Q23). The so-called 'Halakhic Letter' (4QMMT) also refers to the 'book [=scroll] of Moses' alongside the 'books [scrolls] of the prophets and David'. This might well be a reference to the Pentateuch as a single scroll.

Other clues to the recognition of a unified Pentateuch (though not necessarily as a single scroll) are offered in the Temple Scroll, which, among other things, synthesizes laws from Deuteronomy, Leviticus and Numbers. There is also a text knows as 'Rewritten (or 'Reworked') Pentateuch' that includes material from Genesis, Exodus and Leviticus. As for individual pentateuchal scrolls, there are 15 of Genesis, 17 of Exodus, 13 of Leviticus, 8 of Numbers and 29 of Deuteronomy. Although we do not know what proportion of the entire archive has survived, the proportion of pentateuchal manuscripts is high: only Isaiah (21) and Psalms (36) attain totals in double figures. The first-century BCE Book of Jubilees (copies were found at Qumran), the Genesis Apocryphon (first century CE?) and a 'Genesis Commentary' (4Q252) all suggest a particular interest in the Book of Genesis (VanderKam 1994: 29–33, 121–34).

There is also clear testimony to the existence of the Pentateuch in the *Letter of Aristeas*, which claims to describe its translation into Hebrew under Pharaoh Ptolemy, probably Philadelphus, who reigned from 281–246 BCE. The account is legendary and is generally dated to a century later than the events it describes. At the time of its writing, a Pentateuch must have existed—though this conclusion takes us no further back than the Qumran manuscripts, even if it adds a little more evidence. The earliest Greek translation of the Pentateuch is impossible to date more precisely than this, however. While many scholars regard Aristeas' story as substantially correct, our extant Greek translations do not necessarily reflect the translation to which he refers.

The books of Maccabees, in the Apocrypha, provide further evidence. 1 Maccabees, dating from the beginning of the first century BCE, makes several references to the 'law' and 1:57 mentions a 'book of the covenant', though whether this denotes a Pentateuch or the Book of Deuteronomy we cannot say. But 3:4 refers to a 'book of the law', and the possibility, as at Qumran, that the Pentateuch is referred to here in the form of a single 'scroll' is a strong one. 2 Maccabees, from later in the first century BCE, contains a single reference to the 'law and the prophets', indicating the Pentateuch was a recognizable element of the Jewish Scriptures distinguished from the prophetic books (Joshua–Malachi).

Now we come to the interesting problem of the Samaritan Pentateuch. While this differs in a few respects from the biblical version, it has substantially the same contents, and its existence raises crucial questions about the origin of the Samaritans as well as the date of the Pentateuch. The Samaritan tradition sees its own origins deriving from Moses and Joshua and accuses the Judeans as having broken away from the larger group by founding the sanctuary at Shiloh; the Judean ('biblical') view regards the later population of Samaria as descended from the half-pagan and half-Yahwistic society of foreigners transplanted after the fall of the kingdom of Israel (1 Kings 17). Thus, not surprisingly, each tradition dismisses the other as illegitimate.

When did the two communities separate? Josephus, writing at the end of the first century CE, says a schism developed when some rebel Jerusalemite priests established a sanctuary on Mt Gerizim (near Shechem) in the time of Alexander the Great (d. 323 BCE). His chronology may be motivated more by ideological considerations than historical accuracy, however, since he claims that the occasion for the establishment of the new sanctuary was the marriage of a daughter of Sanballat, apparently the opponent of Nehemiah (see Nehemiah 2, 4 and 6). The Book of Nehemiah, which places its hero in the second half of the fifth century BCE, seems to assume that a Judean–Samaritan schism already had developed at this earlier date, but the sharing of the Pentateuch by both groups must point to a previously shared religious tradition. Research has established the likelihood that the Samaritan community did not break with the Judeans until the second century BCE. Ben Sira, a Jerusalemite writing at the beginning of the second century BCE, in describing the population of Palestine in his time, refers to 'those who live in Seir, and the Philistines, and the foolish people who live in Shechem' (50:26); the last reference denotes the Samaritans. Half a century later, the Judean king Hyrcanus destroyed the Gerizim temple (and Shechem) and commenced a policy of Judaizing Palestine. This definitive schism also provides us with a date before which the Pentateuch must have existed in substantially its present form.

Perhaps the work of Ben Sira, written somewhere around 180 BCE, is the closest we can come to the earliest date for the existence of the Pentateuch. Ben Sira refers to the 'book of the covenant of the Most High God, the law that Moses commanded us' (24:23), which could denote the Pentateuch but could equally designate the Book of Deuteronomy. In any case, he certainly is aware of the entire pentateuchal narrative, since he rehearses its contents in a grand review of the history of his people (chs 44–49). He starts with Enoch (4:16), then says a little about Noah, Abraham, Isaac, Jacob, Moses, Aaron and Phinehas before continuing with Joshua and Caleb and other later figures.

At the end, having finished his retrospective summary with Nehemiah, rather curiously, he adds by way of an epilogue Enoch, Joseph, Shem, Seth and Adam—of whom only Enoch had previously been mentioned. Of Adam he says, 'above every other creature was Adam' (49:16). The double mention of Enoch as an outstanding figure (44:16; 49:14) and of Adam as a glorious figure suggest traditions concerning each that are well known in Ben Sira's day but in forms that existed outside and beyond the Pentateuch (e.g. at Qumran). By contrast, all he says of Joseph is 'his bones were also cared for'. Although perhaps not too much should be made of this observation, this might imply that at the time of Ben Sira, the Joseph traditions were still more fluid than other pentateuchal traditions.

We can now continue our track backwards to the Greek writers of the third century. The first Jewish historian writing in Greek, Demetrios the Chronographer, already makes use of the Greek translation of the Book of Genesis in his treatise on Judean kings (ca. 220–210 BCE), of which some fragments have survived in the works of Eusebius and Clement of Alexandria (see Holladay 1983: 51–91). This shows beyond question that at the end of the third century some portions of the Pentateuch had been translated into Greek and were authoritative for the diaspora communities.

Two non-Jewish authors, Hecataeus of Abdera (ca. 300 BCE) and Manetho (mid-third century BCE), both writing in Greek, have left accounts of an exodus of Judeans, neither of which matches the biblical version exactly (for text, translation and commentary, see Stern 1976).

Josephus (*Against Apion* I.73–105, written at the very end of the first century CE) quotes Manetho about an ancient invasion of Egypt by a people called 'Hyksos', understood by him to be the Egyptian term for 'shepherds', who occupied Egypt for 511 years. They were eventually driven from most of the land but maintained a foothold in the area called Avaris. Unsuccessful in capturing this stronghold, the Egyptian king Thummosis came to an agreement with them that resulted in the departure of 240,000 for Syria. They built a city 'in that country that is now called Judea...and called it Jerusalem'.

A second excerpt (*Against Apion* I.228–52) concerns a king Amenophis who, well after the 'shepherds' had been driven out, wished to rid his country of lepers and other diseased persons, 80,000 of whom were sent east of the Nile to work in quarries. Some leprous priests were sent to the old Hyksos capital of Avaris, and these appointed a ruler for themselves called Osarsiph, a priest of Heliopolis, who made them foreswear the Egyptian gods and follow new laws. Osarsiph then wrote to the 'shepherds' in Jerusalem, whose ancestors had been expelled in the earlier episode, and invited them to assist him in a war against Amenophis. Subsequently, the Jerusalemites invaded Egypt, behaving cruelly. Osarsiph, once he had joined the Jerusalemites, came to be known as Moses. Amenophis, having returned from Ethiopia, then drove the shepherds and the lepers back to Syria.

Hecataeus' account is preserved in the work of the first-century BCE writer Diodorus of Sicily (*Bibliotheca Historica* 40.3); another excerpt from his book, 'written entirely about the Jews', is quoted by Josephus, but its authenticity remains disputed. Like the pentateuchal narrative, Hecataeus knows only one story of Judeans leaving Egypt. A pestilence in Egypt at some time (Hecataeus gives no chronological clues) prompted the inhabitants to expel certain strangers who practiced alien rites; of these deportees, some landed in Greece but the larger number went to Judea, which was then uninhabited. They settled under the leadership of Moses, who founded several cities, including Jerusalem, where he established a temple. He also set up 'forms of worship and ritual', laws and political institutions. He divided the people into twelve tribes, forbade images to be made of their sole deity, and appointed priests, who were to be not only in charge of the cult but also political leaders and judges. 'The Jews have never had a king and authority over the people is regularly vested in whichever priest is regarded as superior to his colleagues in wisdom and virtue. They call this man the high priest' (Hecataeus of Abdera, according to Diodorus Siculus, *Bibliotheca Historica* 40.3, quoted in Stern 1976: 28). Moses also instituted a military education and led the people to conquests against neighbouring tribes, after which he apportioned the land equally but reserved larger portions for the priests. The sale of land was forbidden, so as to avoid oppression of the poor by the rich through the accumulation of land. The people were also enjoined to reproduce. Their marriage and burial customs differed from those of others, though their traditional practices were amended under the Persians and Macedonians. The Judeans' laws claim to have been words heard by Moses from God.

It is unclear what we can deduce from these accounts about the state of the pentateuchal text. Both writers know of Moses and hold that the Judeans were once in Egypt and escaped or were expelled. But if either was basing his account even partly on Jewish sources, we cannot assume that the Pentateuch, let alone Joshua–Kings, necessarily existed in its present form at this time and that the Greek-Egyptian writers distorted it. Although Manetho seems to have had an anti-Jewish bias, the same is not true of Hecataeus. It is possible that the exodus story was not yet fixed into a definitive Jewish version when both wrote.

The external evidence then, points to the end of the third century BCE as the latest certain date for the composition of the Pentateuch as a literary unit; prior to that, some of its main components were still evolving. This coheres well with the suggestions we can make on other grounds that the historical horizons in which it was formed cover the fourth–third centuries BCE. So now we can turn to the internal evidence.

4. Internal Evidence for the Dating of the Pentateuch

Dating the Pentateuch on the basis of internal evidence found in other canonical texts is always a difficult undertaking because of the degree of circularity involved; the dating of these other texts is relative and not absolute. Nonetheless, both the Pentateuch and other biblical texts can offer a significant amount of information, and this evidence cannot be simply dismissed. Although the internal evidence is multiple and complex, it is possible to work our way backward to some significant conclusions.

Within the Pentateuch itself, two texts in particular presuppose not only the Babylonian exile but also the perspective of a return from exile. Leviticus 26 ends with a statement promising return from exile; even more pointedly, Deuteronomy 30 describes in some detail a gathering of the diaspora by Yahweh himself: '4 Even if you are exiled to the ends of the world, from there Yahweh your God will gather you and from there he will bring you back. 5 Yahweh your God will bring you into the land that your ancestors possessed, and you will possess it; he will make you more prosperous and numerous than your ancestors' (Deut. 30:4–5). From such texts it is obvious that the final composition of the Pentateuch presumes the end of the Babylonian exile and cannot have taken place before the Persian period. A Persian period dating for the Pentateuch is also obvious from a range of passages that appear to refer to historical realities that are not earlier than the Neo-Babylonian or Persian periods. For instance, the name 'Kasdim', appearing in 'Ur Kasdim' ('Ur of the Chaldeans') in Gen. 11:28 and 31 (see also Gen. 15:7) is not attested before the Neo-Babylonian period. In Gen. 24:3, 7 reference to Yahweh as the 'god of heavens' (*'elohe ha-shamayim*) occurs otherwise exclusively in compositions of the Persian period or later (see Ezra 1:2; Neh. 1:5; 2:4, 20 and 2 Chron. 36:23). Other texts appear to refer to social and cultural realities of the Persian period. A text such as Genesis 10, which depicts the peaceful distribution by the deity of every nation on earth according to its language and to its ethnic origins, is clearly reminiscent of inscriptions from the time of Darius I. On the other hand, it is noteworthy that, contrary to what applies to the Prophets and—especially—to the Writings, there are very few clear references to the Hellenistic time in the Torah itself. The only major exception is the last oracle by Balaam in Num. 24:15–24, which mentions the coming of ships from Kittim (24:24), most likely an allusion to Greek invasions from the time of Alexander the Great (the end of the fourth century BCE) onwards.

In biblical books outside the Pentateuch there are also several indications suggesting that the Torah was composed and promulgated towards the end of the Persian period. Of particular interest in this respect are the books of Ezra, Nehemiah and Chronicles. According to Nehemiah 8, the public reading of the 'Book of the Law of God' (*sefer torat elohim*), which presumably is identical with the *sefer torat mosheh* mentioned at the onset of the account in 8:1, is said to extend over seven successive days (Neh. 8:18). The instruction to read the Torah of Moses in the seventh month, during the Feast of Booths, corresponds to Deut. 31:9–13, but the obligation to build booths (*sukkot*) for the people to reside in during the duration of the festival is not found in Deuteronomy, but in Leviticus (Lev. 23:39–43). Likewise, the conclusion of the seven-day festival with a closing ceremony on the eighth day (Neh. 8:17) derives from Lev. 23:33–36, whereas the indication of the 'great joy' of the people has no parallel in Leviticus but is a recurring motif in the festival legislation of Deuteronomy 16. Thus, there can be little doubt that the Torah read in Nehemiah 8 is already a comprehensive document encompassing the major legal traditions of the Pentateuch. This conclusion is also fully in keeping with the duration of the reading itself, that is, seven days, which appears to imply a fairly long document. In the Book of Ezra as well, it is apparent that the legal traditions referred to comprise both Deuteronomy, on one hand, and Leviticus–Numbers on the other (compare, e.g., Ezra 9:11 and Leviticus 18).

The Book of Chronicles offers more indirect, but no less significant evidence for the closing of the Pentateuch in the Persian period. The genealogies in 1 Chronicles 1–9 are based on the genealogies found in Genesis 1–9. Although there are many interesting differences, it appears that the author of 1 Chronicles 1–9 knows the Genesis genealogies in a form that is not much different from the canonical text of Genesis 1–11 (compare, for example, Knoppers 2003: 285–87 regarding 1 Chron. 1:1–2:2).

Furthermore, the dependence of Chronicles upon the Pentateuch is not restricted to the Genesis genealogies but includes numerous other passages. For example, the Chronicler's account of Solomon's inauguration of the temple in 2 Chronicles 5 is a retelling of the parallel account in 1 Kings 8 that expands the Kings story by introducing a range of references to the wilderness sanctuary as described in Exodus and Leviticus. 2 Chronicles 30 relates the celebration of Passover by King Hezekiah in the second month of the year because of the priests' incapacity to celebrate it in the first month; this practice is actually derived from Num. 9:1–14, a legislation according to which men unable to celebrate Passover at the appropriate time are allowed to postpone the celebration until the second month. There is general consensus today that Chronicles is to be dated in the fourth century BCE (see, e.g., Knoppers 2003: 101–17 and the summary on 116–17); the same likely applies for the first composition of Ezra and Nehemiah, although the textual history of Ezra, in particular, is significantly more complex.

All this means, therefore, that towards the end of the fourth century BCE a first version of the Pentateuch was not only available but that it had established itself as an authoritative document. In this regard, the results obtained by scrutinizing internal evidence for the dating of the Pentateuch are fully in keeping with the overall view achieved in the previous discussion on the external evidence.

5. The History of the Discussion

The question of the authorship and historical location of the Pentateuch already began with the Rabbinic observation that it is difficult to conceive that Moses could have written the report of his own death. They claimed, therefore, that Joshua completed the Pentateuch after the death of his tutor (Babylonian Talmud, *Baba Bathra* 14b). With this proposal, they invented the idea of diachronic investigation. Nevertheless, until the seventeenth century, the main idea held in churches, synagogues and universities was that Moses had written the entire Pentateuch. Ironically, the inventor of source criticism, the French physician J. Astruc (1684–1766), intended it to buttress the traditional view of Mosaic authorship of the Torah. He was aware, as were many others of his time, of the contradictions and differences in style and vocabulary and wished to demonstrate that these arose from two main documents (memoirs A and B) as well as from other fragments that Moses himself compiled when composing the Pentateuch. At the same time and independently, the German scholar H. Witter developed a similar hypothesis in 1711.

An important step was taken when, in 1805, W. M. de Wette argued that the Book of Deuteronomy should be identified with the law book whose discovery is described in the narrative in 2 Kings 22–23. Building on this hypothesis, he proposed that the first edition of Deuteronomy was written at the end of the seventh century BCE in order to legitimate the political and religious reforms of King Josiah's counsellors, who wanted to establish the temple of Jerusalem as the sole sanctuary in Judah. This deduction then became the point of reference that allowed other texts of the Pentateuch to be assigned before or after the 'cult centralization'.

The isolation of Deuteronomy as a document originally independent of the remainder of the Torah was a major step in the elaboration of the so-called 'Documentary Hypothesis'. The presence of different divine names in the Torah had already been used as a major criterion to distinguish underlying sources, which led to the identification of a 'Yahwistic' (J) source written by the Yahwist, who preferred the divine name Yahweh, and an 'Elohistic' (E) source written by the Elohist, who favoured the more generic term *elohim* (God, divinity) to describe the one deity. The classical documentary hypothesis as put forward by A. Kuenen (1828–1891), K. Graf and finally J. Wellhausen (1844–1918) considered J (the Yahwist) and E (the Elohist) to emanate from the early monarchic period, D (Deuteronomy) from the seventh century, and P (the Priestly document) from the end of the Babylonian period (586–538

BCE) or to the beginning of the Persian period (538–333 BCE; for the early history, see the summary in Nicholson 1998).

For Wellhausen, this scheme not only provided a plausible reconstruction of the formation of the Pentateuch but also allowed Israelite religion to be assigned to three major evolutionary stages (Wellhausen 1927). First, during the monarchy, it was related to agricultural needs, there was no priestly hierarchy and a number of independent local sanctuaries were in use (J/E). With the reform of Josiah, the cult was centralized in Jerusalem, the rituals 'historicized' (the Passover, for example, becoming a commemoration of the exodus) and controlled by the Jerusalemite court (D). Finally, during and after the Babylonian period, the priestly class took power and created a ritualized and legalized religion (P). Although this theory reflected the anti-clerical and even anti-Jewish ideology of Protestant liberalism, regarding the evolution of Israelite religion in terms of increasing ritualism and decadence, Wellhausen's intuition that until the Babylonian exile no 'Judaism' existed, only 'Israelite paganism', was basically correct. This insight was subsequently lost and has only been rediscovered in the last few decades.

Wellhausen, with others, introduced another major change in biblical research by postulating that the documentary sources extended beyond the Pentateuch: J/E and P can also be found in the Book of Joshua. As a result, the idea of the Pentateuch as an original, self-contained narrative unit gave way to a Hexateuch instead (i.e. six books running from Genesis to Joshua). Several scholars have since worked with this model; in addition to the source-critical arguments, it has been suggested that an account of Israel's origins would surely have concluded with the conquest of the land.

The underlying idea of the Documentary Hypothesis is that the basic narrative structure of the Pentateuch (or Hexateuch) has been present from the very beginning; the oldest documents (J/E) already contained the entire narrative strand from the origins (Genesis 2) to the eve of the conquest of the land or even the conquest itself (Joshua 24). But M. Noth's highly influential pentateuchal research has challenged this model: since the mid-twentieth century, his two classic traditio-critical analyses of the Pentateuch (Noth 1948) and the Former Prophets (Noth 1943) have been widely accepted and built upon by others in their research. According to Noth, the original 'pentateuchal' complex was contained in the present Tetrateuch (Genesis–Numbers), while an earlier form of the Book of Deuteronomy served as an introduction to a separate 'Deuteronomistic History' comprising Joshua–Kings. In Noth's view, Deuteronomy 1–3 not only opens the Book of Deuteronomy, but a much longer historiographic narrative that ends with the downfall of Jerusalem and the Babylonian exile in 2 Kings 24–25. Only later, during the Persian period, was the Book of Deuteronomy attached to the Tetrateuch, forming a Mosaic corpus. The material in the final chapters of Deuteronomy (chs 32–34) now separated Deuteronomy from the scrolls that followed, leading to the division of the Jewish Scriptures between 'Torah', the five scrolls of Moses and 'Prophets', with Joshua– Kings finally designated as 'Former Prophets' in the Hebrew canon. The five books of Torah gained pre-eminence within Judaism, as is clearly the case in Rabbinic Judaism, but the concept of a Torah is also reflected in the Qumran manuscripts.

Gerhard von Rad was not convinced by Noth's Tetrateuch and agreed with Wellhausen that the original narrative extended through the end of the Hexateuch (von Rad 1938). In his analysis, the idea of a *Grundschrift* (base text) was abandoned and instead he credited the author of the J source, the Yahwist, with a great deal of originality. Von Rad described the Yahwist as an author, a theologian, and the architect of the Hexateuch, whose work reflects the intellectual climate of a 'Solomonic enlightenment'. According to von Rad, the core of his work was a traditional 'little credo', preserved in Deut. 26:5–9:

> 5 A wandering Aramean was my ancestor; he went down into Egypt and lived there as an alien, few in number, and there he became a great nation, mighty and populous. 6 When the Egyptians treated us harshly and afflicted us, by imposing hard labour on us, 7 we cried to Yahweh, the God of our ancestors; Yahweh heard our voice and saw our affliction, our toil, and our oppression. 8 Yahweh brought us out of Egypt with a mighty hand and an outstretched arm, with a terrifying display of power, and with signs and wonders; 9 and he brought us into this place and gave us this land, a land flowing with milk and honey.

On the basis of this 'credo', the Yahwist compiled the pentateuchal story by inserting the Sinai tradition between the exodus and the settlement and by prefacing his work with the addition of the primeval history. He also expanded it into a Hexateuch by what von Rad considered 'perhaps the most important factor of all', the 'integration of the patriarchal history as a whole with the idea of settlement' (1966: 60).

Since the 1970s the traditio-historical model has been challenged from several sides. J. Van Seters (1975), H. H. Schmid (1976) and others have demonstrated that the so-called Yahwist cannot be located at the court of Solomon (if such a king really ever existed); the Yahwistic texts, especially in Exodus and Numbers, seem very close ideologically to 'Deuteronomistic' texts in Deuteronomy and the Former Prophets, some of which likely stem from the seventh or sixth centuries BCE. Van Seters has pointed out that the social contexts described in the patriarchal narratives in Genesis seem to mirror those reflected in Neo-Assyrian and Neo-Babylonian juridical documents (1975). Schmid has shown that the story of Moses' call in Exodus 3, which traditionally was assigned to J and E, builds upon the call stories of Gideon (Judges 6), Jeremiah (Jeremiah 1) and Ezekiel (Ezekiel 2) and cannot be older than those texts (1976). The last two can confidently be dated to the sixth century BCE at the earliest since these prophets are presented as having delivered their oracles on the eve and at the time of the destruction of Jerusalem. The existence of the Elohistic source has become more and more dubious; however, belief in the Yahwistic source remains, though the Yahwist's writing context has been pushed much later, to the Babylonian period or to the beginning of the Persian period.

N. Whybray (1995) and more 'synchronically' oriented scholars have challenged the traditio-historical analysis entirely and posited instead that a single historian is responsible for the creation of the Pentateuch. Yet another process of formation has been put forward by R. Rendtorff (1990), E. Blum (1990) and others. They retain Noth's idea of a cluster of independent traditions but deny the existence of any larger, documentary sources.

In the context of this introduction we cannot present a detailed overview of the present state of the debate. It is nevertheless important to be familiar with the most important developments in pentateuchal research in the last 30 years, which can be summarized as follows.

(a) The 'oldest' literary source of the Pentateuch or Hexateuch, the 'Yahwist', has been redated to the seventh or sixth century BCE. For scholars like J. Blenkinsopp, J. Van Seters and many others, J presupposes the Deuteronomistic literature, which is traditionally assigned to the sixth century. 'J' should not be dated, then, earlier than the Neo-Babylonian period (ca. 605–538 BCE). This new context for the Yahwist, which is becoming more and more adopted in European continental scholarship, was developed primarily on the base of literary analysis. It derives further support from the fact that the historical basis for the entire pentateuchal (or even hexateuchal) complex is now in serious doubt: recent archaeological work seems to suggest definitively that Israel was created from local populations in Cisjordan in the twelfth century BCE onwards and that everything from the patriarchs to the conquest is, to put it very bluntly, fictional. Furthermore, the high culture of the Davidic-Solomonic period, to which von Rad assigned his Yahwist, is now evaporating; indeed, Judah now seems to have emerged as a social and political unit both independently and somewhat later than its northern neighbour Israel (for a succinct presentation, see Finkelstein and Silberman 2001).

(b) The 'Documentary Hypothesis' has been rejected. A growing number of scholars is no longer convinced by the idea of parallel documents and has returned to a 'Fragmentary Theory' (Dozeman and Schmid 2006). They stress the original independence of the traditions and believe that these were combined only at a late stage of the Pentateuch's composition. According to Rendtorff (1990) and Blum (2000), these independent traditions, which include origins, the patriarchs, Moses and the exodus, lawgiving and sojourn in the wilderness, were collected at the beginning of the Persian period by two groups: the Deuteronomistic (D) and the Priestly (P) schools. Following this model, which has gained support in Anglo-Saxon scholarship (see e.g. Carr 1996), the Pentateuch emerges from the combination of these traditions as a sort of compromise intended to provide an identity to nascent Judaism in the Persian period (Knoppers and Levinson 2004).

(c) There are two origin stories in the Pentateuch: the patriarchs and the exodus. The new model that regards the Pentateuch as a combination of 'D' and 'P' texts is problematic in regard to the Book of Genesis, a book that can hardly be considered as having been edited by Deuteronomistic scribes. The patriarchal narrative contains almost no Deuteronomistic stylistic markers or Deuteronomistic ideology (election, segregation, military land promises) and offers a very different account of Israel's origin and relation to the land than the exodus tradition. It promotes a genealogical identity that includes neighbours like Ammon, Moab, Edom and Ishmael, whereas the Moses tradition focuses on Israel's distinctiveness from all other nations, especially the 'nations of Canaan'. For two decades there has been a growing trend to consider the literary link between the patriarchs and the exodus as artificial and late (Schmid 2010). The possibility has been raised that 'P' was the first to conceive of the patriarchal history as a prologue to the Moses tradition. The combination of two independent and even contradictory origin myths could provide one of the most important clues for understanding the Pentateuch.

(d) The extent and character of the Priestly texts is still disputed. As we have seen, the classical documentary hypothesis treated P as a discrete document, on a par with the other pentateuchal sources (J, E and D). Other critics have proposed that P was not a document but the editor of the older sources comprising the Torah; in this case, P would need to be viewed as the actual 'author' of the Pentateuch. However, this hypothesis is generally unable to explain why the Priestly texts, especially in Genesis to Leviticus, not only have a distinct terminology but form a discrete narrative and were obviously intended to be read as a coherent and self-contained story. To give just one illustration of this, P's story of Jacob's departure for Aram starts in Gen. 26:34–35 with an account of Esau's 'foreign' wives, which is continued at the end of Genesis 27 (see 27:46 and 28:1–9); the non-Priestly account of Jacob's theft of Isaac's blessing and his flight to Laban in Gen. 27:1–45 has clearly been inserted in-between at the time of the editing of the Pentateuch, thus breaking the initial coherence of P's account. This example, among many others, clearly shows that P is unlikely to be the editor of the Pentateuch.

A further issue, however, concerns the initial ending of the Priestly document. After Leviticus, it becomes more difficult to follow the Priestly account. In Deuteronomy the texts traditionally assigned to P were so few that they amounted to little more than fragments. In Numbers, it has always been quite difficult to sort out the Priestly elements from the non-Priestly ones and even harder to reconstruct a coherent P narrative in that book. This has led several scholars to argue recently that the Priestly account initially ended either with the Book of Exodus or in the Book of Leviticus.

This new proposal would mean that the so-called 'Priestly' texts in the Book of Numbers would most likely be part of a later expansion of the Priestly document. 'P' should therefore be viewed not just as the creation of a single scribe but rather as a designation for the work of a distinct school in Jerusalem during the Persian period, which gradually enlarged and amplified an original document. At some time during the Persian period, probably in the late fifth or early fourth century BCE, that document was combined with other documents, such as Deuteronomy, to form the Torah. However, this raises the question of the extent of that Torah.

(e) Was the original narrative a Pentateuch or a Hexateuch? It remains a valid observation that some of the major pentateuchal themes reach their fulfilment only in the Book of Joshua. The theme of Joseph's bones that must be buried in his Ephraimite hometown (Gen. 50:21; Exod. 13:19 and Josh. 24:30) clearly presuppose a hexateuchal narrative, and Joshua's second farewell speech in Joshua 24, after his first in Joshua 23, clearly appears as the conclusion to a narrative that began at least with the patriarchs. It is also significant that in ch. 24, Joshua is portrayed as a new Moses, doing the same things Moses did before his death: he erects a memorial stone, concludes a covenant between Yahweh and the people, and writes 'all these words' in the 'book of the Law of God'.

These observations have led some scholars to argue there were two competing literary projects during the Persian period, which can be traced literarily via texts written by 'hexateuchal redactors' (Römer and Brettler 2000) and those from the hands of 'pentateuchal redactors' (Otto 2004; Achenbach 2007). Such a contested authoritative written tradition would make good sense, since the question of the possession of the land was a major issue in the Persian period. A Pentateuch would give quite a different answer than a Hexateuch to the status of the inheritance of the land for emerging Judaism.

Works Cited and Suggested Further Reading

Achenbach, Reinhard. 2007. 'The Pentateuch, the Prophets, and the Torah in the Fifth and Fourth Centuries B.C.E.' In Oded Lipschits, Gary N. Knoppers and Rainer Albertz (eds). *Judah and the Judeans in the Fourth Century B.C.E.* Winona Lake, IN: Eisenbrauns: 253–85.

Barkay, Gaby. 1992. 'The Priestly Benediction on the Silver Plaques from Ketef Hinnom in Jerusalem.' *Tel Aviv* 19: 139–92.

Ben Zvi, Ehud. 1992. 'The Closing Words of the Pentateuchal Books: A Clue for the Historical Status of the Book of Genesis within the Pentateuch.' *Biblische Notizen* 62: 7–10.

Blum, Erhard. 2000. *Studien zur Komposition des Pentateuch*. Beihefte zur Zeitschrift für die alttestamentliche Wissenschaft, 189; Berlin: De Gruyter.

— 2006 'The Literary Connection between the Books of Genesis and Exodus and the End of the Book of Joshua.' In Dozeman and Schmid: 89–106.

Carr, David M. 1996. *Reading the Fractures of Genesis*. Louisville: Westminster John Knox Press.

Dozeman, Thomas B., and Konrad Schmid (eds). 2006. *A Farewell to the Yahwist? The Composition of the Pentateuch in Recent European Interpretation*. Society of Biblical Literature Symposium Series, 34; Atlanta, GA: Society of Biblical Literature.

Finkelstein, Israel, and Neil Asher Silberman. 2001. *The Bible Unearthed: Archeology's New Vision of Ancient Israel and the Origin of Its Sacred Texts*. New York: Free Press.

Hackett, Jo Ann. 1984. *The Balaam Text from Deir 'Allā*. Harvard Semitic Monographs, 31; Chico, CA: Scholars Press.

Holladay, Carl R. 1983. *Fragments from Hellenistic Jewish Authors. I. Historians*. Texts and Translation, 20; Pseudepigraphica Series, 10; Chico, CA: Scholars Press.

Knoppers, Gary N., and Bernard M. Levinson (eds). 2007. *The Pentateuch as Torah. New Models for Understanding Its Promulgation and Acceptance*. Winona Lake, IN: Eisenbrauns.

Levin, Christoph. 2007. 'The Yahwist: The Earliest Editor in the Pentateuch.' *Journal of Biblical Literature* 126: 209–30.

Mathys, Hans-Peter. 2002. 'Bücheranfänge und-schlüsse.' In idem (ed.). *Vom Anfang und vom Ende: fünf alttestamentliche Studien*. Frankfurt am Main: Lang: 1–29.

McCarthy, Dennis J. 1981. *Treaty and Covenant: A Study in Form in the Ancient Oriental Documents and in the Old Testament*. Analecta Biblica, 21A; Rome: Biblical Institute Press, new edn, completely rewritten.

Nicholson, Ernest. 1998. *The Pentateuch in the Twentieth Century: The Legacy of Julius Wellhausen*. Oxford: Clarendon. (Contains all bibliographical indications for the authors not mentioned here.)

Nihan, Christophe. 2007. *From Priestly Torah to Pentateuch: A Study in the Composition of the Book of Leviticus*. Forschungen zum AltenTestament, II/25; Tübingen: Mohr Siebeck.

Noth, Martin. 1948. *Überlieferungsgeschichte des Pentateuch*. Stuttgart: Kohlhammer. English: 1972. *A History of Pentateuchal Traditions*. Trans. B. W. Anderson; Englewood Cliffs, NJ: Prentice-Hall, repr. 1981. Atlanta, GA: Scholars Press 1981.

— 1991. *The Deuteronomistic History*. Journal for the Study of the Old Testament, Supplement Series, 15; Sheffield: Sheffield Academic Press, 2nd edn (German original, 1943).

Otto, Eckart. 2004. 'The Pentateuch in Synchronic and Diachronical Perspectives: Protorabbinic Scribal Erudition Mediating between Deuteronomy and the Priestly Code.' In Eckart Otto and Reinhard Achenbach (eds). *Das Deuteronomium zwischen Pentateuch und Deuteronomistischem Geschichtswerk*. Forschungen zur Religion und Literatur des Alten und Neuen Testaments, 206; Göttingen: Vandenhoeck & Ruprecht: 14–35.

Pola, Thomas. 1995. *Die ursprüngliche Priesterschrift. Beobachtungen zur Literarkritik und Traditionsgeschichte von P^g*. Wissenschaftliche Monographien zum Alten und Neuen Testament, 70; Neukirchen–Vluyn: Neukirchener Verlag.

von Rad, Gerhard. 1938. 'Das formgeschichtliche Problem des Hexateuch.' In Rudolph Smend (ed.). *Gesammelte Studien zum Alten Testament I*. Theologische Bücherei,

8, 48; München: C. Kaiser, 4th edn [repr. 1971]: 9–86. English translation: 1966. 'The Form Critical Problem of the Hexateuch.' In idem. *The Problem of the Hexateuch and Other Essays*. Trans. E.W. Trueman Dickens; Edinburgh: Oliver & Boyd Ltd; repr. 1984. London: SCM Press: 1–78.

Rendtorff, Rolf. 1990. *The Problem of the Process of Transmission in the Pentateuch*. Trans. John J. Scullion; Journal for the Study of the Old Testament, Supplement Series, 89; Sheffield: JSOT Press. German original: 1977. *Das überlieferungsgeschichtliche Problem des Pentateuch*. Beihefte zur Zeitschrift für die alttestamentliche Wissenschaft, 147; Berlin: de Gruyter.

Römer, Thomas. 2000. 'Deuteronomy in Search of Origins.' In Gary N. Knoppers and J. Gordon McConville (eds). *Reconsidering Israel and Judah: Recent Studies on the Deuteronomistic History*. Trans. from French original (1991); Sources for Biblical and Theological Studies, 8; Winona Lake, IN: Eisenbrauns: 112–38.

Römer, Thomas, and Marc Z. Brettler. 2000. 'Deuteronomy 34 and the Case for a Persian Hexateuch.' *Journal of Biblical Literature* 119: 401–19.

Schmid, Hans Heinrich. 1976. *Der sogenannte Jahwist. Beobachtungen und Fragen zur Pentateuchforschung*. Zürich: Theologischer Verlag.

Schmid, Konrad. 2010. *Genesis and the Moses Story: Israel's Dual Origins in the Hebrew Bible*. Siphrut, 3; Winona Lake, IN: Eisenbrauns. German original: 1999. *Erzväter und ExodusUntersuchungen zur doppelten Begründung der Ursprünge Israels innerhalb der Geschichtsbücher des Alten Testaments*. Wissenschaftliche Monographien zum Alten und Neuen Testament, 81; Neukirchen-Vluyn: Neukirchener.

— 2006. 'The So-Called Yahwist and the Literary Gap between Genesis and Exodus.' In Dozeman and Schmidt: 29–50.

Stern, Ephraim. 1976. *Greek and Latin Authors on Jews and Judaism*. 2 vols; Jerusalem: Israel Academy of Sciences and Humanities: I, 20–44.

VanderKam, James C. 1994. *The Dead Sea Scrolls Today*. Grand Rapids: Eerdmans/ London: SPCK.

Van Seters, John. 1975. *Abraham in History and Tradition*. London: Yale University Press.

— 1999. *The Pentateuch: A Social Science Commentary*. Trajectories, 1; Sheffield: Sheffield Academic Press.

Wagenaar, Jan A. 2000. 'The Cessation of Manna: Editorial Frames for the Wilderness Wandering in Exodus 16,35 and Joshua 5,10–12.' *Zeitschrift für die alttestamentliche Wissenschaft* 112: 192–209.

Wellhausen, Julius. 1927. *Prolegomena zur Geschichte Israels*. Berlin: de Gruyter; repr. 2001.

Whybray, Roger N. 1995. *Introduction to the Pentateuch*. Grand Rapids, MI: Eerdmans.

Yardeni, Ada. 1991. 'Remarks on the Priestly Blessing on Two Ancient Amulets from Jerusalem.' *Vetus Testamentum* 41: 176–85.

Zenger, Erich. 2004. 'Das priester(schrift)liche Werk (P).' In E. Zenger *et al.* (eds). *Einleitung in das Alte Testament*. Studienbücher Theologie, 1.1; Stuttgart: Kohlhammer.

Chapter 3

Yehud in the Persian Period

In order to contextualize the creation of the Pentateuch, we need to set forth what can be known about socio-economic, religious and political conditions and currents in Yehud under Persian rule and administration (ca. 538–333 BCE). In light of the likely use of source material from the kingdoms of Israel and Judah in the production of the Pentateuch, it is logical to conclude that these individual books, as well as the larger sequenced collection, were created in Yehud rather than in Babylonia or Egypt amongst the elite of those diaspora communities. Our focus will be, therefore, on the province of Yehud during Persian rule rather than on Jewish communities throughout the Persian empire, although there will be a sketch of what is known of diaspora communities in Babylonia, Syria and Egypt. A review of what is known about the province of Yehud under the preceding Neo-Babylonian rule is necessary to set the stage and understand some of our gaps in knowledge during the control of subsequent world empire, the Persians.

1. Jews/Judeans and Others in Yehud

In 586 BCE the Neo-Babylonians punished their vassal kingdom of Judah for rebellion by ending its independence and making it a province of the empire. Since they used Aramaic as their diplomatic language in the western portions of their empire, they called the new province Yehud instead of Judah. They destroyed the capital of the former kingdom, Jerusalem, and established Mizpah, a site about 12 km to the northwest, as the provincial administrative seat. They established the population that was not deported on farmsteads to continue to produce the traditional agricultural crops of the region, wine and oil (2 Kgs 25:12; Jer. 39:10), which were paid in kind as taxes. In addition, sheep, goats, wool and woven cloth had been part of the annual levy paid when Judah was a vassal and probably remained part of the tax burden on the newly formed province. The region of Benjamin, around Mizpah, had the densest occupation, but settlement continued in the Judean hills as well, and in the Shephelah (see Lipschits 2003; Edelman 2005: 298).

It is hard to determine what geographical limits were set for the new province because there is only circumstantial evidence, but it is likely that they did not correspond to the former borders of Judah in the south and may have been shifted slightly in the north as well (for options, see Aharoni 1979: 413–19; Stern 1982: 245–49; Rainey 1983; Grabbe 1992: 79–81; Carter 1999: 75–113; Edelman 2005: 209–80; Lipschits 2005: 134–84; Wright 2006). The western boundary probably remained the western edge of the Shephelah (against Rainey, Carter, Grabbe, Stern, Lipschits, all of whom exclude the Shephelah) and the eastern boundary probably remained the Rift Valley to the west bank of the Jordan River. The northern border may have been shifted slightly north of where it

Figure 3. Map of the boundaries of Yehud (created by R. Hobson)

had been at the end of the monarchy, to include Bethel and other villages north of the former border at Geba. However, it is uncertain whether that shift had already taken place (1) during the reign of King Josiah (ca. 640–609 BCE) or one of his successors, before the province was created; (2) at the time of the creation of Yehud, to expand the core production area in the fertile area of Benjamin; or (3) after the Persians conquered the Neo-Babylonians and became the new administrators of the province, deciding at some point during their 202 years of domination to readjust the provincial border between Yehud and its northern neighbour, Samerina, the provincial successor to the core territory of the former kingdom of Israel.

Similarly, it is unclear where the southern border of the province was established by the Neo-Babylonians. In the final years of the kingdom of Judah, it appears as though the Negev and Negev highlands were probably included within the sovereign territory; forts there like Aroer, Tel 'Ira, Tel Masos, Tel Malhata, Horvat 'Uza and Horvat Radum were supplied from the capital, as demonstrated by the origin of the clay used to make the vessels found on site. Again, due to the meagre evidence that is solely archaeological, it is possible to reconstruct different scenarios. One would leave the border in place but see this area almost devoid of permanent settlement under the Neo-Babylonians (so, for example, Vanderhooft 1999: 83–86; 104–10; modified in 2003: 255; Stern 2001: 307–11). This approach assumes that the Neo-Babylonians had no interest in administering Yehud by a local provincial government and so were unconcerned about fixing tangible borders for the province.

Another approach would move the border to the northern edge of the Beersheba Valley, at the southern end of the Judean hills, with the valley itself and the Negev highlands being under the official control of Edom, or under the unofficial control of Arabs. Caravans passed through this valley carrying goods from Arabia to the port of Gaza for transport by sea to other destinations. 'Edomite' pottery appears at a number of sites in this region at the end of the monarchy and certain biblical texts, especially Obadiah, imply that Edom broke an alliance with Judah in 586 BCE, leaving the kingdom to face Neo-Babylonian attack alone, or that they actively participated in Judah's demise as Babylonian allies or plundered the area after its fall (e.g. Obadiah; Isa. 63:1–9; Ezek. 25:12–14; 35:5, 10, 12; Mal. 1:4). As a reward for Edom's loyalty as a vassal, Edom's existing overlord, the king of Babylonia, may have ceded official control over the Beersheba Valley region to the king of Edom. Control over the northern portion of the spice trade route would have yielded lucrative returns (see e.g. Edelman 2005: 250–65).

Alternatively, it has been conjectured that the Arabs made themselves unofficial masters of the area in order to benefit from control of the spice trade route and that the Neo-Babylonians did not interfere because they had no interest in this otherwise barren region (see e.g. Dumbrell 1971: 44; Aharoni 1979: 414–15; Blenkinsopp 1988: 329). Those who favour this view tend to assume that there was no definitive southern border for Yehud either, so that the entire area was neglected by the Neo-Babylonians, or that there was a southern border established just south of Beth-Zur.

A final suggestion is that the borders shrank considerably and were set at the fort of Beth-Zur (so e.g. Aharoni 1979: 416; Grabbe 1992: 180; Carter 1999: 98; Stern 1982: 247, map 379; Stern 2001: 431; Lemaire 2003: 291; Lipschits 2005: 183; Wright 2006). This had been the border when the Hasmoneans gained power (ca. 165–137 BCE), with the province of Idumea located south of the fort. Hebron was not Judean according to 1 Macc. 5:65; nor were Maresha (1 Mac. 5:66; 2 Macc. 12:35) or Adoraim (1 Macc. 13:20). Josephus states that Judas Maccabee captured and destroyed Hebron and Maresha after the death of Antiochus VII, ca. 163 BCE (*Antiquites* 12.8.1, 6), but that it was only in 125 BCE that his descendant, John Hyrcanus, conquered Idumea completely and incorporated it into the Hasmonean kingdom, forcing the residents to convert to Judaism (*Antiquities* 13.9.1; 14.4.4). It remains unclear, however, when the province of Idumea was initially created south of Yehud, or by whom.

The earliest reference to the existence of Idumea is often thought to be found in Diodorus Siculus (lived in first century BCE) in his account of events in 312 BCE. Antigonus Monophthalmos, one of Alexander's three generals who played an active leading role in the struggle for power after his death, sent his son Demetrius with an army to force the Nabateans into submission. In narrating the departure of the Greek forces with hostages and gifts and their arrival at the Dead Sea, Diodorus takes the opportunity to digress and describe the characteristics of the remarkable natural feature (*Bibliotheca Historica* 19.98.1). He begins by saying the Lake of Asphalt (=the Dead Sea) lies 'along the middle of the satrapy of Idumaea' (Geer 1954: 99). It appears he is describing what he knows in his day in this digression, not that he was drawing on a source from 312 BCE, so it is more likely that the reference to the satrapy of Idumea reflects the reality of the first century BCE.

The Zenon papyri, found in the Fayyum oasis in Egypt and dating to the middle of the third century BCE, on the other hand, provide incontrovertible evidence that Idumea existed ca. 260 BCE as an independent administrative unit. Zenon, the administrator of the Fayyum estate of Apollonius, the 'finance minister' of Ptolemy II (ruled Egypt 283–246 BCE), had been sent in 260–258 BCE to inspect the Ptolemic province of 'Syria and Phoenicia' and to establish trade relationships. Papyrus no. 59015 mentions that Mareshah and Adoraim were located in Idumea (Edgar 1925: 34), confirming it existed by ca. 260 BCE.

The last body of potentially relevant material is the collection of 1,700+ ostraca found in illicit digging in the area of Makkedah (mod. Kh.El-Qom) in the Shephelah. They have been dubbed the 'Idumean ostraca' (Eph'al and Naveh 1996; Lemaire 1996; 2002; Porten and Yardeni 2007; Stern 2007), even though the term Idumea does not appear on one of them. The ostraca have month dates and year dates on them, which scholars believe correspond to the years 363–313 BCE, spanning the reigns of Artaxerxes II (405/404–359/358), Artaxerxes III (359/358–338) Arses/Artaxerxes IV (338–337) and Darius III (337–330) and continuing into the beginning of the control of the region by the Greek empire (Lemaire 2003: 291). They record the delivery of various foodstuffs, straw, materials and workmen to governmental warehouses and officials. Their identification as Idumean is based on the assumption that the existence of administrative storehouses in Makkedah indicates Idumea already formed an independent administrative unit in the second half of the fourth century BCE when the ostraca were generated. However, the ostraca on their own cannot prove that Idumea was an independent province at this time; they confirm that Makkedah was a local administrative center, but not within which province it lay.

The date of the initial creation of Idumea remains disputed. Some would see it to have begun officially or unofficially as early as the Neo-Babylonian administration, either as a *bona fide* province or as a non-administered buffer zone south of Yehud. Yehud seal impressions from the end of the fifth century BCE are used by some as an indicator to establish the borders between Yehud and Idumea and to argue that Idumea already existed as a separate administrative unit by this time (so Stern 1990: 221). The fact that Idumea apparently was not granted the right to mint coins and did not develop the practice of using administrative seals bearing the provincial name makes it hard to pinpoint when it became an officially recognized administrative unit. The observation that the geographical distribution of Yehud seals 'almost completely coincides' with the lists of settlements found in the books of Ezra and Nehemiah, which often are used to derive provincial boundaries for Yehud during the reign of Artaxerxes I when the rebuilding of Jerusalem took place (Kloner and Stern 2007: 140), rests on two weak methodological assumptions.

The first assumption is that the lists of place names in these books derive from the period they purport to describe rather than the time of their author, which might be more than a hundred years later. A critical evaluation of the purpose and function of the lists in the two books, as well as their likely time of authorship, needs to be undertaken before they can be used as a basis for understanding the political reality during any part of the fifth century BCE (Edelman 2005: 210–33; Lipschits 2005: 154–74).

The second assumption is that the distribution of the Yehud seals should correspond with the borders of the province. Until their specific date range and function are confirmed, which can provide some basis upon which to evaluate the distribution patterns in the archaeological record, such an assumption may well be incorrect, yielding skewed results. Of the 412 known seals in 2007, 96.9 per cent were found at four sites only: Ramat Rahel, Jerusalem, Mizpah and Jericho (Lipschits 2007: 174–81), which should caution against assuming they represent the full territorial extent of Yehud. One was found at Kadesh Barnea in Egypt! The fact that the archaeological results do not fully coincide with the textual claims suggests one or both assumptions are wrong.

A couple of considerations can be brought to bear on this issue of the southern border. First, the assumption that the Neo-Babylonians had no interest in Yehud and would not have established any formal boundaries is naïve; an empire was always interested in extracting whatever it could from its hinterlands. The establishment of a new regional capital at Mizpah shows their intended investment in the area, and the fort at Khirbet Abu Twain, which after excavation is thought to have existed throughout Neo-Babylonian rule, shows some sort of military presence within the southern territory of the province. In order to collect taxes and know who was available for military conscription, official lists of citizens would have been kept, which means that some sort of official boundary or border would have existed on paper, even though it would not have been demarcated by a continuous wall or set of forts at entry points.

Second, in asking when it might have been expedient to create an administrative unit in Idumea, it can be observed that this region became the southern border of the Persian empire every time Egypt revolted. Egypt was effectively lost from the empire in 401 BCE and there were numerous, unsuccessful campaigns undertaken to try to regain it in 385–382 and again in 373 by Artaxerxes II, and in 342 by Artaxerxes III, who finally had success after decades of frustration.

It would have been a logical move for the Persians to create the province of Idumea sometime after 401 BCE, during the period they were continuously preparing for the reconquest of Egypt, which always had involved sending a contingent of the military forces overland. This would have enabled them to ensure that food and supplies would have been stockpiled at the border by the local administration, who were to oversee such tasks as part of their duties, working in conjunction with the administrators of neighbouring provinces, with foodstuffs grown locally being delivered to specified storage facilities as tax obligations to the crown (Sapin 2004: 109–10; Edelman 2011). The proposal this would have been the era because there was finally a sufficient population base and the Qedarites and Nabateans were actively engaged in trade in the area, making it profitable to impose taxation for the first time, is possible, but is based in part on the weak assumption that there had been no taxation prior and that this had been a non-administered frontier region of no interest to the authorities (de Geus 1979–1980: 62).

Jars bearing stamps reading MS(W)H have been thought to have been used in some fashion in Yehud during the Neo-Babylonian administration. The majority has been found at Mizpah, the regional

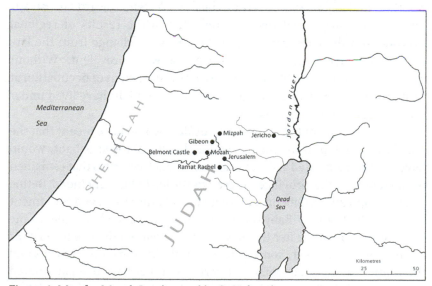

Figure 4. Map for Mozah Jars (created by R. Hobson)

seat, but others have turned up as well at Gibeon, Ramat Rahel, Jericho, Jerusalem and Belmont Castle.

Their specific function is unclear; they probably contained wine or oil produced at the site of Mozah, located ca. 15 km SW of Mizpah, either on a privately owned estate or at a regional processing centre of sorts (see, e.g., Avigad 1958; Zorn, Yellin and Hayes 1994; Stern 1982: 209). They either would have been consumed by family members of the private estate from which they originated, who were living or visiting elsewhere in the province, or were consumed by administrative personnel who were entitled to receive them as food rations. Another possibility is that they contained wine or oil sent to Mozah, which then would logically have been some sort of sub-provincial seat. This option seems less likely, however, because there is no evidence for any other such district seat, and to have only one located so close to the provincial seat at Mizpah would not have been logical. One would have to argue that Mozah was established as a warehouse to store surplus foodstuffs for which there was insufficient space in Mizpah. Yet the limited excavations at Mozah have found only a villa, which might favour the former view, depending on the extent of Persian-era settlement elsewhere on site.

There was no distinctive pottery tradition that developed during the 48 years that the Neo-Babylonians controlled Yehud, so it is very difficult to be certain which sites continued to be occupied after the Neo-Babylonian invasions in 592 and 586 BCE, which were destroyed but resettled, and which were newly established. A trend toward farmsteads rather than villages and towns is reflected in the results of regional surveys from the Late Iron Age, but this is not a change from the late monarchy, when such farmsteads were already prevalent. Without excavation, it is impossible to be able to know the extent of occupation at former village, town and city sites where people might have lived under the Neo-Babylonian administration.

The destruction of the temple in Jerusalem would have meant that the sacrificial worship of the former national deity, Yahweh Sebaot, would have been concentrated at other traditional sanctuary sites that remained in operation in the province. These would likely have included Bethel (Blenkinsopp 2003), Gibeon and Mizpah, and other town and settlement sites as well. The Neo-Babylonians might have made alterations to the monarchic-era temple in Mizpah when they adapted the site to serve as the new provincial seat. Some scholars think that the cultic reforms and the centralization of all worship in Jerusalem that have been attributed to King Josiah in 2 Kings 23 would have left the provincial population with no means to offer legitimate sacrifice once the temple in Jerusalem was destroyed, while others suggest that a limited sacrificial cult was in operation amongst the ruins of the Jerusalemite temple, citing Jer. 41:4–8 in support of this possibility. This text does not specify the ultimate destination of the worshippers from Shechem, Shiloh and Samaria, and the Hebrew would allow one to deduce they were headed to the temple in Mizpah and were diverted to the palace complex once they entered the town as much as to Jerusalem. The Hebrew verb *bo*, used in v. 4 to describe their movement as far as Mizpah, has the semantic nuance of orientation toward a goal; either 'to come', with the origin as endpoint, or 'to enter, arrive, reach' the destination (Polak 2010: 164, 175).

The historicity of Josiah's cultic reforms (2 Kings 23) continues to be debated (see, for example, Ahlström 1993: 770–83; Barrick 2002), and even if they were instituted by this monarch, which is by no means certain, there is no firm indication that they remained in place after the king's death and so would have prevented the continuation or establishment of one or more Yahwistic temples in Yehud under the Neo-Babylonians. The traditional native divine couple, Yahweh Sebaot and Asherah, and various attending local deities, would have continued to be venerated by the population that remained in the land.

In 539 BCE, Cyrus captured Nabonidus and his capital city of Babylon, thereby gaining control over all the territory of the Neo-Babylonian empire, which he joined to his existing holdings in the Iranian plateau and in central and western Asia (the territories of the Persians, Medes, Hyrcanians, Parthians, Saka/Scythians, Bactrians, Elamites and Lydians). The province of Yehud had been part of the larger Neo-Babylonian administrative unit of Across the River, Eber-Nari, and continued to be so in the newly expanded Persian empire.

Initially, under Cyrus, Eber-Nari apparently was joined with the territory of Babylonia and remained so in the early reign of Darius I. Three letters from a private archive from Babylon, dating to years 1–6 of Darius, refer to Ushtani, governor (*pehah*) of Babylon and Across the River (Stolper 1989: 289). Eber-Nari subsequently may have been separated from Babylon later in his reign, as part of administrative reforms. Herodotus claims these took place under Darius I (III, 88–97), relying on a map created by Hecataeus, which in turn was based on a document the latter had probably received from a Persian informant, perhaps from Darius' brother Artaphrenes, who became satrap of Sardis in 514 BCE, with whom he had been friends (Herzfeld 1968: 288). Herodotus claims Darius organized 20 satrapies as his first administrative

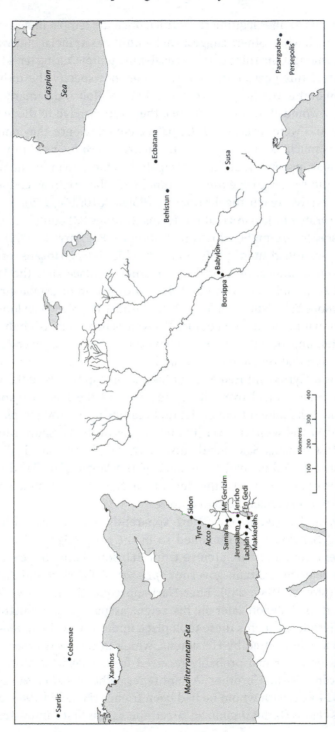

Figure 5. Map of Persian empire (created by R. Hobson)

act after setting up a monument—probably the Behistun inscription (III, 89). The reliability of this information is debated (Herzfeld 1968: 188–349, esp. 304–306; Cameron 1973; Stern 1982: 238–39; Briant 2002: 63–64, 390–94, 487–88); nevertheless, in the list he cites from Hecataeus, Babylon is an independent satrapy from Eber-Nari. Likely confirmation this separation took place sometime after year 6 of Darius I (517 BCE) is provided by a letter dated to 502 BCE, which refers to someone named Ta-at-... as being governor (*pehah*) of Eber-Nari alone (Stolper 1989: 289–91). However, caution is needed, since the title *pehah* could be used for a range of officials, not all of whom were governors.

Cyrus' son and successor, Cambyses (ca. 525–522 BCE), added Phoenicia, Cyprus, the Arabs and Egypt to the empire, though not all became provinces; the Arabs, Cypriots and Phoenicians may have become tributaries or vassals with native kings left in place. We have no information about what sort of changes were made to the inherited administrative practices, but it is unlikely that any sort of major overhaul was accomplished while the expansion was underway (see conveniently, Briant 2002: 49–64). The Behistun inscription of King Darius (520–486 BCE) indicates that the first two Persian kings established garrisons in regions they had physically traversed and conquered and probably also assigned land in newly conquered areas to Persian families, who were then obligated to supply equipped cavalrymen for war, as needed.

Yehud had been inherited by Cyrus but not physically visited by him and probably not by Cambyses either, so it is likely that administrative arrangements and boundaries inherited from the Neo-Babylonians remained in place. While Cambyses had invaded Egypt, he had relied on the Arabs and probably the inhabitants of the coastal plain to supply food and water for his troops en route, who traveled by sea and along the coastal road (Briant 2002: 53). There was no reason for him to have entered Yehud or to have contemplated the establishment of permanent grain storage facilities in the southern coastal plain for future invasions. He would have hoped to be successful on the first attempt at conquest. He may have ordered all surplus grain, wine oil, and animals available within the nearby provinces to have been delivered to Tell el-Erani and Tel Halif, if the large Persian-era facility at the latter site dates to the late sixth–early fifth century BCE, or to a similar site, like Gaza, as an *ad hoc* solution to supplying the food for his intended conquest.

Mizpah remained the provincial seat until the reign of Artaxerxes I, and existing forts were probably re-manned under Persian commanders. No main roads ran through Yehud, so it is unlikely that postal relay

Figure 6. Map of grain storage facilities in coastal plain (created by R. Hobson)

stations were built in the province. The local population would have remained on their farmsteads and paid whatever the annual levies they had borne in the past to the new rulers: in taxes in kind at whatever rates were imposed, any head or poll taxes paid in silver, corvée labour and military obligations tied to land ownership.

The claim in Ezra 1–2 that there was an influx of population to the region from the Jewish diaspora in the first year of Cyrus' reign is unhistorical. A variant form of the census in Ezra 2 appears in Nehemiah 7 but is set under Artaxerxes I, not Cyrus. Most scholars think the setting in Nehemiah is more 'original', whether or not it is a composite list that reflects names and circumstances in two or more periods (see conveniently, Edelman 2005: 175–76). The author of Ezra 1–6 has wanted to show that all prophecies concerning the rebuilding of the temple were fulfilled in historical time; the predictions in Isa. 44:28 and 52:11 that

Cyrus would rebuild the temple and that the temple vessels would be returned led him to set an initial 'return' at this time. He wanted to involve the diaspora communities in the financing and rebuilding activities, to create a 'historical' link between them and the former homeland, where the temple was to become the focus of the cult of Yahweh Elohim and emerging monotheistic Judaism (see Edelman 2009).

Darius' early reign (522–520 BCE) was spent quelling a number of rebellions. Afterwards, he concentrated on conquering the Aegean islands, Greece, Thrace, Macedonia, the Indus Valley, and digging a canal between the Nile River and the Red Sea. He built a new royal city/ capital at Persepolis while continuing the aggrandizement of the royal city/capital at Pasargadae begun by Cyrus and continued by Cambyses. He remodelled Susa to be another royal seat. He also had to deal with the subsequent revolt of Ionia (500–493 BCE) and of Egypt in 486 BCE, shortly before his death (see Briant 2002: 139–61; see Fig. 5, above).

Ezra 1–6 sets the bulk of the rebuilding and completion of the temple in Jerusalem, but not the rest of the city, during years 2–6 of Darius (Ezra 4:4, 24; 6:15). Haggai 1–Zechariah 8 also provides dates for the rebuilding of the temple during the reign of a Darius (Hag. 1:1; 2:1, 10, 18; Zech. 1:1, 7; 7:1). The majority position has been to accept these dates as reliable and to assume they refer to Darius I (522–486 BCE), with a minority position maintaining they refer to Darius II (425–405 BCE; DeQueker 1993:68).

It seems unlikely, however, that he would have concerned himself with such a task, let alone paid for it out of royal treasuries, as claimed in the account (6:8–10), when he had just suppressed a series of revolts in his first year of securing the throne and was not fully in control until year four of his reign. The date given for the dedication of the temple falls at the end of the 70th calendar year from its destruction in 586 BCE by the Neo-Babylonian king Nebuchadrezzar. This date seems to have been derived by the biblical writer from two prophecies contained in the Book of Jeremiah (25:11–12; 29:10) that predicted 70 years of devastation for the land of Judah until its restoration by Yahweh (Edelman 2005: 167–68). A new minority position maintains the temple was rebuilt as part of the general rebuilding of Jerusalem to be the regional seat of the province of Yehud during the reign of Artxerxes I (465–425 BCE) ca. 450 BCE (Edelman 2005).

Darius' son Xerxes (486–465 BCE) quashed the Egyptian revolt after ascending the throne, and another subsequent one in Babylonia in 481 BCE, and then concentrated much effort on invading and subduing

Greece, which began in 480 BCE and led to the defection of Ionian contingents and the formation of the Delian League and temporary loss of control over Aegean islands, but not mainland cities. Cyprus was regained by 470 BCE. He completed building projects begun by his father at Persepolis and Susa and built a residence for himself at Celaenae in Phrygia, which he also fortified (Briant 2002: 515–86).

Artaxerxes I (465–405/404 BCE) was preoccupied with a revolt in Egypt that erupted within a year of his accession and took ten years to suppress. He also is known to have continued the expansion of Persepolis. It is under this king that the Book of Nehemiah places the rebuilding of Jerusalem to be the provincial seat instead of Mizpah. A garrison was built on the former acropolis; the city walls were rebuilt, a palace was built for the governor (2:8), and a civilian population was moved inside (11:1–2). It is logical to conclude that the temple was rebuilt at this time, to serve as the provincial treasury as well as a sanctuary dedicated to the god of the land, a share of whose profits the Persians could pocket. According to the dates given in the book, the fortress was just about completed when Nehemiah was sent to be governor in the king's 20th year, 445 BCE (1:1; 7:2). He completed the remaining tasks after his arrival. There are two 'houses' mentioned in Neh. 7:2 amongst the building projects, allowing for the possibility that the temple was part of the larger plan alongside the palace (cf. 2 Macc. 1:18; Josephus, *Ant.* 11.165). The term 'house' can designate any size human or divine dwelling. If the date of his arrival is reliable, it would mean that the provincial seat reforms were instituted only after the successful suppression of the Egyptian revolt (Edelman 2005: 340–51).

The revolt in Egypt took a long time to end satisfactorily and completely (Briant 2002: 573–77). Before an army could be sent in, food and water supplies needed to be stockpiled en route. It is likely that this time, an assessment was made of the agricultural producing capacities of the provinces in Palestine. Such a move may well have led Artaxerxes to overhaul the inherited administration in this otherwise insignificant region of his empire. Such a decision would have led to its firmer incorporation into the road and postal networks, but more importantly, would have led to the boosting of local food production through the forced resettlement of farmers in the coastal region as well as the underdeveloped hinterlands of Samerina and Yehud, which bordered the main coastal route. The site of Tell el-Hesi, which housed a citadel in str. V-d, has been interpreted to have served as a grain storehouse or depot facility in the period between 500–450, based on the types of

Greek pottery found there (Fargo 1993: 633; see Fig. 6, above). Taxes in kind from the entire province probably were sent there for a few seasons. The introduction of new immigrants onto farmsteads would, at the same time, have provided additional military manpower during the actual campaign, once sufficient food had been amassed after a few harvests.

Bearing the above in mind, the administrative reforms may have been introduced in phases, with the establishment of a permanent garrison in a newly built provincial seat, happening only after the resolution of the Egyptian revolt, when manpower would have become available to rebuild Jerusalem. A series of square buildings that perhaps were fire relay stations have been discovered in regional surveys from the Shephelah and Beersheba Valley leading to Jerusalem and these may have also been built in the aftermath of the suppression of the revolt in Egypt. Many new farmsteads were settled in their immediate vicinities (Edelman 2007).

Any adjustments to the provincial boundaries would logically have been made at this time. The archaeological surveys have revealed limited settlement in the southern Judean hills on the north side of the Beersheba Valley, raising again the question about the date of the founding of Idumea. The patterns suggest that this was not an area of concentrated growth, in spite of its location near the staging area of Gaza. The implication is that it was not made a separate province at this time; its agricultural returns were too variable to be worth investment in an independent administrative structure. It is more likely that the southern boundary of Yehud was set at the Beersheba Valley and that the relay stations in this region were supplied by the Yehud administration.

The building of the palace complex and temple at Lachish may have taken place early in the reign of Artaxerxes I to serve as a residence for the Persian official who oversaw the amassing of the food supplies and then eventually, for the general who would lead the overland troops and for the king himself, should he visit the region. Its unusual use of barrel arches suggests it was not built by locals, who did not know this technique. On the other hand, armies were used for construction projects, and a foreign engineer may well have been included in the general's retinue. O. Tufnell has dated its construction to ca. 450 BCE based on the ceramic evidence (1953: 48, 133). A recent attempt by A. Fantalkin and O. Tal to lower that date to ca. 400 BCE is inconclusive; insufficient information about the pottery and find-spots makes an informed assessment impossible (2006). The suggestion that Lachish served as the seat of an independent province located in the Shephelah

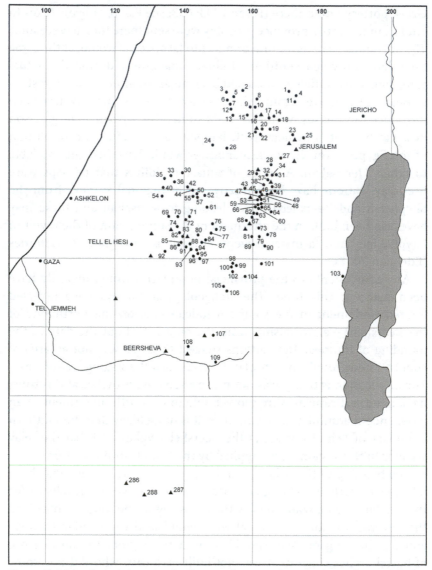

Figure 7. Map of administrative facilities and new settlements (repr. from Edelman, *Origins of the 'Second' Temple*, © Equinox, 2005)

or of Idumea in its early years of existence is less likely (so e.g. Carter 1999: 92–93) though not refutable in light of the scant available evidence. The site lacks the range of administrative buildings one would expect to find in a provincial seat.

Nehemiah 2:8 mentions a royal park or *pardes* from which Nehemiah was to secure wood for the various construction projects around

Jerusalem. The implication is that it would have been located within a fairly close distance. Perhaps the two buildings at Lachish lay within this *pardes*, which would have been established in the opening years of Artaxerxes' reign. There is evidence of a *pardes* located in the 'Valley of Syria' (the Jordan Valley?) that produced balsam at the end of the Persian period, but it might only have been established by Artaxerxes III at Jericho on his return home from Egypt in 342/341 BCE. It is possible that 'En Gedi had served such a role in the early Persian period; besides the natural waterfalls located there that would have attracted wild game, a villa has been found and evidence of perfume manufacture. Yet this region would not have been otherwise heavily forested and so is less likely to have been the *pardes* referenced in Neh. 2:8 (Foerster 1993; Edelman 2005: 229–30). 'En Gedi could have been built by one of the early governors under a land grant from the king as a personal estate modeled after a *pardes* rather than being an official royal *pardes*.

A close look at the list of families that allegedly returned to Yehud found in Nehemiah 7 and in a variant version in Ezra 2 discloses that the population in the Persian-era province of Yehud, whatever the date of the list's components, was of mixed ethnic make-up. The current account in Ezra and Nehemiah portrays the returning community to be Judean, comprised of those whose forefathers had been exiled to Babylonia (the *golah*) and those whose forefathers had remained in their native homes. There is a strong concern to demonstrate continuity in blood-lines between families who had lived in Judah at the end of the kingdom and those still there or returning there under the Persians. Yet the list in Ezra 2 and Nehemiah 7 also includes Elamites (2:7; 7:12), Persians (Bigvai; 2:14; 7:19), and Arameans or another northwest Semitic group (Azgad; 2:12; 7:17) alongside the 'returning Judeans', and Neh. 13:15 claims that Tyrian merchants lived in Jerusalem. Some scholars argue that the names are not true indicators of ethnicity but might have been borne by Jews whose parents gave them names in tune with the local communities where they were living. However, the list purports to register those returning from Babylonia, so it is a bit odd that Babylonian names are in such short supply amongst the Jews bearing assimilated names if this argument is to be invoked.

The Elamites and Persians almost certainly represent the military and administrative personnel settled in the province to oversee the affairs of the king, while the Arameans were probably part of the civilian population that was added to boost food production under Artaxerxes I. We now have proof of a settlement near Borsippa named 'the city of

Judah' that appears in a number of contracts (Pearce 2006; see Fig. 5, above). This is consistent with other evidence of settlements named after ethnic groups that had been resettled outside their original homeland. This practice confirms that the Persian authorities would have been able to 'repatriate' descendants of those exiled to Babylonia in 592 and 586 BCE had they so been inclined. If they wanted to send people back 'home' in fulfillment of standard ideology that considered this a positive thing (Behistun inscription; Cyrus Cylinder), they could have found the appropriate groups easily enough. But the need for a critical mass of settlers to be transferred to Palestine to produce food and become farmers obligated to serve in the military if drafted probably outweighed attempts to send only those known to have historical ties to the region. Thus, it is quite likely that the settlers comprised an ethnic mix.

After 464 BCE, then, the population of Yehud would have been heterogeneous. The books of Ezra and Nehemiah present internal tensions in the province in terms of those whose ancestors had gone into exile and were now returning 'home' (the *golah*) and 'the people of the land', who are usually understood to be those whose ancestors had never left the region but had been given farmsteads by the Neo-Babylonians (the non-*golah*). The authors favour the *golah* and frame the story in terms of those who constituted the true religious community of Israel, which was centred on the newly rebuilt temple dedicated to Yahweh Elohim. Most of the non-*golah* had probably continued to worship Yahweh Sebaot, Asherah and the host of heaven as had been done throughout the monarchy, though a few no doubt accepted the new religious visions and practices associated with the incoming elites who had official backing to regulate the changing administrative and religious policies. The majority of the non-*golah*, however, are rejected in Ezra 1–6 for 'heresy'. The current understanding would have the authors ignore the foreign population groups that also were present in the province, some in positions of authority and influence, who would have continued their non-Yahwistic native religious traditions. It needs to be considered whether these groups might be included in the designation, 'the people of the land', alongside the non-*golah* Judeans. The few horse and rider figurines that have been recovered from Persian-era strata so far show the human in Persian garb and may reflect the worship of Persian military officers, for example, and a cult of Mithra, perhaps. The temple ('solar shrine') at Lachish may well have been dedicated to one or more Persian deities if it had served the army general initially and then had been used by visiting dignitaries, the satrap or the king himself, when on tour, rather than to Yahweh, as has been suggested by Y. Aharoni, for example (1968: 161–63).

The rebuilding of Jerusalem and the temple appears to have marked the beginning of a policy of religious centralization within the province. The sites of Bethel and Gibeon, both of which probably had contained Yahwistic temples, were 'neutralized' about this time (Edelman 2001; 2003). The limited excavations at Bethel suggest an abandonment of the site, which was known to house a temple in spite of its precise location being unknown (Kelso 1993). More indicatively, the defensive walls of Gibeon/el-Jib were pulled down and stones from them were used to block up the interior water system. The fill inside the pool contained *m(w)sh*-stamped jar handles as well as examples of the subsequent animal stamps, which probably date from the early Persian period. There are no Yehud stamps, which probably began to appear from the mid-fifth century BCE after the reorganization of the province, or Yerushalayim stamps, however, which are known from stratigraphic information to date to the third–second centuries BCE. Thus, the site was deliberately made an undesirable place to continue to live sometime after the rebuilding of Jerusalem, and one is hard-pressed to explain this action outside of internal provincial tensions—probably in part religious; there were no external invasions (Edelman 2001; 2003).

Little else is able to be said about subsequent changes in the province when the Persians were in power. The extant biblical and extra-biblical textual traditions report almost no events in Yehud in the reigns of Darius II (ca. 425–405 BCE), Cyrus the Younger (ca. 405–401 BCE), Artaxerxes II (ca. 405/404–359/358 BCE), Artaxerxes III (ca. 359/358–338 BCE), Arses (Artaxerxes IV, ca. 338–337 BCE) and Darius III (ca. 337–330 BCE). Other than the reported capture of Jericho by Artaxerxes III discussed above in connection to the location of royal parks in and around Yehud, Josephus recounts the murder of a third son of the high priest Yeshua under Bagohi's governorship (Grabbe 1992) and the marriage of Sanballat's daughter to a son of the high priest Yaddua in the reign of Darius III, the final king of Persia. Nehemiah 13:28 places the marriage earlier, to a son of the high priest Yoiada/Yehoiada, in the late fifth century BCE, which is more consistent with the evidence that he was governor in the mid-fifth century BCE (Edelman 2005: 66–67).

The intensification of agriculture and possibly of animal husbandry that began under Artaxerxes I would have involved the traditional mainstays of the area: wheat, barley, grapes, olives, sheep and goats. Our inability to know how extensive Persian-era settlement may have been at larger sites precludes our ability to identify possible sub-district seats or regional market towns. It is often argued on the testimony of Nehemiah 3 that Yehud was subdivided into five administrative sub-regions, called *pelakim*, with seats at Jerusalem, Mizpah, Beth-Zur, Keilah and Bet-Hakkerem (see standard commentaries). However, the term *pelek* can also mean 'mandatory annual labour tax', which often took the form of building work, so the references to the teams of workers from these five towns may be a reference to their presence as conscripted rather than voluntary labourers, and to their working status rather than to their origin from sub-district seats (Demsky 1983; Edelman 2005: 212–16).

The highest local authority appears to have borne the title *pehah*, which is usually translated 'governor'. In past decades it was optimistically thought that we could use jar impressions, bullae, seals, coins and texts to reconstruct eight consecutive governors of Yehud who spanned the entire Persian period, from 538–332 BCE. These included: (1) Sheshbazzar ca. 538 BCE (Ezra 1:8); (2) Zerubbabel, ca. 518 BCE (Hag. 1:1); (3) Elnatan, late sixth century BCE (seal and bulla); (4) Yeho'ezer, early fifth century (jar impression); (5) Ahzai, early fifth century (jar impression); (6) Nehemiah in 445–443 BCE (Neh. 4:14); (7) Bagohi/Bagoas in 410 BCE (Elephantine papyrus 30); and (8) Yehezqiyah, ca. 340–312 BCE (coins; so e.g. Stern 1982: 202–206; Meyers 1985). However, we know from the Persian-era Murashu archive from Nippur in Babylonia that the same word could be used to describe an officer in charge of the Simmigar Canal and another in charge of the left side of the Sin Canal (Stolper 1985: 39, 58). Thus, caution needs to be taken in reconstructing the sequence of governors in the province on the basis of seals or bullae bearing the title *pehah*.

The only likely governors we can name are Zerubbabel, in office under Artaxerxes I, possibly Nehemiah, also under Artaxerxes I, unless he was a sub-official under Zerubbabel, Bagohi, known from Elephantine letter 30 to have been in office in 410 BCE, and probably Yehezqiyah, named on a few coins as *pehah* of Yehud, who would have been in office in the closing decade of Persian rule. Bagohi's assumption of power after Zerubbabel (or Nehemiah?) indicates that the Persians were wary of allowing a former native dynasty to become re-entrenched. It is assumed that Yehezqiyah is the 66-year old, highly esteemed Jewish individual named by Josephus in *Against Apion* I.187–89, who tried to meet with Ptolemy I after the battle of 312 BCE. It is possible that he had assumed office in the last decade or so of the Persian era and so bridged the transition to Ptolemaic rule. Thus, he can be provisionally included here as the final governor of Yehud under the Persians, whether the coins were struck in the Persian or Ptolemaic era.

We are better informed about the high priesthood, however, since the Book of Nehemiah gives the sequence of office-holders from the rebuilding of the temple (ca. 450 BCE) to the conquest of Alexander (332 BCE): Yeshua, Yoiakim, Eliashib, Yoiada/Yehoiada, Yohanan, Yonatan and Yaddua. Yohanan and Yonatan are thought by some to be variant references to a single individual, but the names are sufficiently different that they should be distinguished and seen to be brothers, both of whom held the office of high priest in succession. Elephantine letter 30 indicates that Yohanan was in office in 410 BCE (Edelman 2005: 63–69). This produces a plethora of individuals in the first 55 years of the temple's existence and a relative dearth in the last 80, but this is not impossible. Yeshua was apparently quite old when he arrived, and his son would have been mature when he assumed office. Both could have had short careers, and Eliashib may have inherited the office when he already was in his 30s. It is thought that the average lifespan was only about 40-years old for average people in the ancient world, and while priests would have been expected to have had a longer life due to better nutrition and less physical labour, individuals may still have died relatively early due to disease, murder or mishap. Thus, while it would appear that Yohanan and Yonatan and Yaddua probably enjoyed long careers in office, their forebears do not appear to have been so fortunate.

Coinage was first used in Yehud during the Persian period. Two series emulated Athenian coinage in the use of the profiled head of the goddess Athena on the front and her attribute animal, the owl, with or without an olive sprig and with the provincial name Yehud, in Aramaic, on the reverse. Another series, however, bears a lily on the front, or a small

reverse

obverse

Figure 8. Yehud coin (photos by D. Edelman, courtesy of the British Museum)

crowned or helmeted male head in profile, and a bird with spread wings and a hooked beak, with the provincial name Yehud, on the reverse (Meshorer 1982: 13–30). There is a unique coin with the portrait of a helmeted, bearded male in three-quarter profile on the front and a bearded deity seated on a wheeled, winged chair, with a bird perched on his extended hand and a small bearded head, in profile, opposite his feet, on the reverse, with the name Yehud.

This coin has received a lot of attention because of the apparent portrait of Yahweh on the reverse; the imagery has been influenced by that found on Cilician coins (see e.g. Edelman 1995; de Hulster 2009). Finally, the coins of Yehezqiyah feature either the head of Arethusa in frontal pose on the front and Athena's owl on the reverse, with the legends *Yehezqiyah, hapehah,* or at least two different male heads in profile on the front and the forelegs, chest and head of a pouncing, winged lion, with the personal name, on the rear. The first are thought to be Persian in date and the latter, early Hellenistic.

Dating of the earliest coins is difficult since they bear no personal names; nevertheless, it is thought that coinage was minted relatively late in Yehud as compared to neighbouring provinces like Sidon, Tyre and Samerina. While coins may already have been in use in Phoenicia at the end of the sixth century, due to the need to pay rowers in the navy (Wallinga 1987: 71), and in Samerina ca. 440 BCE, minted by Sinuballit/ Sanballat, the two earliest series from Yehud, which copy Athenian coins, seem to date from the fourth century. The coins may have been minted to pay Athenian or other Greek mercenaries of the former Delian League hired by the Persians to be part of the forces sent to quell the long-standing rebellion in Egypt led by Hakoris and his successor, Nectanebo in the 390s–370s BCE. This would account for the decision to emulate images familiar to them.

The governor may have been instructed to pay such salaries by the ruling king, as part of the province's annual tribute or tax burden. The Greek sources (Diodorus, *Bibliotheca Historica* XV.41.2) say that the logistical base for this invasion force had been Acco/Acre (see Fig. 5, above); this may well have been the case for the navies, but not for all the army forces, the Greek components of which were reportedly trained by Iphicrates (Nepos, *Life of Iphicrates* 2.4). If this process of mustering and preparation extended over years, as Diodorus claims, then it is logical that mercenary components of the army would have been quartered in provinces south of Acco in order to spread the burden of their upkeep while placing them en route to the ultimate destination. Those contingents that had been levied on the basis of obligatory service tied to land ownership from *hatru*-estates, bow-estates, and horse-estates were, in theory at least, expected not only to furnish their own horses and weapons, but also to pay for food rations while on campaign and did not draw pay (Briant 2002: 75–76, 597–99).

It is known from comparative evidence that the Persians consolidated scribal and healing arts within temple complexes in their various provinces. According to his inscribed statue, Udjahorresnet was commissioned by Darius I in the opening years of his reign (522–520 BCE) to go from Elam back home to Egypt to establish the offices of the Houses of Life, which had fallen into decay. The House of Life was a combination of library, scriptorium and place of healing where medicine and astronomy were studied. It was sometimes but not always located on temple grounds, but in such cases was separate from the temple library proper (Nordh 1996: 107–13). A primary function was the production and transmission of protective rituals, as well as hymns and texts to be used on public monuments. It is likely that Udjahorresnet's work included the commissioning of sages, priests and scribes to collect the traditional lore relating to the royal court and the temple in use when Cambyses defeated Egypt and incorporated it into the Persian empire, as described in the Demotic Chronicle. This task reportedly took 21 years.

In Mesopotamia, the office of *ashipu*-priest, which specialized in purification and exorcism, holders of which created and maintained 'secret knowledge', was integrated into the temple staff instead of being centred in the palace as in the Iron Age (Sallaberger and Huber Vulliet 2003–2005: 620, 632). All cuneiform knowledge and writing came to be concentrated in priestly staff associated with temples at this time. Thus, it appears that the Persians made temples throughout their empire the guardians and repositories of archival materials relating to local ritual, healing and wisdom, as well as the centres for the ongoing production of such materials.

2 Maccabees 2:13 claims that Nehemiah founded a library and collected the books about the kings and prophets, the writings of David and letters of kings about votive offerings. While these may not all fit within the categories of ritual, healing and wisdom, they still may have been collected as part of a larger Persian initiative that valued archives and centres of learning amongst various subject people and had central temples include a library with such materials.

If the Persians were interested in the collection of the traditional civil and religious knowledge and learning of all of the subject groups within the empire and not just that of recently conquered centres of high culture, like Babylonia, Assyria and Egypt, then Nehemiah's reported initiative in the formation of a library would likely have included the collection of legal and cultic conventions. A reflex of such activity could be seen in the inclusion to various degrees of such materials within the narratives of the books of the Pentateuch. An official Persian demand for their formal collection and public dissemination within the culture could arguably have spurred the writing of certain books that were eventually included within the Hebrew Bible (Blenkinsopp 1987; for discussion, see Watts 2001). On the other hand, as is explained in the section on Torah in Chapter 4 (pp. 93–111), scholars have also proposed that the Pentateuch and other books that eventually came to be within the Hebrew Bible were created to establish a normative account or foundation story for the various groups of emerging Judaism that incorporated sometimes conflicting material in the sprit of compromise. If the Persians were only interested in access to the learning of 'high' cultures, then this alternative explanation is more compelling.

Ezra 7:25–26 claims that Artaxerxes authorized Ezra the scribe to appoint judges to adjudicate among 'all the people in the province Beyond the River who know the laws of your *elohim* (God); and you shall teach those who do not know them. 26 Let judgment be strictly executed on all who will not obey the law of your *elohim* (God) and the law of the king.' The execution of this alleged command is depicted by the author of Nehemiah to have taken place at the opening of the Feast of Booths (ch. 8), when Ezra read aloud to the people assembled in Jerusalem in the square before the Water Gate from 'the scroll of the law of Moses, which Yahweh had given to Israel' (8:3). The Levites then interpreted the read passages 'so that the people understood the reading' (8:7). On the next day, the ancestral heads of all the people are said to have studied the words of the instruction more closely alongside the priests and Levites (8:13). In this biblical version of 'history', Artaxerxes is responsible for the official enactment of Mosaic law, which he recognizes as binding on all residents of Across the River, which would include Yehud and Samerina along with the Galilee, Moab, Ammon, Edom and Damascus-Syria, regardless of their origin. He either declares Mosaic law will be viewed as the official royal law of Across the River, governing both religious and civil matters, or else he declares it will govern religious matters and a separate law of the king will prevail in civil matters.

Earlier, in Ezra 7:6, Ezra is introduced as a scribe from Babylonia who was skilled in the law of Moses that Yahweh, the *elohim* (divinity) of

Israel, had given. The author of Ezra assumes here that king Artaxerxes had authorized the establishment of traditional religious law that would be binding on Jews in the province of Across the River; this law was pre-existent and, by implication, known amongst Jews in Babylonia already and binding on them there. Its description as the law of Moses would point to an association of Moses with divine law-giving and possibly, but not necessarily, the existence of the narratives in the books of Exodus and/or Deuteronomy, where Moses proclaims laws in the name of Yahweh.

The writer of Ezra stresses throughout his narrative how the Jews in Babylonia financially supported the rebuilding of the temple and contributed to its leadership as members of the returning *golah* community, who constituted the true religious community of Israel. His insistence that the Babylonian Jewish diaspora played a central role in the life of the political and religious community in Yehud during the reigns of Cyrus-Artaxerxes (I) could be seen to imply that they were the spiritual masterminds of early Judaism. His advocacy on behalf of the Babylonian Jewish community suggests, however, that there were rival views at the time he wrote that he was trying to overcome. Bearing this in mind, his 'history' of the introduction of the law in Yehud needs to be taken as one version of events, but not necessarily the one that most accurately reflects what transpired. Logically, there would have been two other groups that could have been claiming prominence, who might well have given a different 'history'. These were (1) those whose ancestors had never been deported from Yehud by the Neo-Babylonians, the 'non-*golah*', who would have formed a major component of the group described by the authors of Ezra and Nehemiah as 'the people of the land' and (2) the Egyptian Jewish diaspora. It remains a debatable question whether the 'law of Moses' originated in Babylonia and was secondarily extended to Jews in the 'homeland' or whether it originated in Yehud in response to a demand for the collection of local tradition, including the codification of traditional religious and civil custom, which was secondarily extended to diaspora Jewish communities elsewhere in the empire, including Babylonia and Egypt. A third option would be that it had originated in Egypt and was secondarily extended to the remaining Jewish communities in the Persian empire.

2. Jews/Judeans in Egypt

Various texts in the Hebrew Bible reflect the view that Egypt was seen as a place of safe haven, abundance and political strength (see e.g. Gen. 12:10; 41–43; 1 Kgs 11:4–22; 2 Kgs 24:29; 25:25–26; Jer 41:17–18; 42:14–17; 43:1–7; 44:1, 11–14). Wine and olive oil had been traded from the southern Levant to Egypt from as early as 3,500 BCE, and being the adjoining major political unit to the south of Judah, it is likely that Judahites had sought physical refuge there as well in times of political unrest and drought, in addition to regular trade. Certainly, King Jehoahaz (609 BCE) would have had a sizable entourage of Judahites accompany him to Egypt when Necho deposed him in favour of his brother Eliakim and forced him to take up residence in Egypt (2 Kgs 23:34; 2 Chron.

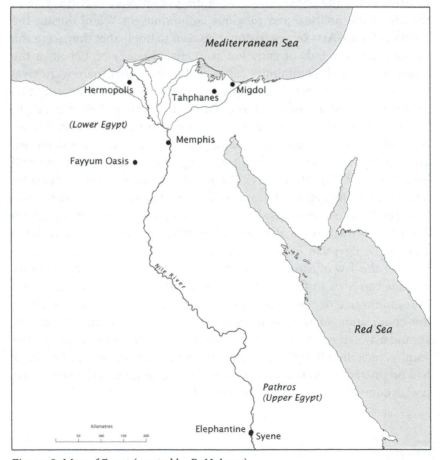

Figure 9. Map of Egypt (created by R. Hobson)

36:4), probably for purposes of 're-education' to ensure his future loyalty as well as that of his brother while he was effectively being held hostage. The fate of these attendants after Jehoahaz's death is not known.

According to Jer. 44:1, there were Jewish mercenaries stationed in forts in the Egyptian Delta at Tahphanes (Daphnae) and Migdol, downstream at Memphis, as well as in the land of Pathros, or southern Egypt, whose ranks were swelled in the 580s with the fall of Jerusalem and the subsequent murder of Gedaliah, the Babylonian-appointed official in charge of Yehud, stationed at Mizpah (41:17; 42:14–17; 43:1–7).

How much earlier Judahites had been stationed in any of these places is unclear. The large amounts of imported Greek pottery that have been found at the first three sites has led to the conclusion that Greek mercenaries were also resident, particularly when the forts were first established in the late seventh or sixth century BCE (Boardman 1999: 33–40). Some would see the mention of Pathros to be an allusion to the military colony at Yeb/Elephantine, which was still in existence in 400 BCE. A fragmentary papyrus found there is dated to 529 BCE, in the 41st year of Pharaoh Amasis, and indicates that soldiers from the southern Levant (*rmt n Hr*) were on active duty, alongside those from Syria (*rmt n 'Iswr*). They could have been stationed on the island of Yeb proper and/ or at the fort at Sewen/Syene, on the northern bank of the Nile opposite the island (see Fig. 9, above). It is known from various papyri that the fort at Sewen/Syene had Arameans and Egyptians resident, possibly with a few Judeans, while that at Yeb included, besides the Judeans, Egyptians, Arameans, Babylonians, Korasmian(s), Medes, Persians and possibly Caspians (Porten 1968: 29).

Our most detailed knowledge of Jews living in Egypt during the Persian era comes from three papyri archives that were excavated inside the fort located at Yeb/Elephantine. They served as mercenaries, earning monthly wages paid in silver as well as receiving monthly food rations. Not only do many of the names from the three family archives include the divine element Yah, which is not always a firm indicator that their bearers were Judeans and worshippers of Yahweh, but the adjective 'Jewish/Judean' is used on many occasions in the papyri to describe a resident of Elephantine. This adjective should be taken literally to mean that the forefathers of the Persian-era Jews had been citizens of the kingdom of Judah, as opposed to citizens of the kingdom of Israel. The title *yhwh sebaot*, 'Lord of Hosts', though not attested in the papyri, occurs once on an undated ostracon and twice again probably on two others, also undated, in the formula, 'May the Lord of Hosts seek your welfare at all times', though both require partial restoration. This was a title used of Yahweh of Jerusalem, not of Yahweh of Samaria or Yahweh of Bethel. It is noteworthy that the element *'el* is attested in only a single name in the papyri, even though it is found more frequently among names on ostraca from Judah at the end of the monarchy and in names in cuneiform documents from Babylonia in the Neo-Babylonian and Persian periods.

There was a temple dedicated to the deity YHW inside the fortress at Elephantine, where meal-offerings, incense and holocaust offerings were made on one or more altars (AP 30). It was destroyed in 410 BCE by the priests of the rival cult of the main deity of the island, Khnum, who colluded with the Persian official Vaidrang/Vidranga in the absence of the governor Arsham. He in turn ordered his son Nephayan, commander of the fort at Sewen/Syene, to destroy the temple (AP 30). Although those who had participated were punished, many with death, the Judean community was initially denied permission to rebuild the temple. In their draft petition dated three years later to Bagohi, governor of Yehud, in an attempt to find a patron with political clout who could secure the desired permission to rebuild, they stated that their temple had been built prior to the Persian conquest of Egypt in the days of the king[.] of Egypt—hence under the twenty-sixth dynasty of Saite pharaohs (664–525 BCE)—and had not been harmed by Cambyses when he had ordered the destruction of temples of Egyptian gods sometime between 524–522 BCE (AP 30; AP 31). After previously unanswered letter(s) had been sent to Jerusalem to Bagohi, Yohanan the high priest and his fellow priests in Jerusalem, Ostanes the brother of 'Anani and the notables of the Jews/Judeans as well as to Delaiah and Shelemiah, the sons of Sanballat, the (former?) governor of Samerina, this one, accompanied by a bribe of gold, elicited a response. A memorandum records that Bagohi and Delaiah instructed the temple leadership to tell Arsham: 'about the altar/sacrifice-house of the God of Heaven, which was built in the fortress of Yeb, formerly, before Cambyses, which Waiderang/ Vidranga, that reprobate, destroyed in the 14th year of Darius the king, to rebuild it in its place as it was before, and they may offer the meal-offering and incense upon that altar as was performed formerly' (AP 32). It is significant that the support given was for the construction of an 'altar-house' or 'house of sacrifice', not explicitly for a 'temple' (*egora*) as the building had been described previously, and, in breaking with past practice, that no holocaust offerings that involved the burning of an entire ox, sheep or goat were to be performed in the new temple; only incense and meal offerings. It is unclear if this was done to ensure no further conflicts with the priests of Khnum, whose sacred animal was a ram, or if it had something to do with a move by officials in the Jewish heartlands of Yehud and Samerina to reserve animal sacrifice to a central altar, in keeping with a recently introduced call for a central sanctuary for Yahweh, as expressed in the Book of Deuteronomy, even if the location of this sanctuary was disputed between the two provinces.

The Judeans of Yeb were not yet Jewish monotheists. They took oaths in the name of Yahu Elohim in the fortress of Elephantine, but also in the name of the Elephantine goddess Sati (AP 14), Anatyahu (AP 44) and Herembethel (AP 7). Opening formulae in their letters seek peace in the name of God of Heaven (AP 38, 40), but also, more generically, the gods (AP 17, 21, 37, 39), and in one instance on ostracon 271, Bel, Nabu, Shamash and Nergal. Blessings are invoked not only by or to Yahweh but also by or to Hn or Khn[m] (ostracon 70). The mention of Anat-Yahu is particularly revealing (AP 44). It suggests that amongst this Judean colony, Anat was honored as Yahweh's consort/partner instead of Asherah, who had been so honoured in the cult in Jerusalem and at Kuntillet 'Ajrud. This variation is easily explained in light of the military background of the worshippers. Anat is described in the Ugaritic literature as a warrior goddess, and mercenaries would have wanted their male deity (Yahweh Sebaot) to have a militarily minded female partner.

Unfortunately, no copies of biblical books were found amongst the papyri. Thus, it cannot be determined if any were known and read in this community or not. The only literature that survived in papyrus form was a copy of the Wisdom of Ahiqar and a copy of Darius' self-justification (the Behistun inscription). Nevertheless, undated ostraca instructions for what is to be done (AP 21), showing that contain three references to Sabbath and two to the keeping of Passover (*pesah*). In addition, there is a partially preserved letter from Hananiah conveying permission from Darius II in 419 BCE to observe the Feast of Unleavened Bread (*matsot*) and giving these colonists were familiar with some Yahwistic and/or Jewish religious practices. The title *elohe hashamayim*, 'God of Heaven', occurs in ten different papyri, indicating that in the Persian period, Yahu was being conceived of in terms of this universal category, perhaps instead of the earlier one mentioned in the ostraca, Yahweh Sebaot, 'Lord of Hosts' (Bolin 1995). The Judeans of Yeb intermarried with Egyptians and Arameans, so the concern voiced in the books of Ezra and Nehemiah (Ezra 9:11–14; 10; Neh. 13:1–3, 23–30) and in Genesis

(24:1–4; 27:46–28:9) to marry others of Jewish heritage or members of the extended clan was not shared or observed amongst this group.

A collection list dated perhaps to 400 BCE, after the rebuilding of the temple, records the names and amounts of silver given for Yahu Elohim. The final summary states that 12 karsh, 6 shekels was for Yahu, 7 karsh for Eshem-Bethel and 12 karsh were for Anat-Bethel (Porten 1968: 162–63). The temple of Yahu, then, seems to have included, besides the worship of Yahu, cults dedicated to Eshem-Bethel and to his female counterpart, Anat-Bethel. The deity Bethel is named in a treaty between Esarhaddon and Baal king of Tyre (ca. 675 BCE), in a religious text written in Demotic, and in Jer. 48:13, where he appears as a principal god of the house of Israel. He had a temple at the fort in Sewen/Syene, as did the deities Nabu, Banit and the Queen of Heaven; all four temples are mentioned in letters found at Hermopolis but written from Memphis to recipients at Syene (Porten 1968: 164–65). Two possibilities are raised here. (1) Perhaps an arrangement had been struck between the resident Arameans in Yeb and the Judeans to share temple space and building expenses. If so, it is unclear if this had been a long-standing arrangement or one that came about only after the temple was rebuilt ca. 405 BCE. (2) Some of the Elephantine community were of Israelite descent and worshipped Bethel either as their main deity or as an important subsidiary deity. If he was seen as their main deity, then he was being equated with the Judahite/Judean Yahu; both male deities were thought to have Anat as their consort. If he was considered a subsidiary deity, then he would probably have been viewed as Yahu's son and a form of the young male warrior and weather deity, Baal, who in the Ugaritic texts was married to his sister, Anat. Philo of Byblos lists Bethel as the second son of Heaven and Earth alongside El, Dagon and Atlas (*Phoenician History* II.16). Bethel appears as a divine component in some of the personal names in the papyri, but it is not possible to tell if the individuals were Aramean or Judean in background.

It is interesting that no money was mentioned on the collection list for the cult of Anat-Yahu, which is likely to have existed as well, given the oath sworn in her name. Two possible explanations for this can be noted. Either (1) it was considered an integral part of the cult of Yahu and so was not assessed separately, or (2) it was eliminated under the emerging influence of Judaism when the temple was rebuilt sometime ca. 405 BCE. The latter might be more likely since there was a separate collection for Bethel's consort Anat in 400 BCE, suggesting a need for separate funding for individual deities. It seems likely, then, that the divine couple, YHW and his warrior-consort Anat, had been worshipped in Elephantine by Judeans until the destruction of their temple in 410 BCE and that after 405 BCE, Yahu alone was honored with incense and meal offerings only, but may have shared his sacred space with the Aramean or Israelite divine couple, Eshem-Bethel and his consort Anat, who were worshipped by resident Arameans or Israelite descendants. In the first case, some sort of compromise might have been reached with the Persian officials about sharing the space in order to secure the final permission to rebuild.

The collection list, which is not an official document but a personal accounting ledger whose figures do not tally correctly, mentions in the final notation that the silver allotted to the three deities was put into the hand of Jedaniah ben Gemariah, who is known from other documents and correspondence to have been the head official of the temple of YHW. He had worked very hard to get the temple restored. This would seem to rule out the possibility that the ledger had been made by an official who happened also to be in charge simultaneously of collecting money for the other two deities who had their own, separate temples(s) in Yeb and who simply appended the note about delivering the silver collected for all three to Jedaniah at the end of his list detailing donations to YHW. Unless Jedaniah had been a royal treasurer, he would only have been responsible for funds collected at the temple of Yahu (Kraeling 1953: 87–88).

It is only because of happenstance and the dry climate at Elephantine that the archives of Judean families living there in the Persian period were preserved. It would be interesting to have similar documents from the Judean families resident elsewhere in Egypt, to learn if temples to YHW existed on other forts and settlements, if Yahweh had a female consort elsewhere, and if they worshipped or acknowledged deities other than Yahweh. It would be particularly helpful to be able to establish if the label 'Jew' was applied to descendants of Israelites as well as to descendants of Judahites, demonstrating its evolution from a geographico-ethnic term marking those who had once lived within the kingdom of Judah and worshipped its national deity Yahweh Sebaot to a religio-ethnic term applied to worshippers of Yahweh Elohim, whatever their ultimate place of origin, in emerging Judaism.

3. Jews/Judeans in Babylonia

The Bible, as well as Neo-Babylonian royal annals, attests to the deportation of many Judahites of the kingdom of Judah to Babylonia in two waves: in 598 BCE (2 Kgs 24:10–17) and again in 586 BCE (2 Kgs 25:1–12). Other than the city of Babylon in 598 BCE (Jer. 29:1–2, 15, 20, 28) and perhaps again in 586 BCE (Jer. 39:9; 40:1–4, 7; 52), the exact location of their new settlements is not given, other than in vague terms: beside the river Habor (Ezek. 1:1–3; 10:15). The Habor was a canal leading off from the Euphrates river above Babylon, passing that city, proceeding through Nippur, and rejoining the Euphrates near Erech/Uruk. Fortunately, the chance finds of various archives of cuneiform tablets from a number of locations around Babylonia allow us to know more about some of the locations where Jews lived in the Persian era. Presumably, they had been settled in these places under the Neo-Babylonians, after the deportations from Judah. Individuals bearing names that include the divine element -Yah, and in some cases, the gentilic 'Judean', lived in Sippar and its environs, including Til Gubbi; Zazanna; Opis; Babylon; Kish, Alu-sha-Nashar, Alu-Yahudu and Bit-Nabu-le', all probably in the vicinity of Borsippa; Marad; Nippur and its environs, including Bit–Eriba, Bit-Gera, Bit-Muranu, Bit-rab-urati, Bit-Abi-ahi, Sha-rese, Bit-Suraya, Gammale, Parak-Mari, Ishqallunu Hashba, Tel-Gabbari, Titurru, Sin-magir canal, Bit-Shula, Sin-belshuni, Enlil-ashabshu-iqbi, Pusaya, Hiduya, Husseti, Naqidim, Nar-Bel-aba-usur; Isin; and at Alu-sha-Bane near Uruk(?).

They included farmers, a royal or commercial agent, a messenger of a royal official, a summoner for taxes and corvée work, an assistant rent collector, a tax-collector, one in charge of the king's poultry, foremen, a gardener, a shepherd, fishermen and an alphabet scribe (writer in Aramaic) and chancellor (Zadok 2002).

Within the list, the existence of al(u)-Yahudu, spelled in a number of ways by different scribes, is of particular interest. It means 'the city of Judah' and represents a newly created settlement of recently deported people from Judah somewhere in the vicinity of Borsippa. The earliest reference to this location, dating to the 33rd year of Nebuchadrezzar, or 572 BCE, only 15/16 years after the deportation in 587/586 BCE, calls it 'the city of the Judean people', clearly demonstrating that it had been named after the point of origin of its settlers (Pearce 2006). By contrast, the other towns in the list appear to have been pre-existing settlements in which the recently arrived people from Judah were assigned land and mixed in with the locals. The possible exceptions are some of the names compounded with *bit*, meaning 'house', particularly Bit-Eribi and Bit-Gera, which might be of Hebrew derivation. The creation of new cohesive settlements of deportees named after their place of origin appears to have been a Neo-Babylonian policy; the Murashu archive from Nippur,

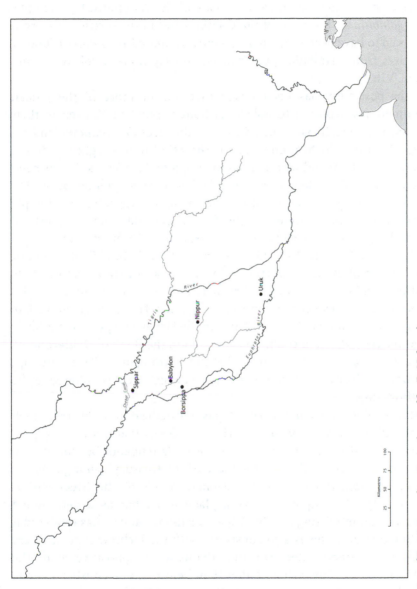

Figure 10. Map of Borsippa and environs (created by R. Hobson)

for example, refers to settlements occupied by deportees from Egypt, Melid, Mushki, Tabal and Sardis in Asia Minor, Hamat in Syria, Tyre in Phoenicia, Ashkelon, Gaza and Arsa in Philistia, and Qedar and the Arabs. This continued an earlier policy of the Assyrians; for example, *uru gambulaia*, 'the town of the Gambuleans' in the district of Harran was said to have been inhabited explicitly by *hubte kur-Gambuli*, 'booty/ captives from Gambulu' (Assyrian Doomsday Book 5 col. II: 26 and 6 col. VII: 4).

The possibility has been raised that one or more of the Judean communities deported to Babylonia built temples to Yahweh in their new settlements. In particular, 'Casiphia, the place (*hammaqom*)' in Ezra 8:15–20, from which 'attendants' (*mesharetim*) were sought to join the group going to Yehud with Ezra in the reign of Artaxerxes (I), has been seen to be a veiled reference to a temple. The term *maqom* can be used to refer specifically to a sacred place, and the reported presence of temple servants (*netinim*) there under the direction of Iddo and his 'brothers' or 'colleagues' might well point to the existence of a functioning temple in Babylonia (Browne 1916; Gamberone 1997: 539–44). Whether or not the version of events as portrayed in the Book of Ezra is historical, its author could have been aware that there had been one or more temples amongst the Judean communities in Babylonia. However, given the late date for the writing of Ezra, probably in the Hellenistic period, it is likely that the centralization tradition expressed in the Book of Deuteronomy had already become the norm so that the wording in v. 17 is an attempt to disguise the existence of other temples, which were prohibited in the author's time.

It is significant that in the parallel passage in the Book of Esdras, which is an independent composition written in Greek that draws heavily on Ezra (1 Esd. 8:45–46), the request is not for 'attendants' but for priests, who are to be secured from 'the place of the treasury' (*en argurio; tou gazophulakiou*) rather than 'in Casiphia, the place'. The Greek author has construed 'Casiphia' not as a place name but as a determined common noun relating to 'silver', *k-s-p*, or money and so has rendered it as 'the treasury'. This is also consistent with the Hebrew syntax, where *hammaqom* stands after *kspy*, functioning as an appositive, as in 'the treasury, that is, "the place"', rather than before it, in a construct chain, which would have given the sense, 'the place of *kspy*'.

But what connection would priests and temple servants have with a treasury? Temples could serve double-duty as royal treasuries. This was the case with the rebuilt temple in Jerusalem (Schaper 1995) and in Babylonian temples, but not the case in Elephantine, where the royal treasury was housed near the temples of Ptah and YHW, but in a separate building. Both the author of Ezra and of Esdras, then, were envisioning the first arrangement of a treasury being located in a temple when they described Ezra's sending to Casiphia/the treasury, the '(sacred) place', for cultic personnel to go/be transferred to Yehud.

Our ability to learn more about Judean diaspora communities is dependent upon the finding of more archives in the future. Unfortunately, archives written in cuneiform on clay are going to survive more readily than those in Aramaic on papyrus or animal skin, and it is likely that transplanted Judeans would have used the services of Aramaic scribes in the first instance, since documents in Judah had been written alphabetically as well, though in Hebrew. The majority of the references to Judeans are to witnesses of transactions rather than to contracting parties, and in both instances, the principles or other contracting party are almost always Babylonians, accounting for the use of cuneiform scribes who wrote in the native language of the parties involved. Of the 50,000+ individuals who are mentioned in the Neo-Babylonian and Late Babylonian private archives, over 98 per cent are urbanite Babylonians and their cronies. In the temple archives, only 2–4 per cent of the named individuals are non-Babylonians (Zadok 2002). It is likely, then, that our knowledge will not increase significantly unless we stumble onto a Judean community that, for some reason, used a cuneiform scribe to record much of the local transactions. The new TAYN texts, which number almost one hundred and are part of a private collection, represent such a grouping. One third were composed in 'the city of Judah' and another third nearby in Nashar, where Judeans also lived (Pearce 2006). Their future publication will allow us to surmise why they used an Akkadian scribe rather than an Aramaic one. We must be careful not to conclude, however, that the largest Judean diaspora was settled in the Nippur region because, fortuitously, the Murashu archive has been found and contained an unusually high number of Judean witnesses and contracting parties.

4. Samarians

Little is known of the places where Israelites/Samarians were resettled after their deportation by the Assyrians in 721 BCE. According to 2 Kgs 17:6, they were exiled to Assyria, and specifically placed 'in Calah, on the Habor River, the river of Gozan, and in the cities of the Medes'. The first

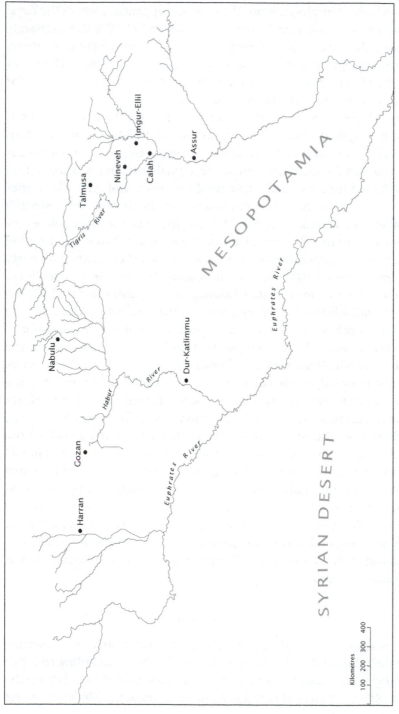

Figure 11. Map of Israelite deportee relocations (created by R. Hobson)

two locations have been confirmed to have received deportees; cuneiform documents mention those of Samarian origin or with Yahwistic names in the first two locations. A troop of Samarian charioteers was assigned to the capital city of Calah and a witness in another document was from Gozan. Other locations where they were assigned land include Zanba, somewhere near Talmusa, Imgur-Ellil, Napisina, Assur, Dur-Katlimmu, Nabulu, Elumu, Qastu, Ma'allanate, Nineveh and Harran.

The professions of the named former Israelites/Samarians include, in addition to charioteers, an archer, a cohort commander, a bodyguard, other military posts, a chief of accounts, an overseer of estates, a prefect, a merchant or commercial agent, a master builder, a subordinate of the chief of construction, slaves, and one in charge of the king's poultry. Only the last one is specifically identified as a Samarian (Zadok 2002).

The inclusion of Harran as a known site where some former Israelites were resettled is of particular interest because it appears to have been the place of origin of Sanballat, the governor of Samerina and contemporary of Nehemiah during the reign of Artaxerxes I. The stories in Genesis that associate Abraham with the region of Harran, from where he leaves to go to the land Yahweh promises to give him and from which he seeks out a suitable wife for Isaac, may reflect traditions designed to acknowledge ties between the Samarian diaspora and their homeland, providing a basis for including them within the definition of the religious community of Israel that was forged when the Pentateuch was created.

Our ability to gain additional knowledge in the future is dependent on the excavation of more sites in the politically troubled regions of Syria, Iran and Afghanistan and the finding of more cuneiform archives. It is highly unlikely that papyri or hide archives will be recovered from these damper climates in the future, and unfortunately, Samarians would have been more likely to have sought out scribes who would have written in Aramaic on papyrus or hide for their necessary deeds and transactions. Thus, we will probably only learn indirectly about other Samarians who also served as witnesses to transactions by Assyrians and other foreign groups.

There is evidence that the Samarian religious community chose to distinguish itself from the Jewish one that accepted Jerusalem as the main sanctuary site in the Hellenistic period, at least, both before and after the destruction of the temple at Mt Gerizim by the Hasmonean rulers. Two inscriptions found on the Greek island of Delos, dated by their style of writing to ca. 200 BCE and 100 BCE, were written by 'the Israelites in Delos who sent an offering to sacred Argarizein' (Kraabel 1984). The identity of those associated with *har gerizim*, the location of the Samaritan temple, as 'Israelites' lays claim by this group to be the true religious community of Israel over against such claims found, for example, in the books of Ezra, Nehemiah and Chronicles, where 'Israel' is used to refer to those who have adopted the cult of Yahweh Elohim and Jerusalem as the sole place where Yahweh has chosen to place his name and have sacrifice offered to him. It is unfortunate that we have no earlier evidence of the use of this gentilic by the community, which might allow us to decide if this was done to counter claims to be the true Israel expressed by the community of Yehud or whether the latter tried to take over the use of 'Israel' from the Samaritans to prevent them from claiming to be the sole legacy of the Israel described in the Pentateuch, which both groups accepted as canonical Scripture. The term 'Jew/Judean' should have been adequate to describe adherents to the form of emerging Judaism that centred on Jerusalem. As we have seen, it was applied by Jews and foreigners alike to those whose ancestors had originated in the kingdom of Judah, both in the heartland and in diasporas in Egypt and Mesopotamia. Yet those from the former kingdom of Israel who were in the diaspora in Assyria or the heartland were known as Samarians, not Israelites. So the use of 'Israel' by the religious community of Mt Gerizim was a deliberate move in some sense. It is unclear whether or not there was any intention to link it specifically to the name of the former kingdom, which had rarely been used to describe the north by its neighbours or conquerors, as a way of claiming more historical continuity.

Works Cited and Suggested Further Reading

Aharoni, Yohanan. 1968. 'Trial Excavation in the "Solar Shrine" at Lachish: Preliminary Report.' *Israel Exploration Journal* 18: 157–69.

— 1979. *The Land of the Bible: A Historical Geography*. Trans. from Hebrew A. Rainey; Philadelphia: Westminster, rev. and enlarged edn.

Ahlström, Gösta W. 1993. *The History of Ancient Palestine from the Palaeolithic Period to Alexander's Conquest*. Ed. posthumously by D. Edelman; JSOTSup, 146; Sheffield: Sheffield Academic Press.

Avigad, Nahman. 1958. 'New Light on the MṢH Seal Impressions.' *Israel Exploration Journal* 8: 113–19.

Barrick, W. Boyd. 2002. *The King and the Cemeteries: Toward a New Understanding of Josiah's Reform*. Vetus Testamentum Supplements, 88; Leiden: Brill.

Bennett, W. J., Jr, and Jeffrey A. Blakely. 1989. *Tell el-Hesi: The Persian Period (Stratum V)*. Ed. K. G. O'Connell, S.J., with F.L. Horton, Jr; ASOR Excavation Reports: Tell el-Hesi, 3; Winona Lake, IN: Eisenbrauns.

Ben Zvi, Ehud, Diana Edelman and Frank Polak (eds). 2009. *A Palimpsest: Rhetoric, Ideology, Stylistics, and Language Relating to Persian Israel.* Piscataway, NJ: Gorgias Press.

Berquist, Jon L. 1995. *Judaism in Persia's Shadow: A Social and Historical Approach.* Minneapolis: Fortress Press.

Blenkinsopp, Joseph. 1987. 'The Mission of Udjahorresnet and Those of Ezra and Nehemiah.' *Journal of Biblical Literature* 106: 409–21.

— 1988. *Ezra–Nehemiah: A Commentary.* Old Testament Library; London: SCM Press.

— 2003. 'Bethel in the Neo-Babylonian Period.' In Lipschits and Blenkinsopp: 93–107.

Boardman, John. 1999. *The Greeks Overseas: Their Early Colonies and Trade.* London: Hudson & Thames, 4th edn.

Bolin, Thomas. 1995. 'The Temple of YHW at Elephantine.' In Diana V. Edelman (ed.). *The Triumph of 'Elohim: From Yahwisms to Judaisms.* Contributions to Biblical Exegesis and Theology, 3; Kampen: Kok Pharos: 127–42.

Briant, Pierre. 2002. *From Cyrus to Alexander: A History of the Persian Empire.* Trans. from French P. T. Daniels; Winona Lake, IN: Eisenbrauns.

Brosius, Maria. 2006. *The Persians: An Introduction.* Peoples of the Ancient World; London: Routledge.

Browne, L. E. 1916. 'A Jewish Sanctuary in Babylonia.' *Journal of Theological Studies* 17: 400–401.

Cameron, G. G. 1973. 'The Persian Satrapies and Related Matters.' *Journal of Near Eastern Studies* 32: 47–56.

Carter, Charles. 1999. *The Emergence of Yehud in the Persian Period: A Social and Demographic Study.* JSOT Supplement Series, 294; Sheffield: Sheffield Academic Press.

Demsky, Aharon. 1983. 'Pelekh in Nehemiah 3.' *Israel Exploration Journal* 33: 342–44.

Dequeker, Luc. 1993. 'Darius the Persian and the Reconstruction of the Jewish Temple in Jerusalem (Ezra 4,24).' In J. Quaegebeur (ed.). *Ritual and Sacrifice in the Ancient Near East: Proceedings of the International Conference Organized by the Katholieke Universiteit Leuven from the 17th to the 20th of April 1991.* Orientalia Lovaniensia Analecta, 55; Leuven: Peeters: 67–92.

Dumbrell, W. J. 1971. 'The Tell el-Mashkuta Bowls and the "Kingdom" of Qedar in the Persian Period.' *Bulletin of the American Schools of Oriental Research* 203: 33–44.

Edelman, Diana. 1995. 'Tracking Observance of the Aniconic Tradition through Numismatics.' In D.V. Edelman (ed.). *The Triumph of 'Elohim: From Yahwisms to Judaisms.* Contributions to Biblical Exegesis and Theology, 3; Kampen: Kok Pharos: 185–225.

— 2007. 'Settlement Patterns in Persian-Era Yehud.' In Y. Levin (ed.). *A Time of Change: Judah and its Neighbours in the Persian and Early Hellenistic Periods.* Library of Second Temple Studies, 65; London: T. & T. Clark: 52–64.

— 2009. 'Ezra 1–6 as Idealized Past.' In Ben Zvi, Edelman and Polak: 178–90.

— 2011. 'Apples and Oranges: Textual and Archaeological Evidence for Reconstructing the History of the Persian Period.' In M. Nissinen (ed.). *Congress Volume, 20th*

International Organization for the Study of the Old Testament Congress, Helsinki.
Vetus Testamentum Supplements; Leiden: Brill [forthcoming].

Edgar, Campbell C. 1925. *Catalogue général des antiquités égyptiennes du Musée de Caire: Nos. 59001–59531, Zenon Papyri.* I. Cairo: l'Institut français d'archéologie orientale.

Eph'al, Israel, and Joseph Naveh. 1996. *Aramaic Ostraca of the Fourth Century BC From Idumaea.* Jerusalem: Israel Exploration Society.

Fantalkin, Alexander, and Oren Tal. 2006. 'Re-dating Lakhish Level I: Identifying Achaemenid Imperial Policy at the Southern Frontier of the Fifth Satrapy.' In Lipschits and Oehming: 167–97.

Fargot, Valerie M. 1993. 'Hesi, Tell el-.' In Ephraim Stern (ed.). *New Encyclopedia of Archaeological Excavations in the Holy Land.* London: Israel Exploration Society & Carta, Jerusalem: II, 630–34.

Foerster, G. 1993. 'Jericho, Hellenistic to early Arab Periods, History.' In Ephraim Stern (ed.). *The New Encyclopedia of Archaeological Excavations in the Holy Land.* London: Israel Exploration Society & Carta, Jerusalem: II, 681–82.

Gamberoni, Johann. 1997. '*maqôm*.' In G. J. Botterweck and H. Ringgren (eds). *Theological Dictionary of the Old Testament.* Trans. from German J. T. Willis; Grand Rapids, MI: Eerdmans: VIII, 532–44.

Geer, Russell M. 1954. *Diodorus of Sicily in Twelve Volumes: X, Books xix. 66–110 and xx.* Loeb Classical Library; London: William Heinemann.

Geus, C. H. J. de. 1979–1980. 'Idumaea.' *Jaarbericht vooraziatisch-Egyptisch Gezelschap 'Ex Oriente Lux'* 26: 53–74.

Grabbe, Lester L. 1992a. *Judaism from Cyrus to Hadrian.* I. *The Persian and Greek Periods.* Minneapolis: Fortress Press.

— 1992b. 'Who was the Bagoas of Josephus (*Ant.* 11.7.1, 297–301)?' *Transeuphratène* 5: 49–61.

Herzfeld, Ernst. 1968. *The Persian Empire: Studies, Geography and Ethnography of the Ancient Near East.* Ed. posthumously by G. Walser; Wiesbaden: F. Stein.

Hoglund, Kenneth. 1992. *Achaemenid Imperial Administration in Syria-Palestine and the Missions of Ezra and Nehemiah.* Society of Biblical Literature Dissertation Series, 125; Atlanta: Scholars Press.

Hulster, Izaak J. de. 2009. 'A Yehud Coin with a Representation of the Sun Deity and Iconic Practice in Persian Period Palestine: An Elaboration on TCT 24.5/BMC Palestine XIX 29.' Available online. http://www.monotheism.uni-goettingen.de/resources/dehulster_tc242.pdf. To be reproduced in *Unity and Diversity in Early Jewish Monotheisms.* Sofjaâ Kovalevskaja Research Project at the Georgâ Augustâ Universitet, Göttingen; Göttingen: 1–16.

Kelso, J. L. 1993. 'Bethel.' In Ephraim Stern (ed.). *The New Encyclopedia of Archaeological Excavations in the Holy Land.* London: Israel Exploration Society & Carta, Jerusalem: II, 674–81.

Kloner, Amos, and Ian Stern. 2007. 'Idumea in the late Persian Period.' In O. Lipschits, G. N. Knoppers and R. Albertz (eds). *Judah and Judeans in the Fourth Century B.C.E.* Winona Lake, IN: Eisenbrauns: 139–44.

Kraabel, A. T. 1984. 'New Evidence of the Samaritan Diaspora Has Been Found on Delos.' *Biblical Archaeologist* 47: 44–46.

Kraeling, Emil G. H. 1953. *The Brooklyn Museum Aramaic Papyri: New Documents of the Fifth Century B.C. from the Jewish Colony at Elephantine.* New York: Yale University Press.

Lemaire, André. 1996. *Nouvelles inscriptions araméenes d'Idumée au Musée d'Israel.* Transeuphratène Supplements, 3; Paris: Gabalda.

— 2002. *Nouvelles inscriptions araméenes d'Idumée Tome II.* Transeuphratène Supplements, 9; Paris: Gabalda.

— 2003. 'Nabonidus in Arabia and Judah in the Neo-Babylonian Period.' In Lipschits and Blenkinsopp: 285–98.

Levin, Yigael (ed.). 2007. *A Time of Change: Judah and Its Neighbours in the Persian and Early Hellenistic Periods.* Library of Second Temple Studies, 65; London: T. & T. Clark.

Lipschits, Oded. 2003. 'Demographic Changes in Judah between the Seventh and the Fifth Centuries B.C.E.' In Lipschits and Blenkinsopp: 323–76.

— 2005. *The Fall and Rise of Jerusalem: Judah Under Babylonian Rule.* Winona Lake, IN: Eisenbrauns.

Lipschits, Oded, and Joseph Blenkinsopp (eds). 2003. *Judah and the Judeans in the Neo-Babylonian Period.* Winona Lake, IN: Eisenbrauns.

Lipschits, Oded, and Manfred Oehming (eds). 2006. *Judah and Judeans in the Early Persian Period.* Winona Lake, IN: Eisenbrauns.

Meshorer, Yaakov. 1982. *Ancient Jewish Coinage.* I. *Persian Period through Hasmonaeans.* Dix Hills, NY: Amphora Books.

Meyers, E. M. 1985. 'The Shelomit Seal and the Judean Restoration: Some Additional Considerations.' *Eretz Israel* 18.33*–38*.

Nordh, Katarina. 1996. *Aspects of Ancient Egyptian Curses and Blessings: Conceptual Background and Transmission.* Boreas: Uppsala Studies in Ancient Mediterranean and Near Eastern Civilizations, 26; Uppsala: Acta Universitatis Upsaliensis.

Oded, Bustenay. 1979. *Mass Deportations and Deportees in the Neo-Assyrian Empire.* Wiesbaden: Dr Ludwig Reichert Verlag.

Pearce, Laurie. 2006. 'New Evidence for Judeans in Babylonia.' In Lipschits and Oehming: 399–411.

Polak, Frank. 2009. 'Verbs of Motion in Biblical Hebrew: Lexical Shifts and Syntactic Structure.' In Ben Zvi, Edelman and Polak: 161–97.

Porten, Bezalel. 1968. *Archives from Elephantine: The Life of an Ancient Jewish Military Colony.* Los Angeles: University of California Press.

Porten, Bezalel, and Ada Yardeni. 2007. 'Makkedah and the Storehouse in the Idumean Ostraca.' In Levin: 127–70.

Rainey, Anson. 1983. 'The Biblical Shephelah of Judah.' *Bulletin of the American Oriental Society* 251: 1–22.

Sallaberger, W., and F. Huber Vulliet. 2003–2005. 'Priester.A.1.' In E. Ebeling and B. Meissner (eds.). *Reallexikon der Assyriologie und vorderasiatischen Archäologie.* Berlin: Walter de Gruyter: X, 617–40.

Sapin, Jean. 2004. 'La frontière judéo-iduméene au IVe s. avant J.-C.' *Transeuphratène* 27: 109–54.

Schaper, Joachim. 1995. 'The Jerusalem Temple as an Instrument of the Achaemenid Fiscal Administration.' *Vetus Testamentum* 44: 528–39.

Stern, Ephraim. 1982. *Material Culture of the Land of the Bible in the Persian Period 538–332 B.C.* Warminster: Aris & Phillips.

— 1990. 'New Evidence on the Administrative Division of Palestine in the Persian Period.' In H. Sancisi-Werdenburg and A. Kuhrt (eds). *Achaemenid History*. IV. *Centre and Periphery*. Leiden: Nederlands Instituut voor het Nabije Oosten: 221–26.

— 2000. 'The Babylonian Gap.' *Biblical Archaeology Review* 26: 45–51.

— 2001. *Archaeology of the Land of the Bible*. II. *The Assyrian, Babylonian, and Persian Periods, 732–332 BCE*. Anchor Bible Reference Library; New York: Doubleday.

Stern, Ian. 2007. 'The Population of Persian-Period Idumea according to the Ostraca: A Study of Ethnic Boundaries and Ethnogenesis.' In Levin: 205–38.

Stolper, Matthew. 1985. *Enterpreneurs in the Empire: The Murašu Archive, the Murašu Firm, and Persian Rule in Babylonia*. Uitgaven van het Nederlands Historisch-Archaeologisch Instituut te Istanbul, 54; Istanbul: Nederlands Historisch-Archaeologisch Instituut te Istanbul.

— 1989. 'The Governor of Babylon and Across-the River in 486 BC.' *Journal of Near Eastern Studies* 48: 283–305.

Tufnell, Olga. 1953. *Lachish III (Tell ed- Duweir): The Iron Age*. The Wellcome-Marston Archaeological Research Expedition to the Near East, 3; London: Oxford University Press for the Trustees of the late Sir Henry Wellcome.

Vanderhooft, David. 1999. *The Neo-Babylonian Empire and Babylon in the Latter Prophets*. Harvard Semitic Museum Monographs, 59; Atlanta: Scholars Press.

Wallinga, H. T. 1987. 'The Ancient Persian Navy and Its Predecessors.' In H. Sancisi-Weerdenburg (ed). *Achaemenid History I: Sources, Structures and Synthesis. Proceedings of the Groningen 1983 Achaemenid History Workshop*. Leiden: Nederlands Instituut voor het Nabije Oosten: 47–44.

Watts, James W. (ed.). 2001. *Persia and Torah: The Theory of Imperial Authorization of the Pentateuch*. Symposium Series, Society of Biblical Literature, 17; Atlanta: Society of Biblical Literature.

Wright, John W. 2006. 'The Borders of Yehud and the Genealogies of Chronicles.' In Lipschits and Oehming: 67–89.

Zadok, Ran. 2002. *The Earliest Diaspora: Israelites and Judeans in Pre-Hellenistic Mesopotamia*. Tel Aviv: The Diaspora Institute, Tel Aviv University.

Zorn, Jeffrey R., Joseph Yellin and John Hayes. 1994. 'The *m(w)ṣh* Stamp Impressions and the Neo-Babylonian Period.' *Israel Exploration Journal* 44: 161–83.

Chapter 4

Key Themes in the Pentateuch

1. Torah

i. Etymology and Semantics

The designation of the Pentateuch as the 'Torah' represents a specialized use of a much more comprehensive term in Hebrew. In the Pentateuch itself, *torah* is used in a variety of ways. It is essential, therefore, that we begin with a brief analysis of the term itself in order to grasp the relationship between the various meanings of *torah* and the canonical 'Torah' as a comprehensive designation.

Hebrew *torah* is derived from the root *yrh*, meaning 'to send/transmit orders or instructions' and, by extension, 'to teach'. It is rendered, therefore, by 'teaching' or 'instruction', even though the specific meaning varies significantly according to context. Former attempts to connect *torah* to the same root, which has a second meaning of 'to throw, hurl', have proved incorrect. Interestingly, the substantive *tertu(m)*, formed in the same way as *torah* by prefixing a 't' to the underlying root, is found in Akkadian texts from Mari and designates an 'omen' or an 'oracle'. Even though an oracular context is not always obvious in the Hebrew Bible, this etymology suggests the term *torah* could be used typically to refer to an individual instruction of divine origin. However, *torah* has taken on different meanings according to the scribal and social contexts in which it has been used. Three such ideological contexts can be distinguished: the temple, prophecy and wisdom, which correspond to the three main classes of specialists for interpreting divine directives: priests, prophets and sages. The semantic nuances developed in these three contexts are all reflected, to different degrees, in the Torah itself.

Various passages indicate that *torah* could be used to denote the form of knowledge distinctive to priests as opposed to other categories of specialists. Jeremiah 18:18 states: 'for the *torah* shall not vanish from the priest, nor the advice (*etsah*) from the sage or the word (*davar*) from the prophet'. Similarly, Ezek. 7:26b notes: 'they shall [in vain] seek a vision (*hazon*) from the prophet, the *torah* shall disappear from the priest, and the advice (*etsah*) from the elders'. Other passages indicate that priestly *torah* was an instruction concerning ritual matters, especially sacrifices and matters of cleanness/uncleanness. The prophet Haggai asks the priests for a *torah* (2:11) regarding a specific point of sacrificial *halakah* (Hag. 2:10–14, esp. v. 12). In Ezek. 44:23–24, it is announced that in the eschatological temple revealed to Ezekiel, the priests will 'teach' (root *yrh* II) the people the distinction 'between sacred and profane' as well as between 'unclean and clean' (v. 23) and that they will 'keep' Yahweh's *torot* and his 'statutes' (*huqqotay*) 'in all his appointed times', his *moadim*. The latter is a term referring to specific, sacred times in the year, such as festivals.

Elsewhere, in Zeph. 3:4 and Ezek. 22:26, priests are reproached for profaning Yahweh's holiness by violating his *torah*. It is not always clear how this priestly knowledge was obtained. Some passages associate the priestly oracle with the Urim and Tummim, possibly two semi-precious (?) stones (Exod. 28:30//Lev. 8:8) used to answer a question with two options (see 1 Sam. 14.41 LXX; Num. 27:21 and Deut. 33:8 for the association between Urim and Tummim and the high priest in an oracular context). However, priestly *torah* need not have always required an oracular procedure; the priests in the temple of Jerusalem, for example, could also refer to the body of ritual instructions they gradually developed over the centuries by this term. In any event, there are indications that the priestly torah, however it was obtained, was thought to be of divine origin; so, for example, Mal. 2:7: 'for he [the priest] is the angel of Yahweh'.

In other passages in the Hebrew Bible, however, the term *torah* can be identified as prophetic instruction. In several places, it is paralleled by the term *davar*, a technical description of a prophetic utterance (e.g. Isa. 1:10; Jer. 6:19; 26:4–5; Zech. 7:12). The two terms probably refer to distinct forms of prophetic revelation, although it is not easy to determine where, precisely, the difference resides. It seems, nonetheless, that *davar* is a more comprehensive term for a prophetic utterance. In several prophetic books, *davar* is used in the superscription to refer to the content of the entire book: see, for example, Isa. 2:1, Hos. 1:1 and Amos 1:1. A few passages suggest, however, that *torah* could occasionally be used to refer to a *collection* of instructions of sorts, probably placed under the authority of a single prophetic figure. This usage occurs in Isa.

8:16, where the prophet commands that the *torah*, apparently consisting of oracles attributed to Isaiah, be 'sealed' among his 'disciples', who are expected therefore to study and meditate on the words of the prophet.

Finally, in the wisdom tradition, *torah* may refer to a specific instruction but most frequently has the general sense of 'teaching' delivered either by the parents or by a wisdom teacher, by which one may live a successful life. This meaning can be seen in Prov. 13:14, 'The teaching of the wise is a fountain of life', as well as in several other passages (Prov. 3:1–2; 6:23; 7:2). Here, contrary to priestly and prophetic *torah*, reference to an oracular background is conspicuously missing. Instead, in agreement with the general attitude that characterizes the wisdom tradition, *torah*'s conformity with the divine will can be evidenced in the blessings or the curses caused by the observance or non-observance of the *torah*. In other passages, however, the term appears to refer more specifically to Moses' law (for example, Psalm 1).

If we turn now to the Pentateuch specifically, occurrences of the term *torah* (in the singular or in the plural) can be classified according to three general categories: (a) a distinct ritual instruction; (b) a general term to designate divine instruction(s) along with other similar terms; or (c) a reference to a specific collection of laws given by Moses to 'Israel'.

a. In the Pentateuch, the term *torah* can be used to refer to specific instructions concerning various ritual matters, such as sacrifices (Leviticus 1–7; see Lev. 7:37–38), bodily uncleanness (Leviticus 11–15),[1] and the *nazir* (Num. 6:13, 21).[2] Usually, *torah* occurs in headings introducing or concluding the description of a ritual, often with stereotyped formulae such as: 'this is the *torah*', followed by the theme of the prescription,[3] or 'this is the *torah* concerning...'[4]

The occurrences of *torah* as 'ritual instruction' are *exclusively* found in passages that scholars have classically assigned to the so-called 'Priestly' source (P) in the books of Exodus, Leviticus and Numbers. In fact, P *always* uses the term in this way. On the other hand, in the non-Priestly portions of the Pentateuch, it is *never* used to designate a ritual instruction. The scribes who composed P belonged themselves to the priestly class or—alternatively—were sponsored by the latter to compose the Priestly document. It is therefore readily explainable that these scribes predominantly use the term *torah* in the traditional sense of a *priestly instruction about ritual matters*, as in Hag. 2:10–14 and related passages. Yet a new development occurs in P: according to this pentateuchal tradition, most of the rituals revealed by Yahweh to Moses at Sinai were actually revealed not just to the priests but to the people as a whole (see Lev. 1:1, and further Num. 1:1). Exceptions include the disposal of sacrificial remains (Leviticus 6–7; esp. Lev. 6:1–2a; 6:17–18a) or the identification of skin disease (Leviticus 13), which are the prerogative of Aaron and his sons.

The notion in 'P' of God's revelation of priestly *torot* to all Israel does not so much reflect a 'democratization' of priestly instructions, as commentators often hold, as *an elevation of all Israel to priestly dignity*. The reference to Israel as a 'kingdom of priests' in Exod. 19:6 expresses the same idea: 'Israel', for the priestly scribes who composed the Pentateuch, is re-defined as a 'priestly nation' among the nations of earth. This means that, for these scribes, 'Israel' is the sole nation chosen by Yahweh to offer him sacrifices and to worship him in his temple. Nevertheless, a clear distinction is maintained between 'priests' and 'laymen' in Priestly texts.

When the Pentateuch was created, the use of *torah* as a specific instruction about ritual matters was necessarily merged with other meanings of the term. Nonetheless, how far this aspect underlies the use of 'Torah' as a comprehensive designation for the entire Pentateuch—in other words, how far the canonical Torah could be viewed by its editors as a priestly teaching specifically—is an important and complicated issue. In his final blessing, when Moses declares that the sons of Levi, the head of the priestly family, are to 'teach' (*yrh*) Yahweh's ordinances (*mishpatim*) to Jacob and his 'torah' to Israel (Deut. 33:10a MT), to which *torah* does he refer: the traditional priestly *torah*, the Torah as a whole, or both simultaneously? We shall return later to this question.

b. So far we have discussed the meaning of *torah* in the 'Priestly' portions of the Pentateuch, noting that P's usage is quite distinctive. Turning now to the *non-priestly* portions of the Torah, we need to distinguish between the first four books, Genesis to Numbers, on the one hand, and Deuteronomy, the fifth book, on the other.

In the non-priestly portions of Genesis–Numbers, *torah* is used infrequently. When it occurs in the plural, it is always in combination with similar terms: *huqqim*, 'statutes' in Exod. 18:16, 20; *mitsvot*, 'commandments' in Exod. 16:28; and, lastly, *mishmeret*, 'observances' or 'service', *mitsvot*, and *huqqot* in Gen. 26:5. In the latter passage, the inclusiveness of the formula reflects an obvious attempt to cover all the commandments given by Yahweh. It is often thought that the use in these three passages betrays the influence of the 'Deuteronomistic' tradition upon Genesis–Numbers. Yet the plural form *torot* is *never* found either in the Book of Deuteronomy or in the Former Prophets; only the singular form. In the three passages cited above, the *torot* clearly refer to specific instructions, although it is difficult to determine precisely what their content would be. It is likely, however, that they are meant to be a form of divine instruction distinct from those presented by the other terms in the list. On analogy with Akkadian *tertu(m)*, the *torot* could refer here to oracular decisions motivated by specific demands that could then become legally binding, as at Mari, for instance. This would make sense, at least, in the context of Exod. 18:16, 20.

In the singular, *torah* is used in Exod. 13:9; 16:4 and 24:12. In the first two occurrences, it refers to a divine instruction, although the context is ambiguous and may suggest the more general idea of a 'norm' or 'standard' for living one's life, as in the wisdom tradition. The last occurrence in Exod. 24:12 is unique and stands apart from the others.

In 24:12, Moses is commanded by Yahweh to ascend Mount Sinai to receive the stone tablets written by God himself containing the '*torah*' and the 'commandment' (*mitsvah*) Yahweh wrote 'in order to teach them' (*yrh*). How the expression *hattorah wehammitsvah* in this passage should be understood is far from clear. The MT begins with the conjunction *w*[e] before *hattorah*; however, this *vav* is missing in the Samaritan Pentateuch (SamP) and in the Septuagint (LXX). The presence of the *vav* before *hattorah* may mean either that the *torah* and the *mitsvah* are 'given' by God to Moses in addition to the two stone tablets; or, alternatively (and perhaps more likely) the *vav* is explanatory, meaning that the tablets are equated with *hattorah wehammitsvah*. In the context of Exod. 24:12 the *torah* and the *mitsvah* should refer to the Decalogue (Exodus 20) and the so-called 'Covenant Code' (Exodus 21–23) respectively. However, other passages in the Pentateuch suggest that the two tables contained only the 'ten words', that is, the *Decalogue* (Deut. 4:13 and 10:3–5), or some rewritten version of the latter, as recounted in Exodus 34 (see 34:27–28). Furthermore, the body of laws revealed to Moses in Exodus 21–23 is never designated as '*mitsvah*' but as the *mishpatim* or 'ordinances' (see Exod. 21:1). It remains difficult to establish with certainty to what, exactly, the phrase *hattorah wehammitsvah* in Exod. 24:12 refers; it certainly includes the Decalogue and, possibly, some additional body of revealed laws. Elsewhere in the Hebrew Bible, the expression *hattorah wehammitsvah* is rare and occurs primarily in very late passages (Josh. 22:5; 2 Chron. 14:3; 31:21).[5]

In the Pentateuch, the singular form of *mitsvah* is found exclusively in Deuteronomy. In some passages, it precedes *huqqim* and *mishpatim*, appearing as a kind of comprehensive designation for all the divine commandments (Deut. 5:31; 6:1; 7:11; *kol hammitsvah* is used in Deut. 6:25; 8:1; 11:8, 22; 15:5; 19:9; 27:1). This summary meaning of *mitsvah* is probably also reflected in the phrase *hattorah wehammitsvah* in Exod. 24:12, since the Decalogue contains the most fundamental commandments. Bearing this in mind, *torah* probably has the same meaning as *mitsvah* in v. 12, even though such a coupling to describe the Decalogue is unique within the Pentateuch and indeed, within the Hebrew Bible.

c. In the Book of Deuteronomy, *torah* occurs exclusively in the singular; apart from Deut. 17:11, it always has an inclusive meaning, referring to the divine revelation disclosed by Moses to Israel. This includes its use in 17:18–19 to describe the *torah* the king is to read and learn 'all the days of his life', which is not restricted to the few conditions incumbent on the king given in 17:14–17, as some scholars would hold. More likely, it refers to Deuteronomy or to the entire Pentateuch. In 17:11, on the other hand, it designates a specific instruction delivered by the priests in the central sanctuary, similar to the use in 'P'. For individual commandments, other terms such as *huqqim/huqqot*, *mishpatim* and *mitsvot* are used. It is in Deuteronomy, therefore, that we find the first systematic use of *torah* as a comprehensive designation for the divine commandments that subsume the other meanings discussed above.

Most scholars agree that, initially, *torah* was not used to refer to the entire Pentateuch but was restricted to designating an early version of the Book of Deuteronomy. The 'Book of the Law' (*sefer hattorah*), reportedly found in the temple under Josiah (2 Kgs 22:8, 11), has traditionally been identified as Deuteronomy. The fact that the Kings account is clearly fictional does not negate this conclusion: indeed, the expression *sefer hattorah* occurs elsewhere exclusively in Deut. 28:61; 29:20; 30:10; 31:26 as well as in two passages in Joshua, Josh. 1:8; 8:34 (MT//9:2e LXX), which clearly derive from Deuteronomy. In addition, Josiah's depicted elimination of Yahwistic cults from the temple of Jerusalem and his destruction of other cultic places in Israel undertaken in 2 Kings 23 conforms entirely to the requirements expressed in Deuteronomy 12, particularly the law of cultic centralization. Many other parallels corroborate this identification; the final notice about Josiah states that there was never before him a king who 'returned' to Yahweh with all his 'heart, his being and his strength', 'according to the *torah* of Moses' (2 Kgs 23:25a).

The three Hebrew terms used in v. 25a, *lev*, *nephesh* and *meod*, occur elsewhere only in Deut. 6:4–5, the first and most important command in Deuteronomy many scholars think may once have opened the book. The result is a perfect *inclusio* or repeated narrative framework between the account in 2 Kings 22–23 and the beginning of Deuteronomy. This need not be seen to imply, however, that Deuteronomy and Kings were part of the same literary collection initially, forming integral parts of the so-called 'Deuteronomistic History' as proposed by M. Noth (1981). What it suggests is that the scribes who composed the books of Kings considered the '*torah* of Moses' (*torat mosheh*; 1 Kgs 2:3; 2 Kgs 2:8; 23:25) to be identical with a former version of Deuteronomy.

It was only at a later stage, when Deuteronomy was included within the Pentateuch, that the expressions 'Law of Moses' and 'Book of the Law (of Moses)' were logically understood by the editors of the Torah to refer to the entire Pentateuch. In the books of Ezra, Nehemiah and Chronicles, this broader sense has become standard. References to the '*torah* of Moses' appear to presuppose the combination of the Book of Deuteronomy with other pentateuchal traditions, especially the so-called 'Priestly' laws. For example, Neh. 8:14 recounts how the people found written in the *torah* of Moses that they should dwell in booths, Hebrew *sukkot*, for the duration of that feast. This explicit command is found in Lev. 23:42 only; it is not specified in the festival regulations presented in Deuteronomy 16. Thus, *torah* here must include the Book of Leviticus.

It remains difficult, however, to determine the exact profile of the Torah at the time Ezra, Nehemiah and Chronicles were composed; particularly, whether it already included five separate scrolls. This matter remains debated, especially in the case of Ezra and Nehemiah (further on this below). Significantly, in both of these books, the designation *sefer torat mosheh*, 'the scroll of the law of Moses', is equated with other expressions that emphasize the divine origin of the Torah: 'the scroll of the law of God', *sefer torat ha'elohim* (Neh. 8:18; used only once elsewhere, in Josh. 24:26) or 'the scroll of the law of Yahweh', *sefer torat yahweh* (Neh. 9:3; 2 Chron. 17:9; 34:14).

ii. Establishing the Pentateuch as 'Torah': Background and Issues

iia. Dating the acceptance of the Pentateuch as 'Torah'. At some point in the history of Second Temple Judaism, the first five books in the Hebrew Bible were defined as comprising '*the* Torah', namely, a collection of scrolls with special authority for the community identifying itself as 'Israel'. This collection provided a legend outlining the origins of

'Israel', from the creation of the world (Genesis 1) to Moses' death (Deuteronomy 34), which was recognized as normative and which was capable of rivalling the founding legends of other nations within the context of the Persian empire. The claim made in Deut. 4:8, 'And what great nation has statutes and ordinances as equitable as this whole Torah that I [Yahweh] am setting before you today?', illustrates the latter function. The establishment of the Pentateuch as 'the Torah' was to be one of the most influential achievements of Judaism during the Second Temple period, even though, as we shall see in the following section, the authority of the Pentateuch as Torah was viewed differently amongst various Jewish groups.

The historical setting of such a development cannot be situated precisely. It is partially connected with the issue of internal and external evidence for dating the Pentateuch, which has been discussed in Chapter 2, but there are other influencing factors as well. Traditionally, it has been linked with Ezra's mission as recounted in Ezra 7 and Nehemiah 8. These chapters tell how Ezra arrived in Jerusalem with a royal decree from one of the three Persian kings named Artaxerxes, who had entrusted him with the responsibility of appointing 'judges' (or 'scribes', according to the LXX) and 'magistrates' 'who would judge all the people who are in (the satrapy of) Beyond the River' and to enforce 'the law (Aramaic *data*) of your God and the law of the king' in the entire satrapy (Ezra 7:25–26).

In Nehemiah 8, Ezra reads the 'Book of the Law of Moses' (*sefer torat mosheh*, v. 1), also designated the 'Book of the Law of God' (*sefer torat haelohim*, v. 18), to the community assembled in Jerusalem. This public reading takes place on the eve of the Feast of Booths, which is then celebrated during the ensuing seven days (vv 13–18). In the course of the festival, the public reading of the Law is repeated.

Even assuming that the 'Torah' mentioned in Nehemiah 8 was the Pentateuch or a first version of it, scholars are usually aware that these two accounts cannot be taken at face value as historically reliable witnesses for the introduction of the Torah into Yehud. The decree of the Persian king in Ezra 7:12–26 has long been suspected of being a forgery. Recent research has shown that the practice of forging documents that claimed authorization from the Persian king was common in the Hellenistic period, and the royal decree in Ezra 7 shares many similarities with such documents (see Grätz 2004 for a detailed history of research). Likewise, the account in Nehemiah 8 is problematic, with its sudden appearance of the figure of Ezra. In addition, there is no real narrative coherence between Ezra 7 and Nehemiah 8, and it is unclear to what extent one should identify the 'law (*data'*) of Ezra's god' in Ezra 7:26 with the *sefer torat mosheh* read by Ezra to the people in Nehemiah 8.

Nonetheless, the fact remains that Ezra, Nehemiah and Chronicles appear to use the designations *torat mosheh*, *torat yahweh* and *torat haelohim* to refer to the main traditions now found in the canonical Pentateuch. In which form those traditions were known is difficult to tell. Chronicles, which is commonly dated to the fourth century BCE, seems to presuppose a form of the Pentateuch not significantly different from the canonical one (see Steins 1996). For the books of Ezra and Nehemiah, however, the evidence is more complicated and the problem remains disputed. These books differ from the traditions recorded in the Pentateuch on a number of points, particularly legal ones (for some examples, see Blenkinsopp 2001: 56–59).

Although the import of such differences may be very variously construed, it appears that in Ezra and Nehemiah, the 'book of the law' putatively brought back by Ezra to Jerusalem cannot simply be identified with the Pentateuch as we know it. On the other hand, there are also several passages that are demonstrably exegetical in nature, which adapt and develop commands 'as written in the Torah', *kakkatuv battorah* (Neh. 10:31–40), meaning 'found in the Pentateuch' (on this formula, see Lange 2005). For example, in Neh. 10:35, where reference is made to the command to 'light a fire upon the altar of Yahweh, as it is written in the Torah', a corresponding instruction for bringing an offering of wood to the temple is added. Later, in the Temple Scroll, this supplemental command will be expanded even further with specific details of what is entailed.

Such a phenomenon presupposes that, by the time of the writing of Ezra and Nehemiah, some form of the Pentateuch was already regarded as authoritative. If we retain a date for Ezra, Nehemiah and Chronicles in the fourth century BCE, we are logically led to conclude that the Pentateuch became 'the Torah' at some point in the second half of the Persian period, after Jerusalem became the administrative centre of Yehud under Nehemiah ca. 450 BCE. However, the books of Ezra and Nehemiah in particular, and Chronicles to a lesser extent, demonstrate that the kind of *textual stability* traditionally associated with the notion of 'canon' is a much later development that did not begin before the end of the Hellenistic period (see further on this below, section iii).

iib. Composing the Pentateuch as 'Torah' in the Persian period. Recently, several scholars have proposed that the promulgation of the Pentateuch as 'Torah' was accomplished by various additions to the Pentateuch itself. This view implies a complete revision of the classical theory that prevailed during most of the nineteenth and twentieth centuries, according to which the redaction of the Pentateuch involved the conflation of various sources without any specific overarching literary or ideological design (so, for example, Noth 1981).

A major concern of the 'pentateuchal redactors', the scribes responsible for assembling the various narrative and legal traditions comprising the Pentateuch into a coherent legend of origins, was to establish the superiority of the Torah of Moses over all other forms of revelation. This is made explicit in the last verses of Deuteronomy, which close the Pentateuch as a whole. They summarize the life and achievements of Moses thus: 'And never again has there arisen in Israel a prophet like Moses, whom Yahweh knew face to face' (Deut. 34:10–12). Also revealing is the declaration found in Num. 12:6–8. When Moses had been criticized by Miriam and Aaron for marrying a Kushite woman (v. 1), they had asked: 'Has Yahweh really spoken through Moses alone? Has he not spoken through us as well?' (v. 2). Yahweh responds directly with the following words:

> If there is among you a prophet, it is in a vision (*bammarah*) that I make myself known to him, it is in a dream (*bakalom*) that I speak to him. It is not so with my servant Moses, he who is in charge of all my house: it is mouth to mouth that I speak to him, publicly (*umareh*), and not by riddles (*behidot*), and he sees the form (*temunah*) of Yahweh. Why, then, do you not fear to speak against my servant Moses? (Num. 12:6–8)

Here, Moses' authority is established definitively over Aaron and Miriam by differentiating between two distinct types of revelation, direct and indirect. Moses alone has been privy to the former. The existence of indirect revelations is not denied, but they are clearly inferior to Moses' Torah, and, in the view of the pentateuchal redactors, must conform to the latter. Yahweh's infliction on Miriam of *tsaraat*, a form of skin disease requiring her expulsion from the community for opposing Moses, emphasizes the message. Only Moses' direct intercessory intervention brings about her cure, which reinforces his uniqueness and authority even further (12:9–15).

In this story, Moses, Aaron and Miriam probably represent different social groups claiming to be the guardians of some form of divine revelation. While Moses represents the editors of the Torah, Aaron logically stands for the priestly hierarchy of the temple in Jerusalem. Miriam's group is harder to pinpoint, but since she is designated a 'prophetess' (*neviah*) in Exod. 15:20–21, she probably represents prophetic groups in and around Jerusalem.

The once popular notion that there existed an opposition between 'free' prophetic groups and the temple needs to be abandoned. Indeed, if we are to judge from the prophetic corpus in the Hebrew Bible (Isaiah, Jeremiah, Ezekiel and the Twelve), the Jerusalemite temple was apparently a central symbol for most prophetic groups; several texts associate the expected restoration with the Temple Mount (for example, Isaiah 65–66; Ezekiel 40–48; Joel 4; Zechariah 14). Thus, there is no reason to posit that prophetic groups were against the temple.

Nonetheless, prophetic texts from the Persian period also indicate that there could be a significant amount of conflict over political and religious issues among certain prophetic groups and other groups associated with the temple, including priestly families. According to Isa. 66:5, sometimes prophetic groups could be (provisionally) 'cast out' or excluded from the temple's precincts.

The principle problem with prophetic groups was probably their strong eschatological expectations (see, for example, Isaiah 65–66; Joel 4; Zechariah 14; Malachi 3)—expectations that were not shared by all groups and parties in Persian-period Jerusalem. Isaiah 66:5 suggests that such eschatological expectations could be ridiculed by other groups. While such expectations are not ridiculed in the Torah, they certainly do not play an important part either. Very few passages reflect eschatological expectations of the kind found in prophetic texts (see, however, Num. 24:10–24), and it seems that prophetic eschatology was not a significant part of the belief system of the scribes who finalized the Torah (see especially Crüsemann 1996: 345–49).

In light of these remarks, Miriam's identification with prophets and the role she is assigned in Numbers 12 probably represents an attempt to 'domesticate' such prophetic groups while simultaneously acknowledging their importance. Similar attempts at 'domesticating' prophecy are apparent in other places in the Hebrew Bible. In Chronicles, for example, prophets are transformed into Levitical singers. In Numbers 12, ecstatic prophecy is tolerated but only insofar as it is entirely obedient to Moses' words.

The use of Miriam, the sister of Moses and Aaron, to represent such prophetic groups reflects the family and legal structures of the day. Being unmarried, Miriam would have been under the social and legal control of her two brothers and her father, were he still alive. The authors of the Pentateuch used this accepted convention to reinforce their view that charismatic prophecy should be controlled by the leading authorities of Jerusalem in the Persian period, the temple and, above all, the Torah.

Thus, the redaction of the Pentateuch and its promotion as 'Torah' was closely tied, from its inception, to the attempt to subordinate other sacred traditions and divinatory mediums to its authority. Torah is presented as the sole, legitimate revelation. Whether this claim was accepted by all groups is another issue, to which we shall return in the third and final section.

iic. The social context and parties involved. The previous observations raise three broader, interrelated issues: understanding the social context in which the Pentateuch was created and established as *the* Torah, the parties involved and the intended audience.

On this matter, much discussion has been devoted to the theory of a 'Persian imperial authorization of the Torah', a theory particularly elaborated by P. Frei (1996, 2001), although it is actually older. In a nutshell, this theory posits that the publication of the Pentateuch and its promulgation as 'Torah' should be viewed as part of an Achaemenid policy of ratifying local laws and customs, so that the Pentateuch was acknowledged by the imperial administration as 'a locally valid imperial law'. The theory was highly influential in the field during most of the 1990s; for some biblical critics, it explains best why rival documents about Israel's origins from the early Persian period (such as the Priestly and non-Priestly traditions mentioned above) were eventually subsumed under a single 'book'. However, the notion of a 'Persian imperial authorization' of the Pentateuch has also been significantly criticized by both Iranologists and biblical scholars and, today, tends to be viewed with caution by a majority of critics (see the essays in Watts 2001).

The main biblical evidence for Frei's hypothesis is the account in Ezra 7 relating how Ezra returned to Yehud from Babylon with a copy of a royal decree from the Persian king Artaxerxes (either Artaxerxes I or II, depending on whether Ezra's mission is dated to 454 or 398 BCE) granting him imperial authorization to enforce 'the law (Aramaic *dat*) of your God and the law (*dat* again) of the king' (Ezra 7:25–26). Here, admittedly, local and imperial legislation are clearly paralleled. However, the authenticity of the imperial edict has often been called into question, and a long scholarly tradition holds it to be a forgery, possibly from the Hellenistic period (Grätz 2004).

Yet independently from this issue, a comparison with other cases of so-called 'imperial authorization' in antiquity, such as the trilingual inscription of Xanthus (the so-called 'Letoon trilingual'), raises several questions. First, the evidence does not support the idea there was a centralized imperial process for the codification of local laws; it suggests instead that Persian officials (such as the satraps) could occasionally react to local queries by endorsing them with their own authority. This is very different from the situation presupposed in Ezra 7, where Ezra is supposed to come back from Babylon with a decree from the Persian king himself and where no reference is made to a previous query from Judean elites in Jerusalem. Second, in the case of inscriptions such as the Letoon trilingual, the official authorization of local customs is not all-encompassing but restricted to specific issues; no legislation matches the scope of the Pentateuch. Furthermore, these inscriptions always are translated into Aramaic, the imperial language. There is no evidence of an Aramaic Pentateuch; Aramaic targums of the Pentateuch are from a later period and belong to a different genre. As noted by Jean-Louis Ska (2001), such a long document in Hebrew, with its unique blending of narrative and legal materials, was of no use to Persian authorities.

In summary, it is probably fair to state that the so-called 'imperial authorization' theory raises too many issues to be taken at face value. This does not mean, however, that the theory of imperial authorization should be entirely dismissed. As some recent authors have noted, the possibility cannot be excluded that Judean elites in Jerusalem were aware of the practice of Persian officials occasionally to authorize local customs (see also the case of Udjahorresnet in Egypt) and sought such authorization for their own legal traditions (e.g. Knoppers 2001), as was the case later in the Hellenistic and Roman periods. In this scenario, the Pentateuch may still have been composed with a *view towards* its official recognition by the Achaemenid administration, even if this was not the sole, or even the main reason for its historical development.

The rejection of 'imperial authorization' as the stimulus for the promulgation of the Pentateuch has resulted in a search for 'internal' explanations for its creation. The dominant trend in the last decade has been to view the Pentateuch as a document of compromise between different scribal schools in Jerusalem in the late fifth or early fourth century BCE (see, for example, Ska 2006: 217–29 and more generally, Knoppers and Levinson 2007). The schools agreed to bring the different traditions they regarded as authoritative—for example, the Priestly writing—and to combine them to create a normative account or, if one prefers, a 'founding legend' of the origins of 'Israel'. That normative account, while it preserved conflicting views, was nevertheless unified by a comprehensive narrative framework stretching from the origins of the world (Genesis 1) to the death of the lawgiver, Moses (Deuteronomy 34).

An example of unresolved conflict is the altar law in Exod. 20:24–26, which permits the existence of multiple altars, and Deuteronomy 12, which presumes a single altar will exist. Later, such contradictions will give rise to a considerable amount of exegetical activity among Jewish scribes in order to harmonize or—at least—smooth over the unresolved tensions. Early examples of this process can be found, for instance, in Second Temple compositions like the group of manuscripts dubbed 'Reworked Pentateuch' (4Q 364–67) or the so-called 'Temple Scroll' found at Qumran (11QT). (For a convenient survey of these and similar compositions, see White Crawford 2008.) The process appears to have begun already in some late portions of the Pentateuch; the so-called 'Holiness Code' (= Leviticus 17–27) may be viewed as a synthesis between 'Priestly' and 'Deuteronomistic' legal traditions. However, although the hermeneutical implications of such tensions were obviously an issue for the scribes who composed the Pentateuch, it was not their central concern. Rather, the major issue, for them, was to create an authoritative account of Israel's origins, whose purpose was to give a sense of overall identity to the diverse forms of emerging Judaism at the time.

Even though the Torah was probably composed in Jerusalem, concessions were made to Yahwistic communities outside Yehud in order to make it acceptable to them. The decision to end the Torah with Moses' death outside of the land (Deuteronomy 34) rather than with Joshua's conquest is significant. It meant that the fulfillment of the central promise of the Torah, Yahweh's gift of the land to the Israelites, remained unaccomplished. This ending is best explained as a concession to the diaspora. It is not necessary to live inside the Promised Land to live in accordance with the Torah. Defining the Torah as a *Pentateuch* rather than a Hexateuch means de facto acknowledging the reality and even the legitimacy of diaspora Judaism; at the same time, however, the overall logic of the pentateuchal narrative implies that life inside the land remains the goal to be attained.

Likewise, the command to build an altar on Mt Gerizim in Deut. 27:4–8 should be viewed as a concession to Yahwists in Samaria. Classically, the building of a sanctuary on Mt Gerizim has been situated in the aftermath of Alexander's conquest of Palestine, on the basis of Josephus' testimony (*Ant.* 11.317–19). However, the archaeological survey of the site conducted by Y. Magen in the last decades has suggested that this is probably too late and that the sanctuary was already built in the fifth century BCE, probably after the resettlement of Shechem ca. 480–475 BCE (see Magen 2000; Magen and Stern 2000). If so, the instruction in Deut. 27:4 for building an altar on 'Mount Gerizim', found in the Samaritan Pentateuch and supported by one codex of the Old Latin, was most likely introduced at the time of the composition of the Pentateuch as a means of acknowledging the legitimacy of the newly built Samarian altar, despite the single altar site prescribed by Deuteronomy 12. One must note, however, it is *not* said the altar in Deuteronomy 27 is meant to be the unique altar of Deuteronomy 12, and the location of the latter at the site chosen directly by Yahweh (in Jerusalem *or* in Gerizim) is left to the appreciation of each community (see further Nihan 2007b). Nevertheless, the introduction of Deuteronomy 27 into the Pentateuch facilitated and led to the adoption of the Pentateuch as Torah both in Yehud *and* in Samaria.[6]

Further instances of concessions vis-à-vis Judean communities outside of Yehud are apparent in other passages. Note, for example, the permission given by Moses in Numbers 32 to some of the twelve 'tribes' to reside on the *eastern* side of the Jordan, outside the boundaries of Yehud, as long as they are ready to offer military assistance to their 'brothers' who have crossed the Jordan river to settle on the western side. Likewise, it has been proposed by some scholars that the Joseph story in Genesis 37–50 was a creation of the Jewish diaspora in Elephantine originally, which was later included in the Pentateuch as a concession to that diaspora. Note, however, that Joseph's treatment in Sir. 49:15 appears to suggest that this story was not well received by the Yahwistic orthodoxy.

Nonetheless, the most likely place for the composition of the Pentateuch and its promulgation as 'Torah' remains Jerusalem. If we try now to identify more precisely the parties involved in that move, we should logically think of the two main institutions in Persian-period Jerusalem: the temple, on one hand, and the lay council presiding over the temple assembly, on the other (for this, see especially Albertz 1994: 466–68).

The existence of a lay council alongside a priestly college is attested by the correspondence with Elephantine (see *AP* 30, ll. 18–19), which mentions, besides the governor, 'the high priest Jehohanan and his colleagues, the priests in Jerusalem' as well as 'Ostanes, the brother of

Anani and the leading men among the Jews'. The council of elders was composed of the *roshey haavot*, the 'heads of the fathers' (houses)', who are repeatedly mentioned in Ezra–Nehemiah. The MT text of Ezra 3:12 makes the equation explicit with its phrase, *roshey haavot hazzeqenim*, 'the heads of the fathers' (houses), the elders'. Significantly, in Deut. 31:9–13, the Torah, after being written by Moses, is entrusted to 'the priests, the Levites, who bear the Ark of the covenant of Yahweh, as well as to the elders of Israel' (31:9), who have the task to read it to the entire community every seven years, during a grand pilgrimage festival (31:10–13). Likewise, in Neh. 8.13, on the second day of Ezra's reading of the Torah in Jerusalem, it is recounted how three groups gather around Ezra 'in order to discern (*skl* hiphil) the words of the Law': these three groups are the *roshey haavot*, the priests and the Levites. The notion that the publication of the Torah was jointly sponsored by the priests and the council of elders appears to be reflected in other passages, for instance, in Exod. 24.9–11, where 70 elders (compare Ezek. 8:11), accompanied by Moses, Aaron and Aaron's elder sons Nadab and Abihu, are authorized to ascend Mount Sinai and contemplate Yahweh immediately after the first revelation to Moses of God's laws (Exodus 20–23).

On the other hand, however, we also have various passages suggesting an attempt by the upper priestly class to claim for themselves authority in the interpretation of the Torah. Thus, in the passage (already discussed above) in Deut. 33:10, teaching (*yrh*) the Torah is presented as the privilege of Levi, the 'priestly' tribe among Jacob's sons. (Note, however, that the Samaritan Pentateuch and Syriac have a plural here, '*torot*'.) Any passage expressing the same view as Deut. 33:10 probably reflects the idea that teaching the *torah* was one of the traditional functions of the priests (see above, and compare Jer. 18:18; Ezek. 7:26; 22:26; 44:23–24; Hos. 4:6; Zeph. 3:4; Hag. 2:11; Mal. 2:7)—except that here, *torah* does not refer to *ritual* rules specifically but has a much more comprehensive meaning.

The same development is even more obvious in Lev. 10:10–11. In this passage, Aaron and his sons are commanded to 'separate' between 'holy and profane, unclean and clean' (v. 10) but also to 'teach' (*yrh*) '*all the statutes (kol hahuqqim)*' communicated to Moses by Yahweh (v. 11). Here, the transition from the traditional duty reserved to the priests to the interpretation of the entire Torah is transparent. This passage is all the more significant because it is, with Numbers 18, the only divine command that is addressed to *Aaron* exclusively. Moreover, a unique account ensues (10:16–20) in which Aaron, after being rebuked by Moses for failing to perform a certain rite (vv 16–18), eventually manages to give a satisfactory explanation based on the Torah that even Moses is forced to accept (vv 19–20). As such, the account exemplifies, in an almost midrashic way, the authority newly conferred on Aaron and his sons to interpret the Law.

Finally, the high priest's authority is illustrated in several passages in the second half of the Book of Joshua, in the story of the division of the land among the tribes (chs 13–24). The division conforms to the instructions found in the Torah, especially in Numbers 32, but it is systematically supervised by Eleazar, Aaron's successor (see Num. 20:22–26; compare Josh. 14:1; 17:4; 19:51; 21:1). Note, furthermore, that the canonical Book of Joshua ends not with the death of Joshua, as one would logically expect, but with the death of *Eleazar*, the high priest.

The conception of Aaronites as teachers of the Law continues to play an important role in several writings from the Hellenistic period (see, for example, Sir. 45:17, or 11QT 56:2–6). It is tempting to situate the emergence of this idea toward the end of the Persian period, in the first half of the fourth century BCE. At that time, the rapid decline in the influence of the Persian administration over the area appears to have led to the development of the power and status of priestly clergy in Jerusalem and particularly to political claims made by the high priest. The first coin minted in the name of a high priest of Jerusalem, a certain Yohanan, is dated ca. 350 BCE. It indicates that at that time, coin minting and, therefore, tax collection came under the control of the high priest in Jerusalem.

In sum, it would appear that there were two important aspects to the composition of the Pentateuch and its promulgation as 'Torah'.

(a) On the one hand, several significant concessions were made at the time of the composition of the Pentateuch so that as many groups as possible could accept it as an authoritative document, including Judeans from the various diasporas (especially Mesopotamia and Egypt) as well as Yahwists in Samaria. The setting of the conclusion to the Torah outside the promised land (Deuteronomy 34); the inclusion of an instruction acknowledging the legitimacy of the newly erected Samarian sanctuary on Mt Gerizim; and the inclusion of the Joseph story, which seems to reflect the concerns of the Judean diaspora in Egypt, all support this view. One could say that the relative *openness* of the Pentateuch was an attempt to cope with the complexity of the religious, ethnic and political situation during the Persian period, when several different groups could claim to be the true heirs to the former kingdom of Israel. Even though the Pentateuch was created in Jerusalem, the conciliating strategy of the temple scribes made it possible for all these distinct 'Israels' to acknowledge its authority and accept it as the 'Torah', thus creating a sense of overall ethnic, cultural and religious identity.

(b) On the other hand, as a counterpart to its religious and political openness, conflicts among different socio-religious groups logically shifted to the Torah's *interpretation*; namely, to exegesis and commentary. The issue of *control* over its interpretation was soon a matter of significant dispute. The passages discussed above suggest this debate was already present at the time of the composition of the Torah, when some groups, especially those belonging to the priesthood, were claiming some form of superior knowledge or authority in interpretation of the Torah.

The struggle continued and developed further during the Hellenistic and Roman periods. Polemics against deceitful teachers of the Torah are commonplace in extra-canonical literature of the Second Temple (e.g. *1 Enoch, Jubilees, Testament of Levi*, the 'Rule of the Community' in Qumran, or the Damascus Covenant). Yet the same phenomenon is already present in some biblical texts dating to the late Persian or early Hellenistic period. In Mal. 2:4–9, Levi, who was charged by Yahweh to give a 'truthful teaching' (*torat emet*), is reproached for 'turning aside' from the (righteous) way and causing 'many' to 'stumble' via the Torah (Mal. 2:8). In other words, the composition of the Pentateuch initiated considerable exegetical discussion in the second half of the Persian period, which continued down to the destruction of the Second Temple and beyond precisely *because* the Pentateuch could be and had been accepted as 'Torah' by so many different groups.

iii. On the Way to the 'Canon': Interpreting the Torah as Authoritative Literature in the Second Temple Period

There are indications that the 'authority' of the Torah was rapidly accepted in varying degrees amongst the various forms of Judaism until the end of the Second Temple period. While this issue is too complex to be discussed at length, a few brief observations may nevertheless be offered.

In the second century BCE the Torah of Moses has become formally identical with the hypostasized Wisdom (Sir. 24:23–24; see also Bar. 4:1) and its foundational role was acknowledged by all major Jewish groups—Samaritans, Essenes, Sadduccees, Pharisees and so on. As early as the third century BCE the books of Genesis to Deuteronomy were translated into Greek. Although such translation may have had many purposes, one of its main functions would probably have been for public recitation at local assemblies in the Jewish diaspora, such as the 'house of prayers' (the ancestors of the synagogues) in Egypt (the first mention of such a 'house of prayer' is in a papyrus connected to the reign of Ptolemy III, 246–221 BCE). Furthermore, the unique status of the 'Torah of Moses' would gradually give rise to a considerable literature consisting of rewritings, paraphrases and commentaries of the Pentateuch, as can be seen from several extra-canonical writings such as the Book of *Jubilees* or the Temple Scroll (11QT).

It would be misleading, however, to speak of the Torah as being already 'canonical' in the second or in the first century BCE. The Torah did not yet have the kind of textual stability generally associated with the concept of 'canon', even if it tends to evince significantly *less* textual diversity than other portions of the Hebrew Bible. Only the Book of Leviticus was relatively stable in antiquity; Genesis, Exodus, Numbers and Deuteronomy existed in various 'text-types', each of which could be more or less harmonistic and expansionistic (see White Crawford 2008). The fact that these different text-types were often preserved side by side in the Qumran library suggests such diversity was not necessarily perceived to be a problem by the scribes during most of the Second Temple period.

Furthermore, compositions such as the Temple Scroll and *Jubilees* show that different groups had different understandings of what was contained within Moses' revelation. For some groups, like the Samaritans and (probably) the Sadducees, the Torah of Moses, and more generally, all Scriptures, were restricted to the Pentateuch. For other groups, however, Moses' Torah could apparently include a further body of revelations. It is generally agreed that *Jubilees* and possibly the Temple Scroll were not composed to replace the Pentateuch but to claim comparable status as authoritative texts (see, e.g., White Crawford 2008). For the groups who create such documents, Moses' Torah was not restricted to the Pentateuch; rather, the Pentateuch formed the basis for other, additional revelations. *Jubilees* claims to have been revealed to Moses on Sinai by an angel; it provides an 'enhanced' account of the history of origins from creation to Sinai, introducing many new divine revelations.

The trend to expand the contents of the body of authoritative texts seems to have gradually come to a halt during the first century BCE. Although the reasons for this diminishing trend are not entirely clear, one may well be the willingness to separate more neatly between the authoritative text and its commentary. As noted by Brooke, the *pesher* genre, which is characterized by commentary separated from the received text, also emerges during the first century BCE (Brooke 2001). It is also toward the turn of the millenium, or a little earlier, that an attempt was apparently made by the temple in Jerusalem to publish a 'standard' version of the Pentateuch, along with some other 'authoritative' texts (see Tov 2005). Subsequently, rabbinic tradition did not accept the canonicity of *Jubilees* and related literature; nonetheless, it furthered the idea of 'additional' revelations made to Moses at Mount Sinai in the form of the Oral Law, which then came to be written down for safe keeping as the Talmud.

2. Ethnicity

The story of the Pentateuch is the formation and definition of a people, 'Israel': in the broadest sense, therefore, it is about ethnicity. Characteristics of ethnicity are geography, descent and custom, which will be dealt with below.

The first point to make, however, is that the Pentateuch itself represents an attempt to *create* a sense of ethnicity among various groups by compiling a single history of a single nation—from different stories and groups that can partly be recognized or inferred from the unified account. Thus, a single line of descent is traced from Abraham onwards; different stories relating to origins and to land occupation are arranged in a sequence, so that a single 'nation' of 'Israel' is created in the past from various social groups and especially, from two kingdoms, Judah and Israel, that later became imperial provinces, Yehud and Samerina. Together with this emerges the notion of a single 'land' given to this 'people' by its single god. But it is significant that the extent of the ethnic territory is both vague and variable, pointing to an ethnicity that, while focussed on well-defined territories, also spreads beyond to neighbouring regions and even further afield. Ethnicity is, indeed, precisely the goal of the Pentateuch.

Geography is an integral factor in determining ethnicity, since the region in which one is born and/or lives is often a primary mark of such identity and generally also determines one's language, a major factor in ethnic recognition. This is an important theme in its own right in the Pentateuch and will be discussed separately.

As for descent, genealogy has long been employed in many cultures as a code in which political and social relationships are expressed, where blood ties that may not always exist in reality are 'created' between 'brothers' or 'sisters', 'fathers' and 'mothers'. Many *ethne* ascribe their name to an eponymous ancestor (such as Israel=Jacob). Finally, customs, or cultural features are also important, especially in multi-ethnic contexts. In large empires, for example, ethnicity is reflected in the use of administrative, especially legal procedures and even more especially in matters of religious affiliation. These aspects of ethnicity are all extensively addressed in the Pentateuch's story, beginning with land (Davies 2007: 1–43, 44–54).

i. Descent

In Genesis, kinship and descent predominate and genealogical relations are paramount. After the Flood, where humanity begins again to populate the world, a genealogical table traces all the nations from the three sons of Noah. The family of Abraham belongs to the line of Shem, apparently comprising the whole of that line, since Shem is named 'the father of all the children of Eber' (10:21). 'Eber' possibly derives from the expression, 'Beyond the River' (Heb. *avar ha-nahar*, Akkadian *ever-nari*, Aramaic *avar-nahara*), meaning that the Abrahamic family constitutes the population of an area 'Beyond the River' (see previous section). The nations of Canaan and the Philistines are both traced in Genesis 10 to the line of Ham, along with Egypt and Mesopotamia, denoting their lack of ethnic affinity with Abraham's descendants.

Once the figure of Abraham is reached, Genesis defines Israel not solely as a single family consisting of brothers who become ancestors of tribes but also as part of an extended family comprising neighbouring peoples. 'Israel' is the family of Jacob, who is given the name 'Israel' in Genesis 32 and 35, while the family of Abraham, of which Israel is a part, comprises the nations of Aram (Abraham's brother Nahor, from whose family came Rebekah, Leah and Rachel), Ammon and Moab (the children of Lot, Abraham's nephew), Ishmael (Abraham's first son) and Edom (from Jacob's elder brother Esau). Abraham also married Keturah, from whom, among others, the Midianites are derived. We must also note some qualifications: Ammon and Moab are the offspring of Lot's incestuous union with his daughters, while both Ishmael and Esau are disinherited (or, as R. C. Heard puts it, 'diselected'; 2001). This ambiguity may reflect disagreement regarding the extent and the status of the Yahwistic community in the period when Genesis was written, reflecting both the wishes of some to exclude these populations from the community of Israel and of others to include them within the larger family community of worshippers of Yahweh.

Excluded from this family, however, are the 'nations of Canaan' or the 'Amorites', whose land is promised to Abraham's descendants, and the Philistines, who were also inhabitants of Canaan but not included among the Amorites. Abraham is represented as dealing peacefully with some of these neighbours and makes no attempt to seize land. The cave for Sarah's burial is bought from a Hittite; later, in Genesis 34, the Shechemites are permitted to intermarry and 'become one people' with the family of Jacob. He deals on apparently friendly terms with the Pharaoh (Genesis 12) and with Abimelech, king of Gerar.

From Exodus onwards, however, the focus shifts to the land to be occupied by the family of Jacob, which has now become a nation (*'am*), and relations with surrounding peoples are generally less cordial. On their way to Canaan, towards the end of Numbers, other nations are confronted. Edom (of the Abraham family) refuses to allow transit, but no hostilities ensue and the land is circumvented (20:14–21). Sihon of the Amorites and Og of Bashan, on the other hand (not Abrahamic), are both defeated and their land occupied, in accordance with the divine bequest. This land is later assigned to the tribes of Reuben, Gad and part of Manasseh. While encamped near Moab, Israelites begin to have sexual relations with Moabites and Midianites both, again, of the Abraham family. The Moabites are said to be idolaters and the Midianites are apparently also implicated in the same cult of Baal-Peor. But nothing is said of warfare with, or of the capture of land from, these nations until Numbers 31, when Midian is despoiled in revenge.

ii. The Twelve Tribes

The twelve sons of Jacob that constitute the genealogical element of Israel's identity are enumerated several times. First, their births are recorded in chronological order in Genesis 29–30. Leah, Jacob's first wife, bears Reuben, Simeon, Levi, then Judah; then, since Rachel is barren, her maid Bilhah bears Dan and Naphtali; Leah is now past childbearing age and her maid Zilpah bears Gad and Asher; but subsequently, Leah bears Issachar, Zebulun and a daughter, Dinah. Finally, Rachel bears Joseph and dies after bearing Benjamin. In 35:23–6 the summary lists them by their mothers—Leah, Rachel, Bilhah then Zilpah; not in order of birth. All the sons are said to have been born in Paddan-Aram—though this contradicts v. 16, which puts Benjamin's birth near Ephrath. The matriarchal groupings may reflect political or cultural affinities (Joseph [Ephraim and Manasseh] and Benjamin, Judah, Reuben and Simeon), but attribution to secondary wives might reflect status. The order of birth is more difficult to interpret. In the Joseph story, Reuben, who always is the firstborn elsewhere, sometimes appears as the spokesman for the brothers but at other times Judah takes this role, as if he were the eldest. But the twelve-tribe scheme of Genesis remains almost completely consistent (see also 46:8–27 and ch. 49 with slight variations in order). Exodus opens with another listing of those who came to Egypt: the six Leah tribes, then Benjamin (Rachel's other son, Joseph, being already in Egypt), then the sons of the secondary wives (6:14 gives a truncated list of tribes containing only Reuben, Simeon and Levi).

In Leviticus, where cultic criteria weigh more heavily, the constituent tribes of Israel are not mentioned at all (not even Levi!), but in Numbers they play a very important role. At the outset, a census is taken with the aid of twelve tribal representatives. Levi is now explicitly exempt from the census; in order to maintain twelve tribes, Joseph is divided into Ephraim and Manasseh. When twelve spies are sent out to reconnoiter the land of Canaan subsequently in ch. 13, Ephraim and Manasseh are 'tribes'; there is no further mention of Joseph.

The census is of men eligible for warfare, and thereafter the nation is reconceived as an army on the march and camping in military fashion (see the slightly fuller description below). The order of enumeration follows Gen. 46:8–27: Leah, Rachel, then the children of Bilhah and Zilpah mixed together. These tribes camp around the tent in four groups of three: to the east Judah, Issachar and Zebulun; to the south Reuben, Simon and Gad; to the west Ephraim, Manasseh and Benjamin; and to the north Dan, Asher and Naphtali. The arrangement is strange, reflecting a mixture of genealogical and geographical criteria. The Rachel tribes are grouped together, and the northernmost tribes in the land of Canaan, who are also from secondary mothers, occupy the northern side of the camp. The tribe of Levi is likewise divided into the four points: Aaron to the east, and the three Levitical families of Gershon, Merari and Kohath on the other sides.

A new census is taken in Numbers 26, again by tribes, but now in the order Reuben, Simeon, Gad, Judah, Issachar, Zebulun, Manasseh, Ephraim, Benjamin, Dan, Asher, Naphtali—reflecting closely but not precisely the distribution of the camps around the Tent.

The Numbers census also reveals a pattern of social organization: the tribe (*matteh*), at the first generation, named after the ancestral eponym, then the paternal houses (*bet av*) named after the sons of the ancestor, and then the clan (*mispahah*), named by the sons of the heads of the *bet 'av*. Thus, the social structure is further fixed into a strict genealogical code, spread over three generations, so that Israel as a social entity is entirely defined during the wilderness period—as it is in every other way except in its landholding. The extent of Israel's own land is also described for the first and only time in the Pentateuch, beginning with the southern edge bordering Edom, the Mediterranean, a northerly line from the sea to Hazar-Enan, and the eastern boundary embracing Gilead, then running down the Jordan (Numbers 34). The Levites are to have 42 cities, plus six refuge cities.

iii. Custom

The issue of idolatry underlines that on the way to this land, Israel has also acquired a law that imposes on it a distinctive way of life, one not inherited or customary, not 'natural', but pledged in a contact with a deity and prescribed by laws revealed and handed to it. Thereafter, armed with this new way of life or 'constitution', the nation is prepared to capture its land.

Deuteronomy forbids cultural contact with the 'nations of Canaan' and commands them to be exterminated; the danger is not so much that Israel would lose its genealogical distinctiveness by intermarriage, but rather lose its divinely given culture. But this applies to certain nations. Although after Genesis the emphasis is on exclusiveness rather than inclusiveness, segregation rather than integration, other kinship groups are included: Moses marries the daughter of Jethro the Midianite, a priest of Yahweh, and takes a Cushite wife in Numbers 21, while among those who escape with the Israelites from Egypt are a 'large mixture' (Exod. 12:38; Heb *erev rav*), usually interpreted as meaning other population elements. 'Israelite' identity is never *exclusively* determined by descent (see Genesis 34). Intermarriage with foreign women is not generally forbidden in the pentateuchal law: foreign slaves and prisoners, for instance, may be taken as wives.

Israel's exclusivity, in effect a separation from all other nations, is already more a matter of cult and culture than descent in Leviticus and parts of Numbers. Here, Israel's wilderness 'camp', which stands for the territory it occupies and thus, its future land, is a cultically defined area of divine presence, focused on the tent in the middle, the divine meeting place. Because of their proximity to the deity, the Israelites are exhorted to remain pure, and to control carefully the various forms of impurity that may possibly affect them (see Leviticus 11–16). In this regard, Israel must live in a pure land and cannot share it with impure non-Israelites.

As Exod. 19:6 has it, 'you shall be for me a priestly kingdom and a holy nation.'

The shift of perspective between kinship and religion as defining the essence of Israel within the Pentateuch is quite considerable. Israel's 'customs' are not developed naturally over time nor culturally embedded in its geographical or social environment as customs inevitably are. They are presented as being divinely *given*. In that sense, Israel is 'artificial', while the culture of Canaan is represented rather as being 'natural' and, for that reason, corrupt.

Some mention should be made of customs that especially came to define Judaism in the eyes of non-Jews. Circumcision, which later became one of the most distinctive features of Judaism, was in fact practised by Semites (Babylonians, Assyrians, Syrians as well as Israelites and Judeans) and Egyptians; interestingly, it is instituted with Abraham (Gen. 17:11), the father of several of these 'nations'. It is, however, also referred to in a strange way in Exod. 4:26, apparently in connection with Moses. But there are no pentateuchal laws concerning this practice.

The Sabbath/*shabbat*, another prominent feature of Jewish practice, is included among the 'ten commandments' either as a day of rest, commemorating the divine rest after creation (Genesis 1; Exod. 20:8–11) or as a reminder of the Exodus (Deut. 5:12–15). The notion of Sabbath was also extended to seven-year (Deut. 15:1) and 49/50- (7 × 7) year cycles (Leviticus 25). In Leviticus, too, the Sabbath is marked by certain cultic observances. While *sabbatum* designated the middle of the (lunar) month in Mesopotamia, the origin of the Jewish Sabbath observance is rather obscure.

A third major Jewish ethnic marker is certain dietary laws, deriving partly from a division between 'clean' and 'unclean' food. Laws such as the 'cooking of a young animal in its mother's milk' (Lev. 19:19) have been elaborated into general rules about mixing meat and dairy products, to which can be added not wearing clothes made of both wool and linen (Deut. 29:9–11). This kind of distinction is likely to have become more important as an ethic marker following the loss of national sovereignty and the spread of Judean and perhaps Samarian practices over a wider area in the Persian and Hellenistic periods. Thus, the process of ethnic formation in the Pentateuch continued to be elaborated, partly by means of extending the scope of the scriptural laws.

Finally, while the Pentateuch refers to several different kinds of religious festivals, the centralization of the cult of Yahweh that is particularly commanded in Deuteronomy and gradually took effect from the late fifth century onwards led to the emergence of three great festivals at the central sanctuary (Passover, Weeks and Booths/New Year/Yom Kippur). The geographical dispersion of 'Jewish' (=Yahwistic) populations led to these centralized festivities becoming times of pilgrimage. But Exodus 12, for instance, reflects a time when celebration of the Passover was still located in the household. The Pentateuch itself therefore shows us the beginnings of a process of explicitly 'ethnicizing' certain customs. This process was still under way long after the Pentateuch was completed. The Jewish custom of the wearing of tassels on prayer shawls, for example, is mentioned (in passing) in only one verse, Deut. 22:12, where it seems to be a permanent injunction and there is no mention of prayer shawls.

iv. Reflections

For whom does the story of Israel's foundation of Israel in the Pentateuch speak? We can only say that there are multiple voices. We know that it is the foundation document for both Jews and Samaritans, and this corresponds to the notion of a twelve-tribe united nation, in which traces of a separation between Israel and Judah are minimal and probably late touches (see earlier on Jerusalem; also, the Joseph story shows some signs of special Judean interest). Common descent and common land (Canaan) reflect a deep sense of unity between the two societies. But there are also aspects of a 'greater Israel' encompassing Edom and parts of Syria, and these might suggest awareness of a wider participation in the cult of the 'god of Israel', while the patriarchal travels point even more widely to an awareness of diasporic 'Israelite' communities in Mesopotamia and Egypt. In Genesis, moreover, there are no cultural antipathies between the Israelite ancestors and the 'Canaanites', suggesting that local 'non-Israelite' inhabitants of Canaan are not an issue. They are effectively either adopted, as in the Book of Ezekiel, or benignly ignored.

But with this more ecumenical vision of Israel and its land we must also compare other parts of the Pentateuch that, while maintaining the unit of the nation, fix firmly on land possession and on cultural alienation from others, and especially other inhabitants of the land. The presence of both tendencies in the Pentateuch suggests—as does, indeed, the notion of a united 'Israel'—a degree of compromise between differing visions of what constitutes the 'nation' of Israel. It is not too dramatic to speak of 'inclusionist' and 'exclusionist' programmes being equally represented here or indeed, to consider that within the Pentateuch, the Book of Genesis stands somewhat apart from the others.

These indications suggest a certain time-frame. The notion of a single 'nation' postdates the Neo-Babylonian or 'Benjaminite' period, in which the communities of Judah and Samaria/Samerina came together (Davies 2007) and in which Edomites now residing in formerly Judean territory were 'Judaized' and became brothers to Israel. The ambiguity of Transjordan possibly makes sense in that these territories become both politically separated but religiously connected—there seems to be a significant Yahwistic population here, too.

As for the Philistines, whose absence from most of the Pentateuch is so curious except for a few references in Genesis and Exodus, we should note that their presence on the coast and in the Shephelah is constant throughout the Iron Age and into the Persian and Hellenistic periods. But it may be indicative that after the end of the seventh century BCE, the label 'Philistine' ceases to exist and is replaced by references to the three individual cities that had once been part of the Philistine region, which had continued to be inhabited after 600 BCE: Ashkelon, Asdod and Gaza. Their failure to be included among the 'nations of Canaan' is interesting, especially since their 'land' certainly lay within the pentateuchal definition of 'Canaan' (e.g. Gen. 21:32). The *terminus ad quem* is determined mainly by the deteriorating relations between Samaria and Jerusalem that were initiated in all probability by the Judean closure or destruction of Bethel and its subsequent replacement by the Gerizim temple, around 450 BCE, constituting a clear cultic separation and possibly a rivalry between two centres of the same cult claiming an exclusive status, either of which could be justified by a reading of Deuteronomy. Such rivalry might also have been affected by changes in the political and thus religious arrangement of all of Palestine under the Ptolemies, but of this we have very little certain information.

v. Israel's 'Constitution'

A very important way to understand the self-definition(s) of Israel among those who produced the Pentateuch is to examine those portraits they present of the ideal society they think Israel ought to be. Within the story of Israel's formation as a nation, during the desert-wandering that occupies most of the Pentateuch, we find three coherent but differing descriptions of what Israel ideally should be, how it should be constituted. Leviticus defines it according to the categories of holiness and ritual correctness, clustered around a most holy centre where the deity is (supposedly) present. Nevertheless, the 'camp' is also surrounded and threatened by the power of uncleanness. An underlying principle of *order*, expressed in terms of holy/profane and clean/unclean, embraces everything from the taxonomy of human sexual relations and bodily emissions to animals and to sacrifices. The book opens with sacrifices and the priesthood, culminating in the ordination of Aaron, then deals with matters that affect other Israelites (food, childbirth, disease), the slaughter of animals, sexual relations, cultic offerings, festivals and the sabbatical and jubilee years. But all these are viewed and prescribed wholly from a cultic point of view. The correct management of purity and impurity is the responsibility of both priests and non-priests, and governance of Israel seems to be in the hands of the high priest, the representative of Aaron. Only at the end (ch. 26) of Leviticus is the relation between Yahweh and Israel explicitly defined in terms of a contract (covenant) that applies to each individual as well as to the nation corporately.

This contractual definition of 'Israel' is elaborated at length in Deuteronomy. In that book, the relationship between deity and nation is consistently defined as one of patron and client, and there is no priestly (or royal) representative making the covenant on behalf of the people. Moses acts only as an *intermediary*, not as a representative here, and his profile is that of a prophet, a go-between. While Deuteronomy shares some ritual and cultic concerns with Leviticus (compare, e.g., the clean diet defined in Deuteronomy 14, and compare with Leviticus 11), the laws aim primarily at the social order of Israel. Religious behavior (festivals, heeding prophets, cities of refuge) is considered within the dominant context of social relations: property, warfare, murder, the treatment of women and children, marriage and slavery. Familial relations are also covered: marriage and divorce. More than Leviticus, Deuteronomy insists on a strict separation from the dangerous culture of the surrounding Canaanites (Ammonites and Moabites, who are not 'Canaanites', are not absolutely excluded from membership of Israel but cannot join 'even to the tenth generation'; 23:3).

Israel is ruled by what we would recognize as a constitutional monarch, something entirely alien to the ancient Near East (Deut. 17:14–20), but elders, judges and Levites, who are not differentiated from priests, are entrusted with the daily administration of society. Overall, Leviticus and Deuteronomy overlap only slightly in their content and they differ in their conception of how Israel is organized and, indeed, what it *is*.

Contrary to the case in Leviticus and Deuteronomy, the Israel of Numbers is expressed not only in speech but also in various narratives. The narrative moves the nation from Sinai to the edge of Canaan and is characterized by organization for warfare. The book opens with a census of those 'able to go to war' (1:3), and Israel is on the march towards a destination to be conquered, living off the terrain and on the alert for attack. The disposition of the camp and the order of marching are detailed, the latter led by the ark: when it moves, Moses says, 'Arise, Yahweh, let your enemies be scattered and your foes flee before you', and when it stops, 'Return, Yahweh of the massed armies of Israel'.

The entire nation is a militia; families and tribes of Israel are reconfigured as military units. Towards the close of the book, attention moves to the imminent occupation of the land and its divisions and the disposition of tribal allotments is given, followed by allotments for the Levites. The geography of the camp is thus converted, in anticipation, into the geography of the land, the new home, the permanent 'camp'.

The military character of Israel is also reflected in the attitude towards discipline. 'Rebellion' is a constant theme (see chs 14, 17 and 20), and the issue of Moses' leadership and the challenges to it by Miriam (ch. 12) and by Korah, Dathan and Abiram (ch. 16) form one of the book's motifs. Disobedience is harshly punished.

These different portraits of Israel suggest that within a single story several different configurations of that ethnic group are open for negotiation. They suggest a certain open-endedness, an ongoing debate about the real character of Israel. We can read these portraits as exercises in imagination, with the wilderness as a kind of ideal or the matrix of all ideals, not a space or a historical time. Or, they might reflect the interests of different constituencies within the one society: Leviticus for the priests, Deuteronomy for the legal scribes, Numbers for soldiers (?). Each construction promotes a clear differentiation from neighbours and outsiders that ranges from exclusion from the divine realm (Leviticus) to rejection (Deuteronomy) to military aggression (Numbers). Differentiation of this kind is nowadays recognized as a major component of ethnicity, and these portraits, however we read them, make an important contribution to the process of nation-formation that the surrounding narrative describes in bringing Israel all the way from family to political state.

In all these three definitions of 'Israel', ethnicity is never exclusively defined through genealogy, but presupposes a complex set of customs that, from one book to the other, are actually construed quite distinctively. Furthermore, genealogy itself plays a different role in the books of Leviticus, Numbers and Deuteronomy. The Book of Numbers is structured by complex lists of Israelites tribes (Numbers 1–4 and

26) that emphasize the importance of this social structure for the self-definition of 'Israel'. In Deuteronomy, on the contrary, the twelve-tribe system plays virtually no role, if we except the final blessing of Moses (ch. 33).

In Deuteronomy, the promise of the land to 'your ancestors, Abraham, Isaac and Jacob' links the conditional covenant promise of Deuteronomy with the unconditional promise to the patriarchs. The juxtaposition indicates that the patriarchal promises have been not so much fulfilled as superseded by being conditional on the requirements of Deuteronomy for living inside the land. Furthermore, in most cases the word 'ancestors' ('fathers') omits the three names Abraham, Isaac and Jacob and actually refers either to those generations who entered or left Egypt (Lev. 26:40; Num. 14:23) or who trekked the wilderness.[7] Deuteronomy fittingly brings the Pentateuch to an end with Moses' blessings on the twelve tribes (Deuteronomy 33), yet these blessings make no reference to the tribes' descent, but rather celebrate tribal characteristics.

For a foundation document, the Pentateuch is extremely fluid. Indeed, it took the Mishnah, after the loss of the temple cult, to create a new 'Judaism' from a combination of the covenant (Deuteronomy) and holiness (Leviticus) perspectives. On close inspection, kinship, despite its prominence in Genesis, really plays a minor role, while the land has not even been won. Even within the 'law' itself, there are considerable differences. What these features highlight is a large amount of dissent about what constitutes the real essence and purpose of the newly created 'nation' of Israel.

3. Geography

The occupation of a promised land is arguably the major narrative theme of the Pentateuch, beginning with the story of the Garden, in which the first humans are set to farm and enjoy their life, via the dispersion of humanity to its allotted lands (and languages), and then to the promise of land to Abraham and his descendants. Thereafter, the narrative moves, though not directly, towards the occupation of that land, though significantly, the narrative ends before that takes place.

It is important to understand what conceptions of the nature and extent of the land are present and, indeed, the relationships between people and that land. Two points need to be made at the outset. First, the land is not unambiguously a 'homeland'. There are always other nations there, some having been there longer than others. Second, Abraham and the family of Jacob both enter the land from outside; this means also that the land is not Israel's 'birthplace' nor a natural or an unconditional possession, but a divine gift and as such it acquires a very important role within the cultic scheme, as a 'sacred space'.

i. *The Definition of the 'Promised Land'*

Despite its importance, the precise delimitation of the 'Promised Land' is unclear. In Gen. 11:31, the family of Abram sets out from 'Ur of the Chaldees' to go to the 'land of Canaan', though they settle instead in Harran on the Upper Euphrates, in Aram/Syria. But in 12:1 Abram is called to go to a land that God will show him, which he understands to be Canaan. At the 'oak of Moreh' he is promised 'this land' for his descendants (12:7). In Genesis 13, at an unspecified place (Bethel?) he is invited by God to look round, and his descendants are promised all the land that he can see. On a third occasion (15:18), God promises 'this land, from the brook of Egypt to the Euphrates'; in 17:8 we find 'all the land of Canaan'. Isaac also receives similar promises: 'the land that I will show you' in 26:2; in 28:4 'the land I promised to Abraham'. The promise is reiterated to Jacob in 35:15 without further definition. The 'land of the Canaanites', according to Gen. 10:19, extends 'from Sidon, in the direction of Gerar, as far as Gaza, and in the direction of Sodom, Gomorrah, Admah and Zeboiim, as far as Lasha'. Although many of the places are unknown, its extent lies between Sidon and Gaza on the Mediterranean coast and the Rift Valley (the Jordan and the Dead Sea). Numbers 34:2–12 has a similar but more detailed definition of the 'land of Canaan', though the northern boundary is unclear, while Exod. 23:31 follows Genesis 15: 'I will set your borders from the Red Sea to the sea of the Philistines, and from the wilderness to the Euphrates; for I will hand over to you the inhabitants of the land, and you shall drive them out before you'. Finally, in Deuteronomy 3, Reuben, Gad and half of Manasseh are given territory east of the Jordan in Gilead and Bashan, while Deut. 34:1–4 includes Gilead in Moses' view of the land.

The definition of the 'Promised Land', Canaan, is not entirely consistent, but neither is it without other problems. Most of these definitions exclude Transjordan; all include Philistia but do not mention the Philistines among the 'dispossessed nations'. Indeed, in Genesis 21 and 26, the 'land of the Philistines' seems to be a separate place, even *outside* the territory in which the patriarchs habitually live. But clearly Philistia *is* in Canaan, though not, according to Josh. 13:2, actually possessed. Then there is Edom, which is sometimes included and sometimes not—a problem

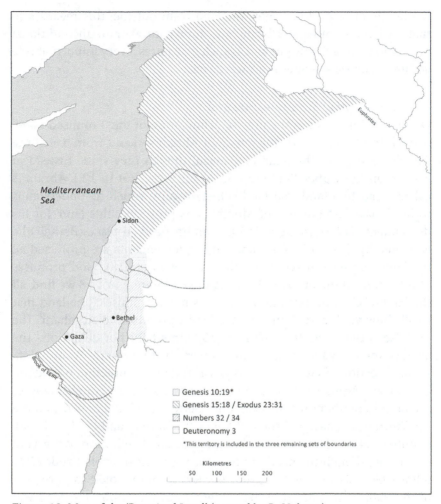

Figure 12. Map of the 'Promised Land' (created by R. Hobson)

complicated by the shifting boundaries of Edomite territory during the Iron Age (Edelman 1995b).

If we now try to map the pentateuchal 'Promised Land' against its historical populations, we arrive at the following results. From the beginning of the Iron Age (1200 BCE) onwards, the territory between the Mediterranean and the Dead Sea rift valley (Cisjordan) was not occupied by any single political unit, let alone any wider area. The 'united monarchy', if historical at all, is highly exaggerated in its extent; it can never have covered even all of Cisjordan, and the separate kingdoms of Israel and Judah together never occupied the entire Mediterranean coastal plain, where Phoenician and Philistine cities dominated. But during the Late Bronze Age (1550–1200 BCE), all of Cisjordan had been ruled by Egypt, and under the empires of Assyria, Babylon and Persia it was divided into imperial provinces and vassal cities. It may, however, have been unified under the Egyptian Ptolemies again at the end of the fourth century BCE, with its capital at Acco. But it was always an arena for many different societies, including Phoenicians, Philistines and Edomites as well as Judahites/Judeans and Israelites/Samarians.

The observation that 'Canaan' is in some cases larger than the land said to be settled by the Israelite tribes leads to another: the importance of foreign origins and foreign travel, as well as the relationship between the land and its neighbours. Abraham comes from Ur, then from Haran (leaving family behind, implicitly the first time and explicitly the second); he wanders to Egypt, and later (as does Isaac) to the land of the Philistines. Jacob lives for many years in Aram (Syria) and the entire family of Jacob finally leave for Egypt. The descendants of Jacob even travel to Canaan by a lengthy route that brings them through the Sinai peninsula, across the Negev and via Transjordan. It is as if all these wanderings anticipate a diaspora, taking in on the way places where 'Israelites' (or Judeans) may settle, thus bringing them into the ancestral orbit. If that is the point, it provides some indication of the date and context of the Pentateuch's geography; it shows an awareness that there are parts of 'Israel' not in the 'land of Israel', apart from Gilead and Bashan—just as there are non-Israelites (Edomites, Philistines) in the land.

What do we make also of the larger territory in Genesis 15 and Exod. 23:31, from Egypt to the Euphrates, which is also reflected in the extent of the Davidic realm in 1 and 2 Samuel, which included the Transjordanian territories of Aram, Ammon and Moab? Perhaps significantly, this came to be a distinct geo-political region. Under the Assyrians, then Neo-Babylonians and the Persians, it was designated 'Across the River' (i.e. seen from the eastern side of the Euphrates). The Persian satrapy is several times so named in Ezra and Nehemiah and, interestingly, the term is also found in Joshua 24.

This is a more precisely defined area. It reappears in the idealized extent of the kingdom of David and Solomon, where Jerusalem also stands as the capital of the entire area. As formally 'Judean' territory, it corresponds most of all with the Hasmonean kingdom of the late second and early first centuries BCE, but that kingdom itself perhaps deliberately embodied some kind of religious or cultural unity that may have begun to form as a result of centuries of imperial administration—plus the use of a common language, Western Aramaic.

Genesis 15:19 defines this territory as 'the land of the Kenites, the Kenizzites, the Kadmonites, the Hittites, the Perizzites, the Rephaim, the Amorites, the Canaanites, the Girgashites, and the Jebusites'. Deuteronomy 7:1 similarly refers to the displacement of 'the Hittites, the Girgashites, the Amorites, the Canaanites, the Perizzites, the Hivites and the Jebusites, seven nations mightier and more numerous than you'. The two texts show that the concept of 'Canaan' and its inhabitants in the Pentateuch is far from exact; 'Canaanites' and 'Amorites' form distinct elements *within* slightly different listings. In addition, the extent of Canaan is inconsistent; though the Deuteronomic definition of Canaan is nowhere provided, it does not include Edom, and it is also incomplete, since the Philistines are always ignored.

ii. Landmarks

A significant feature of the land is the sites mentioned. In Genesis, the patriarchs settle at sites of religious rather than political significance. Absent are the great cities of Megiddo, Hazor, Lachish or Gezer; since the stories neither relate themselves to any clear historical context nor can be archaeologically or historically related to one, we cannot apply any chronological considerations to the geography. The major sites of residence are Shechem (including Moreh), Bethel, Hebron and Beersheba. Dan is mentioned once (Gen. 14:14), but only incidentally and not as a place of residence.

The capitals of the two kingdoms, Jerusalem and Samaria, are not mentioned, although 'Salem' in Genesis 14 is a possible allusion to Jerusalem. Its ruler, Melchizedek, is both king and high priest. If Jerusalem *is* meant, as it was later clearly understood, perhaps even in other biblical texts (Ps. 76:2; 110), then this figure is possibly symptomatic of a political and religious claim on behalf of Jerusalem. In Samaritan tradition, Salem is identified with the site of Kiriath Aqraba, adjoining Shechem and near the chosen place Mt Gerizim (Gammie 1971: 392–93). The ancient name seems to be preserved in the modern village of Salim, located on the slope of Jebel el-Kebir, and has been extended to the basin between Mt Ebal, Mt Gerizim, Jeel el-Kebir and Taanath-Shiloh.

Shechem plays a prominent role in Gen. 33:18–20; 34 and 35:1–5. The town is consistently claimed in these passages to have been originally non-Israelite. However, Gen. 33:18–20 relates that Jacob erected an altar at that place. The story of Genesis 34 is more polemical; the eponymous

Shechem is 'avenged' by Simeon and Levi, yet they are reproached by their father Jacob (34:30). In Gen. 35:1–5, the 'great tree' near Shechem is acknowledged as a major cultic place (compare Joshua 24), but the reference is also ambiguous since the 'foreign gods' are said to have been buried there by Jacob.

Some tension between Jerusalem and Shechem as rival religious centres might thus be indicated in these passages, though only slightly, for, as already noted, the Pentateuch is strongly pan-Israelite and does not intervene in the Judah-Israel polemics that appear in almost all the rest of the Bible, including cult centralization.

The major centres of patriarchal 'settlement', Shechem, Bethel, Hebron and Beersheba, rather suggest a joint recognition of religious centres in what are to be both Israel and Judah, though Hebron is unknown outside the Pentateuch as a centre of any religious significance and Beersheba likewise, except for Amos 5:5; 8:14. The prominence of Bethel, historically a neighbouring rival to Jerusalem and elsewhere in the Bible a place of opprobrium, is especially significant. In this context we can only say that Genesis, like the entire Pentateuch, bears no traces of any separation between Israel and Judah (with the possible exception mentioned above). Genesis does not reflect a clear ideology of cult centralization, but seems on the contrary to acknowledge the plurality of sanctuaries in the Persian period. It should nonetheless be noted that the different altars that the patriarchs build are usually not used for sacrifices, with the exception of Genesis 22. The situation is different in the Book of Deuteronomy.

It is generally assumed that Deuteronomy calls for a single sanctuary and that Jerusalem is the intended site in the Deuteronomistic literature and in Chronicles. However, the law of centralization in Deuteronomy 12 could equally be applied to the central sanctuary in the Persian province of Samerina, as will indeed be the case (see further below, section 5).

iii. Land and Ancestors
In many cultures, past and present, an important function of the ancestors was and is the lineal transmission of property, land-use rights and family authority. The association of landholding with a particular family is embedded in the biblical understanding of ownership, but while such hereditary rights are usually associated in traditional societies with a divine grant to a family ancestor, in the Pentateuch, individual grants and ancestral recipients are subsumed under the notion of a single grant to the entire nation through a single line of ancestors. Thus, in Gen. 13:17

Abram is ordered to 'Rise up, walk through the length and the breadth of the land, for I will give it to you'. However, in most occurrences of this formula of land-promise, it is emphasized that the *descendants* are the recipients and that the possession of land by every single 'Israelite' is grounded in his descent from the same ancestor. The 'land of Israel' thus belongs to the 'children of Israel'.

In Deuteronomy, we find numerous references to the 'land' that Yahweh 'promised' or 'swore' to the 'ancestors' (*avot*); yet, in only four places do the names of Abraham, Isaac and Jacob appear (1:8; 6:10; 9:5; 30:20), probably as secondary additions. In the Book of Deuteronomy, there are only seven references by name, in total, to any of the three 'patriarchs', and in the view of many scholars, these names were not originally supplied; other 'ancestors' were meant (see Loretz 1978: 191–92 and Römer 1992). But in the Pentateuch, all land is subject to the one promise and the one genealogy. The Pentateuch does not deal in detail with the allocation of this land to tribes and families (see Numbers 32); this topic is developed in the second half of the Book of Joshua (chs 13–21). However, the jubilee legislation in Leviticus insists that land is inalienable and that should it be mortgaged because of debt, it shall be returned in the jubilee year (Leviticus 25).

4. Yahweh and Other Deities

i. Monolatry and Monotheism in the Hebrew Bible

In the present form of the Hebrew Bible, before they constitute a sovereign nation within the land of Canaan, the biblical community of Israel agrees at Mt Sinai/Mt Horeb to worship Yahweh ahead of any other gods and not to make any divine images. A small number of texts, found primarily in the prophetic books, assert that Yahweh is the only god who exists and is to be worshipped by all nations, but these are a minority; the majority of texts impose the strict worship of Yahweh alone on Israel but seem to acknowledge that other deities exist and can be legitimately worshipped by other groups and nations. The minority position can be labelled 'monotheism', while the majority position is usually termed 'monolatry'.

Yet, from the well-intentioned beginnings depicted in the Pentateuch, a story of constant 'backslidings' by the people and their leaders unfolds in subsequent books (Joshua–Kings), in which Yahweh is abandoned over and over in favour of 'other gods', thereby breaking the terms of the covenant to which their ancestors had agreed. Infighting leads the former twelve tribes to become two kingdoms, Israel and Judah, with Yahweh honoured as the main deity in each. Eventually, he punishes the inhabitants of both kingdoms by allowing foreign kings to conquer them, convert their former territories into provinces of their empires, and send many of them into exile.

Eventually, God ends their punishment and gives his people another chance. He does not give them back their two sovereign kingdoms but keeps them as his special people who now form the religious community of Israel. It is centred in the original homeland around the temple in Jerusalem but has members scattered throughout the known world in the diaspora. The geographical dispersion is testimony to the universal nature of Yahweh, who can be worshipped anywhere his people call on his name.

This story of Israel and its relationship with Yahweh over time is the result of theological reflection and the combination of a number of originally independent writings and traditions to form a sequenced 'epic'. It presents a view of the past from particular points in time, where contemporary debates and developments helped shape the presentation and interpretation so that they addressed current events and views. The authors espouse the exclusive worship of Yahweh as the only correct way to conceive of their god in their own times, and accordingly, portray it to have been Israel's religion in the distant past as well, from the time of the ancestor Abraham in the Book of Genesis, or from the covenant at Mt Sinai/Horeb in the books of Exodus and Deuteronomy. It does not correspond to the religion as practised during the Iron Age in the kingdoms of Israel and Judah. Even in the Persian period, significant evidence testifies to the persistence of a polytheistic worldview among Yahweh-worshippers.

ii. Yahweh and Asherah

During the time of the two kingdoms, Yahweh was consistently associated with a female deity, Asherah. Together, the divine couple was the main source of animal, agricultural and human abundance. Inscriptions from a way station located in the Sinai desert at Quntillet 'Ajrud invoke blessings from 'Yahweh of Samaria and (his?) Asherah' and from 'Yahweh of Teman [the south] and (his?) Asherah'. The site dates from ca. 850 BCE. A tomb located at Khirbet el-Qom in the Shephelah, within the territory of the kingdom of Judah, from about the same time period as the way station, asks for blessings from Yahweh and (his?) Asherah (Zevit 2001: 359–405).

A wooden symbol of Asherah was part of the official cult conducted in the temple in Jerusalem (2 Kgs 18:4; 23:4, 6) and there was a dedicated staff at the temple that wove in her honour (2 Kgs 23:7). Hundreds of female figurines with prominent breasts have been found in Judah, and it is generally assumed that they represent the efforts of women to petition Asherah for healthy children and an adequate milk supply to ensure their survival (Kletter 1996).

iii. Yahweh Sebaot

Yahweh Sebaot was the main male deity in Judah. The epithet Sebaot, 'hosts' or 'armies', can have two implications. One is royal, in the sense of a king who is surrounded by a large retinue waiting to do his slightest bidding and to enact his decisions. The other is military, in the sense of a commander-in-chief who leads troops into battle. Both would emphasize Yahweh's role as king of heaven, since ideally, the king served as commander-in-chief in war and final judge and arbiter in peacetime. In a divine context, the epithet would refer to Yahweh's heavenly retinue in his palace or to his heavenly troops.

The Bible does not indicate what epithet(s) might have been used of Yahweh in Israel because the texts have been written in the south and their authors wanted to give the impression that their understanding of Yahweh was the only legitimate one. In the north, Yahweh was probably associated with the bull as his attribute animal. He may have been depicted as a male god standing on the back of a bull or represented simply as a bull (1 Kgs 12:28). In the south, he may have been represented iconographically as an enthroned male god inside the temple in Jerusalem (Isaiah 6; Ezekiel 1) and, possibly, in a portable form carried inside the ark. The ark's association with Yahweh in the Judahite cult was maintained in later tradition, but its contents were 'neutralized'. The ark became the container for the tablets of law that recorded the divine prescriptions Yahweh gave Israel at Mt Sinai/Mt Horeb instead of a chest containing a portable image (*efod*) of Yahweh that could be consulted before engaging in battle or any other time a divine oracle was needed away from home.

iv. Yahweh, El and Baal

In the biblical texts, Yahweh is ascribed characteristics typically associated with two well-known types of male deities: the aged creator god who was the male head of the divine pantheon and father of the gods and all life on earth, human, animal and vegetal (the El-type), and the young male god associated with animal and agricultural fertility and war (the Baal-type). Both are best known from the cycle of myths found at Ras Shamra, on the coast of Syria. This was the seat of the kingdom of Ugarit, and the texts were found in the destruction of the settlement, usually dated during the twelfth century BCE. In the texts, El is depicted as an aged, bearded male seated on a throne. He is called father of the gods, and he is the one who created earth and heaven. Baal, on the other hand, is a young, virile, potent male weather god. Baal is often associated with the bull, although this could also be the case for El. As bringer of the rain, Baal is responsible for the growth of crops and survival of animals. Population groups living throughout the ancient western Levant were dependent on rain to water their herds and crops; there were not enough perennial rivers to use for irrigation. A stele of Baal from a temple in Ugarit shows him standing with one foot in front of the other and with an upraised arm brandishing a mace and an outstretched arm grasping a thunderbolt. According to the Ugaritic Baal myths, he is the military leader of the younger generation of the gods who defeated his rival, the sea-god Yam, and became king of the younger generation in heaven (Dietrich, Loretz and Sanmartín 1995).

Yahweh is depicted as an El-type deity in various biblical texts. The deities known to the patriarchs in the Book of Genesis are either manifestations of El or represent traits associated with a generic god since *'el* can be the common term used to mean 'a god': *el elyon* (Gen. 14:18–20, 22), *el roi* (Gen. 16:13), *el shadday* (Gen. 17:1), *'el olam* (Gen. 21:33), *el elohe yisrael* (Gen. 33:20) and *el bethel* (Gen. 35:7). Yahweh is equated individually with most of the various El/els in Genesis and subsequently, with *el shadday* of the patriarchal stories, in Exod. 6:2–3. He is an aged, patriarchal god who sits on his throne in heaven.[8] He is called 'the creator'[9] and 'father'[10] and is the source of great wisdom in Job 15:7–8.

Yahweh also is depicted as a Baal-type deity in many biblical texts. Especially noteworthy is the Greek text of Deut. 32:8–9, where *el elyon* assigns territories to various deities on earth and Yahweh is given Jacob as his portion. Here, Yahweh is one of the younger generation of national gods. Yahweh's role as the giver of rains is emphasized,[11] particularly in 1 Kings 18, where Yahweh proves his superiority to Baal on Mt Carmel and then sends rains. His status as a divine warrior is widespread in the Hebrew Bible[12] and twice he is depicted as taking his stand on Mt Zion, his holy place, to fight off enemies who will assault the location (Isa.

31:4–5; Zech. 14:1–9). His defeat of the cosmic water monster in various manifestations parallels Baal's defeat of the sea god, Yam. In biblical tradition, Yahweh fights Sea,[13] Leviathan,[14] Rahab,[15] Tannin[16] and the waters.[17]

v. Other Deities/Roles Associated with Yahweh

In addition to the head divine couple, the potency of a range of deities who comprised lesser members of the divine family in the heavenly court and who oversaw special domains assigned to them by Yahweh was acknowledged. Examples include Shemesh ('Sun'),[18] Yareah ('Moon'),[19] Resheph ('Burning Heat'),[20] Deber ('Pestilence'),[21] Nehushtan ('the Copper One'),[22] or female deities such as Anat (warrior goddess)[23] and Astarte (female fertility god).[24]

The status of Molech as a deity or as a type of sacrifice remains disputed. Various passages indicate that child sacrifice was practiced *lemolek*, either 'to or for Molech', a deity, or alternatively, 'for a *molek*', a category of sacrifice or offering known from Punic inscriptions. However, this second interpretation is unlikely in the case of the Hebrew Bible since the majority of passages imply the term refers not to the sacrifice itself but to the deity to whom it was offered. The sacrifice 'for Molech' is described in some texts as a 'passing over/dedication' (Lev. 18:21) or more specifically, as a 'passing over/dedication by fire' (2 Kgs 23:10; Jer. 32:35); elsewhere, the verb 'to burn' is used, making it clear the child was offered as a holocaust sacrifice (Jer. 7:31; 19:5; Isa. 30:33).

The child sacrifices were made in a precinct called a *tofet*, located in the Valley of Hinnom outside Jerusalem (2 Kgs 23:10; Jer. 32:35). It is unclear if this was the only place they were made or the only one that has been mentioned in the biblical texts. Worship of Molech is also characterized as a 'whoring after Molech' (Lev. 20:2–5 [5]), which parallels the condemnation of the people for 'whoring after other gods' elsewhere (for example, Exod. 34:15–16; Lev. 17:7; Deut. 31:16; Judg. 2:17; 8:33; Jer. 2:20–25; Ezek. 6:9), and Jer. 32:35 claims the deity so worshipped was a form of Baal. Some scholars think he might have been an underworld deity instead (Isa. 57:9), although the two are not mutually exclusive (for more details, see Day 1989). A few scholars think the sacrifices were made to Yahweh during the monarchic era and then later condemned as a form of illegitimate worship in the Persian period: see especially Ezek. 20:25–26; Genesis 22; Jer. 7:31; 32:35 (Stavrakopoulou 2004). Most likely, Molech was a title or epithet of a deity; it is associated with the Hebrew root for kingship, *m-l-k*, and probably meant 'the king', as in Isa. 57:9.

At a later time *melek* was probably changed to *molek* by substituting the vowels from the term *boshet*, 'shame'. Elsewhere in the Hebrew Bible, the title *baal* was changed to *boshet* by pious scribes who considered it a reference to a deity other than Yahweh. For example, the name of Saul's youngest son is Eshbaal in 1 Chron. 8:33; 9:39, but Ishboshet in 2 Sam. 2:8, 10, 12; 3:8, 14–15; 4:5, 8, 12, and Eisbaal in the Greek text of 2 Sam. 2:8, 10, 12.

In the kingdom of Israel there was another figurine type featuring a female playing a drum or possibly a tambourine. It is uncertain which deity was being petitioned and for what reason with this figurine. It might have been a means women used to ask for victory for their men from the warrior goddess Anat or might have been connected with an annual agricultural festival in which Astarte woke up the dead male agricultural god with music to ensure a good planting that would yield an abundant harvest. Anat appears to have been worshipped as the female consort of Yahweh in the Jewish military colony located on the island of Yeb/ Elephantine in the Nile River just south of the First Cataract and the modern Aswan Dam in the Persian period.

There appear to have been other created orders of good and evil spirit-beings as well who acted as divine messengers, as guardian angels, and who also took over human bodies and caused illness. The first are called 'messengers' in the biblical texts, *malakim*, which is often rendered 'angels' in English versions. Other benevolent spirits existed in addition to the messengers of the gods, who functioned in a way similar to guardian angels, protecting individuals from evil spirits. Phantoms or demons were another, malevolent form of invisible created beings. They liked to lurk in the desert, mountains, sea or graveyards (see, for example, Isa. 34:11–15), lying in wait for humans to whom they could cause evil or illness by casting their eye on them or entering their bodies. They were keen to possess dead bodies as well as live ones, so caution had to be taken to prevent such a misfortune when burying the dead. Amulets and shiny objects like beads were placed on the interred bodies to ward off evil spirits. It was possible for humans to cross-breed with gods or other invisible spirits and create a half-human, half-divine (or half-spirit) entity. Genesis 6:2–4 speaks of the creation of such beings as the result of sexual unions between humans and the lesser gods.

vi. The Cult of the Dead
Finally, the ancestors formed a link in the chain between the living and the divine realms. They may have been conceived as low-level divinized

beings after their death or simply as another potent order of spirit-beings now divorced from their former physical bodies. They are called *elohim*, 'gods', in 1 Sam. 28:13 and Isa. 8:19, and *qedoshim*, 'holy ones', in Ps. 16:3, but elsewhere they are described as 'those who pass over' (*avarim/ovrim*; Ezek. 39:11, 14, 15), 'beings' (*nefesh*; Lev. 19:28; Num. 5:2; Hag. 2:13) and 'ghosts' (*ovot*; Isa. 29:4). It is unclear if the *terafim* were representations of family ancestors or some sort of minor house deities or spirits, like the Roman *lares* and *penates*. In Gen. 31:30, they are called *elohim*, which, as seen above, could refer to ancestors as well as lesser gods.

The ancestors looked after the interests of their descendants and, in particular, guaranteed land rights and could be turned to for assistance in securing children, general success in life and healing. The last function might be seen in their characterization as the *refaim*, 'healing ones', if this term derives from the root *r-f-'* (Isa. 14:9; 26:14, 19; Ps. 88:11; Job 26:5; Prov. 2:18; 9:18; 21:16). Michal's attempt to stall Saul's discovery that David had fled by staging a healing ritual that involved the family *terafim* to make the royal messengers think that David was lying in bed, ill, across the room, would tend to support the view that the *terafim* were connected to the family ancestors, who were being invoked as healers (1 Sam. 19:11–18).

In Israel and Judah, the dead were laid to rest in a family tomb in which the bones of the various generations were literally intermixed in heaps as space was made to lay out new corpses on the few benches cut into the interconnected chambers. In the countryside, such tombs lay on family land and physically marked possession from generation to generation (Josh. 24:30; Judg. 2:9). In towns and larger walled settlements, by contrast, it appears that family tombs were located outside the settlement proper. Even so, the ancestors were in all cases seen to have influence over the living generations and, like other spirit-beings, could act benevolently or malevolently toward them. Their designation as *yiddeonim*, 'knowing ones' in Isa. 8:19, and as *ittim*, 'mutterers' in Isa. 19:3, highlights their ability to be consulted by the living about matters otherwise beyond human knowledge, which they would know because they belonged to the divine realm or had access to it.

The dead were dependent on their living relatives to feed them and give them drink after their burial and their passing into *Sheol*, the realm of the dead. Even the humblest burial included a bowl and a jug, which were deemed essential dining equipment for the dead, and Isa. 5:13 indicates that *Sheol* was a place where one could experience great thirst. Evidence that the dead were fed regularly by their living relatives is found in the later oath, which affirmed that no portion of the agricultural tithe owed to Yahweh had been offered to the dead (Deut. 26:14). It is also reflected in the reference in Ps. 16:3–4 to the pouring of drink offerings of blood and the naming of the dead, the 'holy ones', which will no longer occur because Yahweh has become the psalmist's sole divinity and guarantor of his boundary lines and heritage (v. 6). Finally, Isa. 57:6–7 condemns the Judeans for continuing to pour out drink offerings and making cereal offerings to the dead in the seasonal riverbed, and Isa. 65:4 expresses Yahweh's displeasure with those who sit among graves and pass the night in protected places eating pork and a broth made of abominable things, which may refer to rituals conducted in honour of the dead ancestors. It is thought that the feast of David's family that was to be held at the new moon in the ancestral home of Bethlehem reflects the widespread monarchic custom of honouring the dead at regular intervals (1 Sam. 20:5–6, 19).

In exchange for being given food and drink regularly and having their names pronounced in remembrance, the ancestors became favourably disposed towards their living descendants, as allies, not enemies, and served as channels to knowledge not otherwise accessible. The prohibition of consulting the dead through the medium or 'knowing one' (*yiddeoni*), the wizard or 'ghost-inquirer' (*ov* or *shoel ov*), or the necromancer, that is, 'answer-seeker from the dead' (*doresh el-hammetim*; Lev. 19:26, 31; Deut. 18:9–13) indicates that this had been a custom before the rise of monotheism. In Isa. 8:19–20, Yahweh warns Isaiah not to listen to those who are counselling the prophet to 'inquire of the ghosts and knowing ones that chirp and moan; for a people may inquire of its divine ones (i.e. the dead) for instruction and a message'.

vii. Yahweh Reconceptualized

As monotheism developed, it was only natural that Yahweh would have had to assume all the roles formerly associated with his wife, the lesser gods and the divinized ancestors. As the only divinity in heaven, he had to take control of a wide range of functions: the natural order, justice, rainfall, animal fertility, human fertility, plague and other death-causing agents, death itself, healing, and protecting family lands and interests. The lesser orders of invisible spirit-beings, on the other hand, maintained their independence and the benevolent ones became the only members of the heavenly court who praised the sole deity and carried out his commands. They had no independent volition (Handy 1994).

The loss of the monarchy allowed Yahweh's former conception as the main male god who was tied to a given territory and its people (Israel and Judah), for whom the ruling king served as earthly vice-regent, carrying out the will of the god on earth, to be altered. With the dispersal of a significant number of former Israelites and Judahites to other lands, the continuation of his worship would have been predicated on the assertion that his influence and power were not limited to his home territories in the western Levant. This eventually led to the recognition of his status as a universal deity. As a corollary, it was only logical to maintain that he cared for all people and nations on the earth, all of whom were his people. Even so, Jewish tradition emphasized that he viewed Israel as his 'special people' among the inhabitants of the earth, because of his long-standing relationship with them. Thus, as Judaism developed, it was unable to abandon its Yahwistic roots completely and never fully resolved the tension between Israel's special status as the former inhabitants of Yahweh's territory and his free access to all people, as the only deity in existence.

5. Theories of the Cult in the Pentateuch

The above sketch of Israel's and Judah's religious background as well as of the transformations that took place in connection with the rise of monotheism in the Persian period are reflected in the Pentateuch itself. In many ways, the Pentateuch offers different, at times competing conceptions of how and where the unique deity, Yahweh, should be worshipped. Three conceptions, in particular, emerge from the Pentateuch: first, in the Book of Genesis, in connection with the origins of humankind and the time of the patriarchs; second, in Exodus, Leviticus and Numbers, where the cult is closely tied to the wilderness sanctuary; and lastly, in Deuteronomy, where the emphasis lays on the central sanctuary.

i. Genesis

References to the cult and to the offering of sacrifices in the history of humankind (Genesis 1–11) are sparse but occur at strategic places. Significantly, the creation of the world in Gen. 1:1–2:3 does not conclude with the building of a temple and the installation of sacrificial cult, as it does in the Mesopotamian creation myth, the *enuma elish*, but rather, with the institution of Sabbath/*shabbat*. Also, in Genesis 1, man is not created to 'serve' the gods, as he is in the latter myth, but as the 'statue/

image' of the deity, thus taking over the function classically associated with kingship in the ancient Near East. In a second account focusing on Adam (*adam*), the first man (Gen. 2:4–3:24), man's function is redefined; he is to 'serve/labour' (*avad*) the ground (*adamah*). This prepares for the account in Genesis 4.

In Genesis 1–11, the two main forms of sacrifices described occur in Genesis 4 and at the end of the Flood account in Genesis 6–8. After the expulsion from Yahweh's garden, Adam's sons present for the first time two types of sacrifice as a *minhah* or gift/tribute offering for Yahweh: fruits from the ground (Cain) and animals from the flock (Abel). However, only the latter finds the deity's favor (4:4). The offering of animals recurs at the end of ch. 8, where Noah's sacrifice from every type of ritually acceptable animal at the end of the Flood symbolizes the reconciliation between Yahweh and humanity.

The only other reference to some form of cultic worship in Genesis 1–11 occurs at the end of ch. 4, where it is said that in the generation of Adam's grandson Enosh (whose name means 'humankind'), people began to call upon the name of Yahweh (v. 26; *liqro beshem yahweh*). This expression refers probably to a non-sacrificial type of worship. It is used again in the stories of Abraham, where twice, the patriarch calls upon Yahweh's name after building altars for Yahweh. He is said to have built three altars in the land of Canaan, at Shechem, in response to Yahweh's theophany (Gen. 12:6–7), between Bethel and Ai, where he subsequently calls upon the name of Yahweh (Gen. 12:8), and at Hebron near the oaks of Mamre after another divine encounter (Gen. 13:18). He also plants a tamarisk tree in Beersheba after another divine reassurance that he will receive the land and have offspring; there again he invokes Yahweh's name (Gen. 21:33). Even when he tithes himself to Melchizedek at Salem in Gen. 14:18, he is blessed in a ritual that involves bread and wine; there is no mention of meat explicitly. Although it would be possible to argue that *lehem* is here being used in a more generic sense of food rather than to designate bread specifically, the avoidance of meat can also be a significant and intentional device.

The remainder of the patriarchal narratives evinces the same tendency to avoid a depiction of animal sacrifice. Like Abraham, Isaac builds an altar for Yahweh at Beersheba after a divine theophany and calls upon the name of Yahweh afterwards (Gen. 26:23–25). Jacob is twice presented as the founder of the sanctuary in Bethel, where his cultic activity consists in the pouring of oil on a sacred stone/pillar (Gen. 28:10–17); also, he builds an altar after burying foreign gods brought from Aram under the oak near Shechem, where his grandfather Abraham had already set up an altar for Yahweh (Gen. 35:1–7). As for Joseph, no cultic activity is mentioned. However, he is represented as becoming the son-in-law of an Egyptian priest. The reader also finds out that he can even talk with Pharaoh about God (*elohim*), a feature that already appeared in an earlier account about Abraham and the king of the Philistines in Genesis 20.

The only exception to this consistent omission of animal sacrifices in the patriarchal stories is in Genesis 22. Abraham first receives the command to sacrifice his own son, Isaac; at the end of the story, however, the human sacrifice is replaced by the offering of a ram. The entire story has traditionally been interpreted as an etiology for the substitution of animal sacrifices for human sacrifices. The fact that this is the only place in the patriarchal stories where animal sacrifice is recounted may have to do with the fact that the place of the sacrifice, Moriah, was understood as a veiled reference to Jerusalem, the temple city and the centre of the sacrificial cult (see also 2 Chron. 3:1).

ii. Exodus–Numbers

Contrary to the patriarchal stories, the establishment of the sacrificial cult forms the very centre of the books of Exodus, Leviticus and Numbers. Leviticus consists primarily of various instructions for offering sacrifices to the deity (esp. Leviticus 1–7; 17; 22:17–30) and for cleansing the central sanctuary by means of various offerings (Leviticus 16). It is framed by the account of the building of a portable tent-sanctuary for the deity in Exodus 25–31; 35–40 and by additional instructions regarding the cult in Numbers 1–10. In Leviticus, immediately after the building of the sanctuary, the main types of offerings that may be brought to the deity are defined (the burnt offering, cereal offering, well-being offering, 'sin' or 'purification' offering and reparation offering; see chs 1–5). Also, the division of the sacrificial matter between the deity, the priests and the offerer is systematically settled (chs 6–7). The conclusion of the account of the institution of the sacrificial cult in Leviticus 8–9 also emphasizes that the offering of sacrifices at the sanctuary is the privileged channel of communication between Yahweh and his community (see Lev. 9:23–24).

This representation in Leviticus, however, stands in tension with the account in Exodus 19–24, where the revelation to Israel of the Decalogue and of various additional rules (*mishpatim*) constituting the 'covenant' (*berit*) between Yahweh and his people concludes with the representatives of the tribes offering burnt offerings and well-being offerings in 24:3–6, even though the tent-sanctuary had not yet been built. Nonetheless, the lack of priestly mediation is possible because in Exod. 19:6 all Israel has been defined as a 'kingdom of priests' and a 'holy nation.' The sequel to the story, Exodus 32–34, suggests that if Israel needs a specific class of priests—as per the instructions given in Exodus 29 and accomplished in Leviticus 8—it is because the people have violated Yahweh's covenant by transgressing the prohibition of cultic images of the deity (Exodus 32; see Exod. 20:4, 23).

The focus of the books of Exodus, Leviticus and Numbers on the institution of the sacrificial cult at Mt Sinai is prepared from the very beginning of the exodus story. There is repeated emphasis that the purpose of the exodus is to make a pilgrimage (*hag*) to the wilderness (Exod. 5:1) in order to offer sacrifices to Yahweh (5:3; see 3:18 and 10:9; Exod. 7:16 similarly speaks of 'serving' Yahweh in the wilderness). The Book of Numbers also contains ritual instructions for offerings to be made at the wilderness sanctuary, given to Israel after the stay at Mt Sinai, such as Numbers 15 (additional instructions for the sin/ purification offering appear in Leviticus 4), Numbers 19 (purification in case of corpse pollution) and Numbers 28–29 (sacrifices to be offered at appointed festivals, completing the festival calendar in Leviticus 23). In addition, there are a few rites not connected with the sanctuary, which apparently can be practised away from—and independently of—the latter; this the case, in particular, for Passover and Unleavened Bread in Exod. 12:1–13:16.

iii. Deuteronomy

The main concern of the central law collection in Deuteronomy (chs 12–26) is with the centralization of the cult in a single place or sanctuary (*maqom*), an idea unparalleled in the first four books of the Pentateuch. This ideology and its concomitant implications are detailed in the first law that opens the central collection of instructions in Deuteronomy 12–26. A related understanding is introduced in the statement of Deut. 6:4, which insists on the fact that Yahweh is 'one' (*ehad*), with the logical implication that if Yahweh is one he should be worshipped at only one place. In addition, there is a clear connection between 6:4–5 and ch. 12, especially vv 13–18:

> *Deut. 6:4–5*
> 4 Hear, O Israel! Yahweh is our God, Yahweh is one (*ehad*)! 5 You shall love Yahweh your God with all (*kol*) your heart and with all your soul and with all your might.

Deut. 12:13–14
13 Be careful that you do not offer your burnt offerings in every (*kol*)
place that you see, 14 but in the place that Yahweh will chose in one
(*ehad*) of your tribes, there you shall offer your burnt offerings, and
there you shall do all (*kol*) that I command you.

The concern for cult centralization in Deuteronomy is not restricted
to Deuteronomy 12 (in connection with 6:4–5), but can be found in other
legal instructions. Like Exod. 23:14–17, Deut. 16:1–17 gives detailed
prescriptions for the three pilgrimage festivals to be made during the
year; however, contrary to Exodus 23, the text of Deuteronomy 16 now
makes clear that these festivals have to be held at the central sanctuary.
The same applies for the bringing of the tithe according to Deut. 14:21–
23; see further 26:1–15. Lastly, according to Deut. 17:2–13, legal matters
that cannot be settled by local (town) judges must be brought before the
main tribunal in the central sanctuary.

Although the authors of Deuteronomy make clear the worship
at the central sanctuary includes sacrifices, Deuteronomy does not
contain precise instructions about the classification and organization of
sacrifices, contrary to the detailed legislation found in Exodus, Leviticus
and Numbers. The major concern of the Book of Deuteronomy as a
whole lies in the transmission of Yahweh's laws and commands from
generation to generation, as well as in polemics against the cults of 'other
gods'.

iv. Three Competing Cultic Ideologies in the Pentateuch

The foregoing overview allows us to distinguish three major ideologies
concerning Israel's veneration of Yahweh that coexisted during the
Persian period and were accepted by the editors of the Pentateuch
as possible ways to construct the identity of nascent Judaism. The
concepts of cult and worship in Genesis and Exodus–Numbers seem
to presuppose the Deuteronomistic ideology of centralization and
represent elaborations of the latter. For this reason, with respect to the
question of the cult, we need to reverse the canonical order and to start
first with Deuteronomy.

iva. The edition of Deuteronomy in the Persian period. The emphasis on
the fact that Yahweh is 'one' (*ehad*) in Deut. 6:4 is directed against the
prevailing notion in the ancient Near East that deities are worshipped
under various manifestations at different cultic sites. In Mesopotamia,
Ishtar was worshipped as 'Ishtar of Akkad', 'Ishtar of Arbela', 'Ishtar of

Uruk, 'Ishtar of Kish' and 'Ishtar of Nineveh'; likewise, inscriptions from Kuntillet 'Ajrud testify to the fact that Yahweh was worshipped in the Iron Age as 'Yahweh of Teman' and 'Yahweh of Samaria', and it is likely that he had other manifestations as well (Zevit 2001: 370–405).

A central tenet of the Deuteronomistic ideology resides in the notion that the exclusive worship of Yahweh (monolatry) implies worship at a single, central sanctuary, as required by Deuteronomy 12. Even though Jerusalem is not explicitly named in Deuteronomy 12, it seems obvious that the reference to 'one place', as well as 'one tribe', refer to Jerusalem and Judah respectively. This means that Deuteronomy 12 was certainly conceived in Jerusalem initially, and that it reflects the ideology of the central administration.

A possible origin for this ideology of centralization is the second half of the seventh century BCE. That period witnessed a relative growth of Jerusalem, related in some way to the integration of Samaria into the provincial system of the Neo-Assyrian empire (734–722 BCE) and possibly to transfers of population following the loss of the southern part of Judah at the beginning of the seventh century. The last decades of the seventh century are also a time of political change, with the decline of Neo-Assyrian presence in the entire Levant and the concomitant rise of the Neo-Babylonian empire. Against that background, the cult centralization in Deuteronomy may reflect an attempt to establish the royal sanctuary in Jerusalem as the only administrative, economic and religious centre (so, for a example, Römer 2005: 67–106). How far and to what extent this attempt might have been effectively enacted at that time, however, is difficult to tell.

The capture of Jerusalem, the sacking of the temple, the deportation of elite parts of the Judean population, and the probable destruction (or deportation) of Yahweh's statue (597–587 BCE) also had significant implications for the theology of Deuteronomy. Under the political rule of the Persian (Achaemenid) administration, the theology of the central sanctuary remained but was nonetheless significantly reinterpreted. In the Persian province of Yehud, the ideology calling for a central cult found in Deuteronomy now served to support Jerusalem's claim to become the economic and religious centre of the province, which effectively occurred during the second half of the fifth century BCE (see above, Chapter 3). Alternatively, some scholars prefer to situate the origin of Deuteronomistic theology only in this later period, with no precursors in the Iron Age (see, for example, Edelman 2008). In any event, there is general consensus that the law of centralization of Deuteronomy 12 and related passages elsewhere in Deuteronomy were effective in the Persian period.

The major modification vis-à-vis the cult theology of the late monarchic period in Jerusalem was the abandonment of the royal iconography representing Yahweh as a god enthroned inside his temple (see above) and the gradual elaboration of an aniconic conception of Yahweh's presence in his sanctuary. In the Second Temple, Yahweh's statue was never replaced; instead, in the Persian period we witness the development in Deuteronomy and related literature (Joshua–Kings) of the idea it is only Yahweh's 'name' or 'fame' (*shem*) that dwells inside the sanctuary.

In the present form of Deuteronomy 12, the first occurrence of the notion of the 'central place' chosen by Yahweh is accompanied by the qualification that the deity should be sought 'at the place that Yahweh your God will choose from all your tribes, to establish his name there' (Deut. 12:5a). Sometimes it has been argued that this formulation parallels an Akkadian expression referring to a claim to possession (Richter 2002). However, this interpretation does not do justice to the use of that expression in a passage such as Deut. 12:5, or in 1 Kings 8, as Richter herself must admit. Instead, on the basis of Neo-Assyrian parallels (see the expression *shumu shatru*, 'the written name' which in royal inscription replaces the king or the deity), it is more plausible that Yahweh's 'name' is a hypostasis, or a substitute, for the deity itself. Because the Hebrew term for 'name' also means 'reputation', it could also be argued that the so-called 'name theology' in Deuteronomy reflects an attempt to connect the central sanctuary with the regular recitation of authoritative accounts of Yahweh's deeds on behalf of Israel such as are found in the Torah (see Edelman 2009). In any event, so-called 'name theology', which is distinctive of Deuteronomy in the Pentateuch, is a means to maintain a revised version of the old tenet of the divine presence inside the temple while emphasizing the greater distance between humankind and a deity dwelling in heaven. For instance, Solomon's prayer repeatedly states that 'the earth cannot contain Yahweh' and that Yahweh exclusively dwells in heavens (see 1 Kgs 8:27–30).

For Yahwists living outside the Persian province of Yehud, on the other hand, Jerusalem and its temple become more a symbol of the unity of Yahweh's cult despite the loss of geographical cohesion. Solomon's prayer in 1 Kgs 8:44–51—a text with many links to Deuteronomy 12— exhorts Yahwists living outside the land to direct their prayers towards Jerusalem and its temple (exactly like Muslims and the Mecca today).

The emphasis in Deuteronomy on transmission of divine laws as well as regular recitation of Moses' torah should probably also be explained in the context of diaspora Judaism. Even though it is difficult to specify the origins of the first synagogues, it is likely that the general concept of communal readings of the Torah probably originated in the Persian-period diaspora. The somewhat striking notion in Deuteronomy that the divine commands should be written on the doorposts of every house (Deut. 6:9) also makes sense in that context: the reading of the Law tends to become a substitute for the sacrificial cult; likewise, any house can potentially replace the temple—at least outside the province of Yehud.

What we see, therefore, in the Book of Deuteronomy in the Persian period is the parallel development of two cultic systems, one for Jerusalem, the temple and the province of Yehud, the other for the Yahwists of the diaspora. These two co-existing systems, however, converge in the idea of a religious and cultural exclusivism. Not only does Deuteronomy maintain that Yahweh is the only god to be worshipped by Israel, but this exclusive worship goes along with exclusive customs and leads to an ideal of total cultural segregation from other ethnic groups. Deuteronomy 7:1–6 forbids any kind of interaction with the nations in the land, be it economic transactions or intermarriage, both being equated with abandonment of Yahweh. The same language recurs at the beginning and the end of Deuteronomy 12, where, however, the emphasis lays upon the segregation of Yahweh from other gods, in accordance with the topic of ch. 12. Deuteronomy 12 concludes with the following words (vv 29–30):

> 29 When Yahweh your God cuts off before you the nations you are going to dispossess, and you dispossess them and dwell in their land,
> 30 beware that you are not ensnared to follow them, after they are destroyed before you, and that you do not inquire after their gods, saying, 'How do these nations serve their gods, that I also may do likewise?

ivb. The Priestly school in Exodus–Numbers. The coherent depiction of the wilderness sanctuary and its cultic organization are commonly accepted to be a product of the same milieu of Persian-period Jerusalem, reflecting the ideology of a 'Priestly' school. This school (usually labeled 'P') also created stories about the origin of the world and of Israel, which have been gathered into a great narrative stretching from the creation in Genesis to the wilderness narratives in Numbers. The fact that this Priestly school contributed to the Book of Genesis accounts for the presence of distinct cult conceptions inside that book, as outlined above. The Priestly school appears to accept the idea of cultic centralization as advocated in Deuteronomy. The wilderness sanctuary may be viewed as an image, or an archetype, of the central sanctuary in Jerusalem— although this fictional sanctuary could also be claimed as an archetype by various cultic centres in Persian-period Yehud simultaneously, such as Bethel or Gerizim. In some Priestly texts such as Leviticus 17 (the opening of the so-called 'Holiness Code'), the legislation of Deuteronomy 12 is clearly presupposed.

Cultic centralization does not appear to be the major concern of the Priestly scribes, however; they are much more interested in elaborating a form of Yahwistic cult that may be described as 'inclusive monotheism'. This conception is based on a distinctive theory regarding the revelation of Yahweh to humankind, in which three successive stages are identified that correspond to the organization of humankind into three spheres. In the Priestly account of Genesis 1–11, the creator god is known to humankind as *elohim*, a term that, interestingly, can be understood either in the singular or the in the plural. This deity then reveals itself to the patriarchs Abraham and Jacob as *el shadday* (perhaps meaning 'god of the wilderness', see Gen. 17:1 and 35:11). It is only to Israel it reveals itself as *yahweh* at the beginning of the Exodus narrative. Compare Exod. 6:3, where Yahweh says to Moses, 'I appeared to Abraham, Isaac, and Jacob, as *el shadday*, but under my name, Yahweh, I did not make myself known to them.' This complex theory of revelation implies that, even though all nations unknowingly worship the same god, Yahweh, only Israel knows the personal name of the creator god and can worship him in the right way, with the appropriate cultic organization. In that respect, the Priestly theory of revelation in Genesis and Exodus prepares for the establishment of the wilderness sanctuary and the sacrificial cult in Exodus to Numbers.

In this way, Israel is redefined as the 'priestly nation' in the universe, the one in charge of the sanctuary of the unique god. This can easily be understood in the context of the Persian period. The notion that all peoples are gathered under the supreme authority of one creator god, Ahura Mazda, is a central aspect of imperial Achaemenid propaganda, as can be seen, for instance, in the relief and inscription of Darius I at Behistun. The same conception is apparent in Genesis 10, where the creator god 'Elohim is responsible for the peaceful distribution of every nation on earth according to its language and to its ethnic origins. From the perspective of the inclusive monotheism promoted by the

Priestly scribes, this means Ahura Mazda was probably interpreted as a manifestation of the Jewish deity for all the nations in the Persian empire.

Overall, the Priestly narrative in Exodus–Numbers implies the basis of Israel's identity under Achaemenid rule resides in the sole institution that survived the crisis of the exile: the temple. In this respect, Israel's redefinition as the 'priestly nation' of the Persian empire appears to reflect the religious, political and economic interests of the priestly class in Jerusalem. The detailed sacrificial legislation in Leviticus and Numbers also implies this legislation was not purely speculative but was conceived for actual cultic activity. Contrary to Deuteronomy, where sacrificial legislation plays a minor role, the organization of the sacrificial cult is now integrated into the founding document of 'Israel'.

Although the Priestly writings are clearly focused on the temple and the sacrificial cult, there is nonetheless concern for ritual practices that may be performed outside of the land. In particular, instructions for circumcision (Genesis 17) and for the celebration of Passover (Exodus 12) are entirely detached from the temple cult and may apparently be practiced anywhere. As in the case of Deuteronomy, this should probably be understood as a means of taking into account the existence of a large Yahwistic diaspora. A letter from a Judean official, Hananiah, written to the colony of Elephantine in Egypt in 419 BCE, witnesses to the ongoing practice of celebrating Unleavened Bread (and possibly Passover) in the diaspora at the end of the fifth century.

Besides inclusive monotheism—as opposed to monolatry—another major difference between P and Deuteronomy concerns the representation of the divine presence. The notion that Yahweh's 'name' dwells in the temple is consistently missing from P. Instead, the Priestly writings reassert a more direct form of divine presence, which is designated as the *kavod* ('glory') of Yahweh. This idea has a parallel in the prophetic Book of Ezekiel, which was also strongly shaped by priestly circles in Jerusalem. In the Priestly texts of the Pentateuch, the *kavod* of Yahweh is always described as a burning 'fire' surrounded (or covered) by a 'cloud' (see for example, Exod. 24:15; 40:34–35). Interestingly, cloud and fire can be viewed as a reminiscence of two of the traditional attributes of the storm god in Syria-Palestine. The major point, however, is that the Priestly texts explicitly establish that this *kavod* dwells (Heb. *shakan*) inside the sanctuary (Exod. 25:8; 29:45–46 and 40:34–35), contrary to the conception that surfaces in 1 Kings 8, for instance. Because the Priestly authors are keen to emphasize the sacrificial cult as the very place where Yahweh and his community can meet, as is made clear at the end of the account of the institution of the sacrificial cult in Lev. 9:23–24, such a conception necessarily required the reaffirmation of the divine presence inside the sanctuary.

ivc. Patriarchal traditions in Genesis. Finally, a distinctive conception of the cult is perceptible everywhere in the narratives about the patriarchs Abraham, Isaac and Jacob. In the opening part of Abraham's story, the patriarch stops at major cultic sites in Israel and Judah (Gen. 12:1–13:18), first Shechem, then Bethel and lastly Mamre/Hebron. The very fact that Abraham builds altars in every one of these sites clearly appears to imply some form of recognition of their legitimacy as sanctuaries. Jacob is also strongly associated with Bethel as a cultic site (Gen. 28:10–22 and 35:6–15) and, to a lesser extent, with Shechem (Gen. 33:18–20).

Read in the context of the Persian period, this depiction should be understood as a rejection of the Deuteronomic ideology of centralization as well as a plea for cultic diversity within 'Israel'. On the other hand, it was observed above that Abraham never offers sacrifices on such altars but instead 'calls upon' the divine name. Likewise, although Jacob is once described as offering a libation in Bethel (Gen. 35:14), he never offers animal sacrifices at all. This must probably be understood as a concession to the Deuteronomic and Priestly cultic ideologies: even though there may be several sanctuaries, only in the central sanctuary may animal sacrifices be offered. The Elephantine correspondence testifies to the same notion. The Judean and Samarian authorities granted the Elephantine community permission to rebuild its temple after the latter had been destroyed with the specific condition that no animal sacrifices be offered there. The most likely explanation is that they wanted to reserve the offering of such sacrifices in the sanctuaries of Jerusalem and Gerizim respectively.

The only passage where Abraham offers animal sacrifice, Genesis 22, can be interpreted along the same lines. As mentioned earlier, the name Moriah could easily be understood—from a Judean perspective—as a reference to the temple mount in Jerusalem, as per 2 Chron. 3:1 already; from a Samarian perspective, the association of Shechem with *Moreh* in Gen. 12:6 could also favor a reference to Mt Gerizim, the central sanctuary of the province of Samaria built ca. 450 BCE, which was precisely located in the area of Shechem.

v. Strategies of Conciliation at the Time of the Composition of the Pentateuch

On the whole, it appears that the three cultic systems that surface in the Torah tend to agree upon the idea of a central sanctuary for the patron deity of Israel, even though these systems considerably differ as regards the nature of the presence of that deity inside the sanctuary or the deity's relationship to other gods (monolatry vs monotheism). In addition, the previous discussion suggests the tradents of these three constructs knew each other and sought somehow to take each other's constructs into consideration. Further efforts at synthesizing these competing conceptions were made at the time of the composition of the Pentateuch, when these traditions were grouped together to form a single authoritative document, the Torah of Moses. For example, Deuteronomy 4 introduces into Deuteronomy a monotheistic statement that revises the monolatry of the book. Chapter 4 takes up monotheistic assertions from Genesis 1 (the Priestly creation account) and from Second Isaiah to establish there are no other gods than Yahweh (see especially vv 32–40). Many other examples could be enumerated, which testify to an attempt to align more closely 'Priestly' and Deuteronomic conceptions of the cult. For instance, the same list of clean and unclean animals can be found in Leviticus 11 and Deuteronomy 14; or Deut. 12:20–26 introduces within ch. 12 a prohibition of profane, non-sacrificial slaughter that has its closest parallel in Leviticus 17.

Such conciliatory attempts were not restricted to competing conceptions of the cult in Yehud. Because the Torah was also intended to be accepted by Yahwists in Samaria, a reference to the sanctuary on Mt Gerizim had to be introduced in the last chapters of Deuteronomy in Deut. 27:4–8.

6. Treaty, Loyalty Oath and Royal Grant

i. Terminology and Semantics

In several passages of the Pentateuch, one finds the idea of a formal pledge made under oath by one party to another that creates a self-imposed, voluntary obligation or a mutual obligation. While the parties involved are often human and can be equal in power and importance (this may be the case in texts such as Gen. 21:27, 32; 26:28; 31:44), usually one is more powerful than the other. In the majority of pentateuchal uses, Yahweh is the more powerful party who commits to obligations, with one or more humans the weaker ones who also commit, on their side, to perform stipulated obligations. Two different terms can express the notion of pledge or formal agreement made under oath in Hebrew: *berit* and *edut*; the former dominates.

The etymology of the noun *berit* is unclear. It has often been connected with the verb *brh* that, in Hebrew, can mean either 'to eat' (2 Sam. 3:35; 12:17; 13:5, 6, 10; Lam. 4:10) or 'to choose, designate' (1 Sam. 17:8). However, there are no passages in the Hebrew Bible where the verb *brh* is used in a treaty context, so this etymology remains entirely hypothetical. Another, more interesting parallel is with the Assyrian verb *baru*, 'to bind', and the related substantive *biritu*, which can mean either the 'space-in-between' (in-between two fields, for instance), or a 'link' or 'fetter'. The Hebrew noun would then refer to the relationship made between the two contracting parties. The connection between *berit* and the notion of 'bond' or 'binding' is obvious in some passages of the Hebrew Bible (see, e.g., Ezek. 20:37), but not in all so that the derivation may not be established with certainty (Weinfeld 1975; Kutsch 1997). Nonetheless, this derivation appears to fit with the main expressions for establishing a treaty or a covenant, such as 'to give' (*ntn*) or 'establish' (*qwm* hiphil) a *berit*.

The case of the expression 'to cut' (*krt*) a *berit* is less obvious. This expression may refer to a treaty ritual in which animals were cut into pieces, through which one of the contracting parties passed so as to symbolize the solemn acceptance of the stipulations contained in the treaty (see Jer. 34:18, further Gen. 15:17). However, the ritual implies some form of bond between the contracting parties and, moreover, it delimits a sort of 'ritual space' in which the treaty is established, so that this use of *berit* is also consistent with the basic meanings of Akkadian *biritu* as noted above.

The term *edut* is cognate with Aramaic *'dy* as well as Assyrian *ade*, two terms referring either to an oath taken in the context of a treaty or to the written document containing the treaty itself (Simian-Yofre 1999). In Aramaic the term is found in the Sefire treaties from the eighth century BCE. In Assyrian and Aramean usage, the term describes different types of political pacts or obligations concluded under a range of circumstances for various purposes, all of which included the swearing of an oath by one or more of the contracting parties. The involvement of divine witnesses is central, and while it is likely that oaths were sworn in their presence, they equally were invoked to oversee the agreement and punish either party should they break the stipulations with the series of stated curses. Examples include bilateral and unilateral treaties, nonaggression pacts, peace and friendship treaties or parity treaties, mutual assistance pacts, alliance treaties, treaties with exiled foreign royalty or with Assyrianized foreign royalty, treaties with submissive adversaries and loyalty oaths. Thus, it is a broad term that could apparently take many specific forms (Parpola and Watanabe 1988; Kataja and Whiting 1995). One such example of a Neo-Assyrian *ade* is the loyalty oaths that Esarhaddon imposed on members of his Median bodyguard in 672 BCE to execute his decision to make Asshurbanipal the crown-prince of Assyria and Shamash-shum-ukin the crown prince of Babylonia. These oaths were imposed as unilateral agreements to ensure a smooth succession to the throne in the context of a political situation (Liverani 1995).

Some scholars have also proposed connecting so-called 'royal grants' by which the king grants land to a loyal vassal with the loyalty pacts of the *ade*-type. This parallel has especially interested biblical scholars because of the close connection in the Pentateuch between the Sinai/ Horeb covenant and Yahweh's gift of the land to Israel and God's promise of land to Abraham and his descendants. However, royal land grants are never designated by the term *ade*, and the stipulations in the two sets of documents are quite distinct, so that the parallel is general at best (Knoppers 1996). It is important to note, however, that a type of document existed in Assyria that is conveniently called a royal grant and that it had a few differences from a treaty.

ii. Treaties

Ancient treaties were elaborate oaths that set forth something to be performed by one or both parties, which was usually accompanied by a sworn vow that called for divine vengeance in case the promise was broken. Treaties in the ninth–seventh centuries BCE usually included (1) stipulations, (2) a violation clause specifying the consequences for disobedience, and (3) traditional curses. Also, additional elements could also be found, such as a preamble or introduction defining the nature of the pact and the parties involved, a list of divine witnesses to the agreement, an oath clause, a brief history of the past relationship that existed between the two, or ceremonial curses, some of which probably were enacted before the party to drive home the point.

In the Iron Age II (ca. 950–500 BCE), *ade* treaty-pacts included the stipulation that the vassal was to keep a copy of the text and was to relate the stipulations agreed to under oath to his sons, grandsons and posterity, adjuring them to maintain the treaty. It was standard practice to make two copies of a pact so that both parties involved would each have a copy. The international treaty form given above for pacts is not a complete invention from the Iron II period, however, but is already found in several Hittite treaties from the second millennium that were discovered in the palace at Boghazköy. However, the study of biblical treaty ideology is heavily dependent on the Neo-Assyrian treaty form, as is obvious in the case of the Book of Deuteronomy especially. The entire treaty ideology in the Hebrew Bible, as well as specific terms such as *berit* and *'edut*, cannot be understood without due consideration of the ancient Near Eastern—and especially Neo-Assyrian—background.

iii. Treaty and Loyalty Oath in the Pentateuch

In the Pentateuch, *berit* is used to describe agreements between individual patriarchs (Abraham, Isaac and Jacob) and local kings or other powerful individuals (Gen. 14:13; 21:27, 32; 26:28; 31:44), pacts between God and individuals (Noah in Gen. 6:18; 9:9–17; Abraham in Gen. 15:18; 17:2–21; Exod. 2:24; and Phineas in Num. 25:12–13) or between God and Israel (at Sinai: Exod. 19:5; 24:8; 34; at Horeb: Deut. 4:13, 23; 5:2–3; 7:9, 12; 8:18; 9:9–15; in Moab: 29; 31:16, 20). The extension of what is normally a formal agreement between humans witnessed by gods to an agreement initiated by a deity with one or more humans is an innovation of the biblical writers. It was a logical development, however, which allowed them to eliminate the usual 'royal' middleman, as it were, the king, who served as the god's earthly vice-regent, and have the god grant favours directly. Instead of overseeing the terms stipulated by human contracting parties, the god became a contracting party directly.

As far as treaties, or 'pacts' between God and Israel (or individual ancestors) in the Pentateuch are concerned, it is relatively easy to distinguish two major types. One is found in the Book of Deuteronomy and in the Exodus account of the covenant at Mt Sinai (Exodus 19–24 and 32–34). The other is found in the so-called 'Priestly' texts of the Pentateuch.

The first conception is closer to the traditional treaty ideology found in the ancient Near East. In a general way, several key passages in the Book of Deuteronomy are reminiscent of Neo-Assyrian treaties, insofar as the dominant issue in that book is the exclusive loyalty to Yahweh, who has taken over the role traditionally assigned to the king. Such exclusive loyalty is concretely manifested through the various stipulations contained in the centre of the book (chs 12–26). Also, these stipulations are themselves concluded by a detailed list of the curses Israel could expect in the case of disobedience, which employ several motifs from curses found in Neo-Assyrian treaties. These curses would have become standard scribal language within the Assyrian empire and amongst its vassals and they remained part of the international repertoire of curse phraseology taught to scribes operating in subsequent empires. Yahweh himself is consistently depicted as a Neo-Assyrian suzerain who grants occupation of the land to his vassal, Israel, upon condition of the people's exclusive loyalty.

Although the language used is partly different, the same general conception underlies the account of the *berit* concluded at Mt Sinai in the Book of Exodus. As in Deuteronomy, the covenant made by Yahweh with the people consists of several stipulations (the Decalogue and the so-called 'Covenant Code' in Exodus 21–23) whose observance is mandatory for the maintenance of the relationship defined by the covenant. The negative consequences of failure to observe these stipulations are illustrated in the account of the 'golden calf' in Exodus 32–34, where Yahweh threatens to exterminate the entire people.

The conception of the *berit* in P presents some significant differences. First, P no longer relates the conclusion of a *berit* at Mt Sinai; at most one passage, Exod. 31:12–17, presents the Sabbath as the 'sign' of the *berit*. Instead, the making of the *berit* is reported to have occurred in primeval times (Noah; Genesis 9) and the time of the patriarchs (Abraham; Genesis 17). While the covenant with Noah after the Flood concerns humankind as a whole, the covenant with Abraham concerns his offspring, Ishmael and Isaac. It is usually thought that in both texts the concept of *berit* in P is 'unconditional', a view that seems to be supported by the fact that, in P, the *berit* is always referred to as a *berit olam*, an 'everlasting covenant'. Such an interpretation, however, does not entirely do justice to the formulation of Genesis 9 and 17. Both texts also contain covenantal stipulations: Gen. 9:4–6 forbids the 'eating' of blood as well as murder, whereas Gen. 17:10–14 requires every member of Abraham's offspring to be circumcised.

The difference with the Deuteronomistic tradition is that the transgression of these stipulations by an individual leads to the condemnation of the offender alone but does not abolish the covenant itself. In other words, the *berit* in P is still conditional, but for the individual, no longer for the group as a whole, and this is why the *berit* may be termed a *berit olam*. This Priestly conception of covenant may reflect a shift from the idea of collective to individual responsibility, which appears to be characteristic of Priestly circles during and after the exile (see Ezekiel 18).

Also, it may be viewed as a Priestly reinterpretation of the motif of the 'everlasting covenant' made with David in Samuel–Kings, which is now transferred to the people as a whole. The same notion recurs in other early postexilic texts, like Isa. 55:3. In a few other Priestly passages, however, we find the notion that Yahweh also made an everlasting covenant with the high priest and his dynasty (see Num. 18:19 and especially Num. 25:10–13). In these passages, therefore, the promise to David of an everlasting dynasty is now reinterpreted and reapplied to the high priest after the exile.

In addition, contrary to the Deuteronomists, the Priestly writer makes significant use of the term *edut* in connection with the revelation at Mt Sinai. In P, the term *edut* appears to refer to a sort of 'charter' given to Israel and placed inside the Ark (Exod. 25:16, 21–22 and related passages). However, the contents of this 'charter' are not entirely clear. According to Deut. 10:1–5 and 1 Kgs 8:9, the Ark contained the two tablets with the Decalogue, so that the 'charter' placed inside the Ark according to P has often been understood to refer to a version of the Decalogue, especially the 'Priestly' Decalogue in Exodus 20. If so, it means that the Priestly writers use *edut* to describe the formal agreement made at Sinai, where the obligations were incumbent upon Israel, the weaker party, but not on God, and essentially reserved the term *berit* for the earlier covenant made with Noah and Abraham.

In the present shape of the Pentateuch, Deuteronomistic and Priestly conceptions have been juxtaposed and, in a few cases, we see attempts to harmonize these two concepts of the covenant. Thus, in Leviticus 26, disobedience to the *berit* leads to the exile, yet it is said that Yahweh will eventually 'remember' (*zkr*) his *berit* with the patriarchs and bring back the people from exile. Despite the people's disobedience, the *berit* has not been entirely broken. The same notion appears in Deut. 4:25–31. Genesis 15 may possibly represent a different sort of synthesis between the Priestly and non-Priestly covenants since it uses the expression *krt berit*, which occurs exclusively in non-Priestly texts in the Pentateuch, to characterize the conclusion of a covenant that anticipates the Priestly covenant of Genesis 17, yet is devoid of any stipulations. Still, it may be noted that, contrary to what is the case with other central themes of the Pentateuch, this harmonizing strategy does not appear to have been extensively developed.

iv. Royal Grants

In a royal grant, the king voluntarily placed himself under an obligation towards his servant to reward him for his loyalty, usually by granting him land and a tax-exempt estate. In form, the royal grant contains most or all of the following elements: (1) historical introduction, (2) border delineations, (3) stipulations, (4) witnesses, and (5) blessings and curses. It is quite similar in its formal structure to the treaty form detailed above. Examples of sealed land grants recorded on tablets, on the other hand, include (1) an introduction naming the king and stating the acts of loyalty performed by the other party, (2) boundary delineations if it involves a gift of property, (3) stipulations of exemptions from taxation, military levy and corvée and choice of burial site, and in some instances, (4) an oath overseen by selected deities that no future royal descendant will set aside the words of the tablet, and if he does, the gods overseeing the oath will hear the prayer of the injured recipient of the grant (Kataja and Whiting 1995: 4–64). The recipient is to be punished if he is found guilty, after a full investigation, but one is not 'to act negligently against the seal' (Kataja and Whiting 1995: 27–28). Thus, in these variant forms, gods serve as witnesses to an oath and there are no explicit blessings or curses, though there is an implication that the gods will hear the prayers of the wronged and act in his interest against the reigning king.

There are a few differences between a royal grant and a treaty. In the grant, the curses are directed against anyone who violates the rights of the king's servant, not the servant himself, as in the treaty. In addition, the grant is a reward for the loyal actions that the vassal has already performed, while a treaty is premised on future loyalty between the contracting parties. This is the case even if a past relationship had already existed between the two; details of such a prior relationship were optionally recorded in Assyrian treaties. While a past association can set up a sense of obligation in the present and future, a treaty is still regulating future behaviour between the two parties. In the grants recorded on tablets, the reward is usually limited to the servant/vassal himself, most of whom were eunuchs, without children. In those found on *kudurru* stones, which are stones erected by a recipient of a grant and placed on the boundary of the granted property, the privileges are granted to descendants, on condition of loyalty, or can be made in perpetuity with no further strings attached.

In reality, a royal grant was only enforceable during the lifetime of the king who made it; his successor could overturn it at will, even with the terms specified in writing, under royal seal. He was a law unto himself and could act as though no past obligations were binding during his reign, not honouring the commitments of the previous generation. This can be inferred by the oath the king makes on behalf of his descendants and the failure to stipulate the specific consequences the offending future king will suffer.

v. Royal Grants in the Pentateuch

The pentateuchal pacts that God makes with Noah, Abraham and Phineas, like the one with David in the books of Samuel, are modeled after royal grants, where Yahweh assumes the role of the human king and voluntarily commits to give rewards for loyalty. In Assyria, the king making a royal grant is routinely given the ancient title *uklu* (OA *waklum*), 'overseer', which is always used when he is acting as head of state, not as an individual. This implies he is acting as steward of the national god's estate. It can be argued that Yahweh is portrayed to be acting on his own, without an intermediary, in his pacts with Noah, Abraham and Phineas. However, the terms of the pacts with Noah and Phineas do not involve the usual reward of land, as does the one with Abraham; and the pact with Abraham also offers a slight variation to the norm because in its present form, God promises land to Abraham in exchange for his future loyalty, not because of prior acts of loyalty. Nevertheless, Yahweh is committing to act in a certain way toward his 'property' in the two other pacts: the earth and all its life forms (Noah) and Israel (Phineas).

7. Moses

Besides Yahweh, Moses is the most important figure in the Torah, and the Pentateuch may justifiably be understood as a 'biography of Moses' (Knierim 1985). The Book of Exodus opens with the birth story of Moses (chs 1–2) and Deuteronomy ends with his death (ch. 34). In the last verses of the Torah, Moses is explicitly presented as outweighing all the other heroes or prophets in Israel's history:

> 10 And there has not arisen a prophet since in Israel like Moses, whom Yahweh knew face to face, 11 in all the signs and the wonders that Yahweh sent him to do in the land of Egypt, to Pharaoh, to all his servants, and to all his land; 12 and in all the mighty deeds and in all the great terror that Moses wrought in the sight of all Israel. (Deut. 34:10–12)

This final statement introduces a clear separation between the Pentateuch and ensuing books. At the same time, it characterizes the majority of the Pentateuch as the story of Moses, with Genesis forming a prologue. The major division within the Pentateuch thus is to be found between Genesis and Exodus.

If we look at references to Moses in the Hebrew Bible outside the Pentateuch, he appears frequently in the so-called Deuteronomistic History, especially in Joshua and Kings (ten times) and in Chronicles and Ezra–Nehemiah (21 times). Yet only four prophetic texts and six Psalms mention him (Isa. 63:11; Jer. 15:1; Mic. 6:4; Mal. 3:22; Pss 77:21; 90:1; 99:6–7; 105:25; 106:16, 23, 32–33), and the psalms have a postexilic setting. This seems to indicate Moses' alignment with the Deuteronomistic school, which may well have invented the biography of Moses.

There is no doubt that the deliverance from Egypt is the central, defining event in the story of Moses; it appears in every 'historical summary' and in all the 'historical psalms' of the Hebrew Bible. Surprisingly, however, Moses is not mentioned in a number of these summaries (e.g. Deut. 6:21; 26:7–8; Amos 2:10; Psalms 80; 136). According to the texts, it is Yahweh himself who brought Israel out of Egypt; there was no need for a mediator. This, then, raises the question if there might have been an older exodus tradition without the figure of Moses.

Hosea 12 presents the first use of a go-between figure in connection with the exodus event. In this oracle, the prophet criticizes the ancestor Jacob as a trickster, a liar and a man interested mainly in women. The Jacob tradition is here devalued in favor of the exodus tradition (de Pury 2001). 'Jacob fled to the land of Aram; there Israel served for a wife, and for a wife he guarded sheep. But by a prophet Yahweh brought Israel up from Egypt and by a prophet he was guarded' (12:12–13). The sharp critique of Jacob found in Hos. 12:4–7 and 13 is often understood as a justification for the fall of Samaria in 721 BCE, but it might well be a much later attempt to shed negative light on Israel's ancestral traditions. Whatever its purpose, it is clear that Jacob is rejected as a mediator. The addressees of the prophetic statement are thereby warned not to rely on genealogy; instead, they are invited to turn to the prophet who appears as Yahweh's agent in saving Israel from its bondage. The prophet intended might be Moses, but it is noteworthy that he is not named explicitly. The author of Hosea 12 knows the Jacob epic well, but offers no details regarding the exodus tradition except that it involved prophetic mediation.

The question of the relation between Moses and the exodus tradition is linked to the question of the origin of Moses, the so-called 'historical Moses'. Since the focus of this chapter is on the different presentations of Moses in the Torah, not his historicity, a few remarks should suffice.

There is no clear evidence for a historical person who would correspond to the biblical Moses (Assmann 1998). There is evidence in Egypt for many contacts between the Nile kingdoms and Asia Minor during the second and first millennia BCE and Egyptian sources mention a number of important ministers (chancellors, chamberlains) with a Semitic background. However, efforts to identify one of these individuals with Moses have not won endorsement since the evidence is so scanty and inconclusive. For a while, the most attractive candidate was a Semitic chamberlain named Bey or Beya (Knauf 1988; de Moor 1990). About 1187 BCE, he was involved in a civil war and seems to have escaped from Pharaoh Sethnakht with a group of *hapiru*, who robbed Egyptians of their gold and silver. However, a newly discovered papyrus fragment shows he was executed in Egypt and so could not have led an 'exodus' (Grandet 2000).

There is no doubt that the name Moses is Egyptian. It contains the same element found, for instance, in Ramses, 'son of the God Ra/Re'. The name Moses means 'son of...' The Hebrew narrator of Exodus 2 knows this meaning; contrary to all other biblical birth narratives, Moses' mother does not name her child after his birth, so the name eventually assigned him by the narrator is simply the generic local term for 'son'. However, if a historical individual underlies the current biblical figure, it is possible that his name has been deliberately shortened to its generic element 'son' to eliminate the name of an Egyptian deity, particularly once it was decided to use the figure as the recipient of the Torah of Yahweh. Interestingly, other people related to Moses in the Pentateuch also carry Egyptian names, especially Aaron and Phineas. One could argue that if Moses were a totally invented figure, he would not bear an Egyptian name, so there might be some historical memories behind the Moses traditions.

It may be that the worship of the desert-god Yahweh had been introduced in some Israelite tribes by a man called Moses. It has been proposed that before becoming the lawgiver par excellence, Moses might have been the eponymous ancestor of a group of oracle priests, the Mushites, who perhaps were involved in a healing cult and may have had some Egyptian connections (Edelman 2007). The Pentateuch contains several texts in which Moses engages in magic and healing activities.

The open question that remains is that of Moses' association with the exodus. It may also be that the biblical and extra-biblical traditions about Moses and the exodus constitute a kind of 'patchwork quilt' sewn from various fabrics taken from the store of 'cultural memory' (for this term, see Assmann 1998), in which a new history has been constructed out of different elements like Asian ministers, the expulsion of the Semitic Pharaohs, the Hyksos in the sixteenth century BCE, or even of the so-called monotheistic revolution of Akhenaton. Tentatively, one could imagine that this story-line was constructed in the seventh century BCE, when the exodus story was written down as a counter-history in reaction to Assyrian propaganda (Otto 2006). Though the primary role assigned to Moses in Exodus to Deuteronomy is that of the quintessential mediator for nascent Judaism, he is portrayed as playing a number of different roles. He appears as a royal figure, the first of Israel's prophets, a judge and lawgiver, the founder of the cult, an intercessor, a general, a hero and a tragic figure. Each will now be reviewed in turn.

i. Moses as a Royal Figure

In the ancient Near East, the king is the traditional mediator between the gods and the people. According to this royal ideology, the king can be considered the 'image' of the deity. In Egypt, Pharaoh is the son of Re and priest of all temples in the land. The title 'pharaoh' means the 'great house'; this Hebrew adaptation of an Egyptian phrase refers to the place where the Egyptian king lives rather than to the king himself.

In Mesopotamia, the political ruler is often also first among all priests because of his special relation to a particular deity. The king receives his power and its symbol (sceptre, crown, throne) from the god. He is said to have been created or engendered by the god, or fashioned or chosen by him while still in the womb of his mother. He is the 'servant' of the gods, the 'vicar'. He is also considered to be 'shepherd' of his people. In Assyrian iconography, the king and his god are depicted in an almost identical way, with the same clothes and gestures (see, for instance ANEP: 180, n. 534; 154, n. 447).

In Israel and Judah, kingship was established according to the ancient Near Eastern pattern; the king is above all mediator between the territorial, dynastic god and the people. Upon accession to the throne, the king becomes 'son of Yahweh' (Psalm 2) and could be considered *elohim* (Ps. 45:7–8). He is elected by the god (Ps. 78:70) and loved by him (so, for example, the name David, 'beloved', and Solomon's other name, Yedidiah, 'beloved of Yahweh'; Naram-Sin means 'the beloved of Sin').

The king is Yahweh's servant (Ps. 18:1, 89:4); this title is frequently used of David in the books of Samuel and Kings. His accession to kingship is symbolized by his anointing, which was understood to reflect the divine gift of health, strength and *ruah*, 'spirit'. Like Mesopotamian and Egyptian kings, Israelite and Judahite kings build or renovate temples, select priests for cult and sacrifices and pray for the people and their welfare.

In the Pentateuch, Moses takes over all these royal functions. This assigning of royal traits to the figure of Moses may have begun as early as the seventh century during the so-called Josianic reform, which was not organized by the king but by his counselors. They took control of the capital, limiting the king's power. Since Deuteronomy 17 subordinates the king to the law of Moses, the text might have been written as a means to justify the actions of the counselors and enforce their desire to limit royal power then and in the future. This idea remains hypothetical. There is, however, no doubt that the fall of Jerusalem (587 BCE), the loss of political autonomy and the deportation of the royal family to Babylon provoked the transfer of royal ideology to the figure of Moses during the sixth and fifth centuries BCE.

In the Book of Exodus, Moses is presented as a king from the very beginning. The story of his birth and exposure shows literary dependence on the birth legend of Sargon, the legendary founder of the Assyrian Empire:

> Sargon, strong king, king of Agade, am I. My mother was a high priestess, my father I do not know... My mother, a high priestess, conceived me, in secret she bore me. She placed me in a reed basket, with bitumen she caulked my hatch. She abandoned me to the river from which I could not escape. The river carried me along: to Aqqi, the water drawer, it brought me. Aqqi, the water drawer, when immersing his bucket lifted me up. Aqqi, the water drawer, raised me as his adopted son. Aqqi, the water drawer, set me to his garden work. During my garden work, Ishtar loved me (so that) 55 years I ruled as king. (quoted from Lewis: 1980)

The text of Exodus 2 evinces clear parallels with this legend; this is all the more so if one considers the possibility that the figure of Moses' sister is a later addition.[25] Sargon and Moses are exposed for obscure reasons by their mothers, both of whom are in some way related to the priesthood. Sargon's mother is a priestess and Moses' mother is the daughter of Levi, the ancestor of Israel's priestly tribe. Their fathers do not intervene. They are set adrift on a river in a basket, found and adopted. In both cases, the adoption alludes to the royal adoption of the king by his divine father.

Even if the Sargon story is about a third-millennium king, it was written under Sargon II, his namesake, at the end of the eighth century; it contains Neo-Assyrian orthographic forms and idiomatic expressions attested only in this period (Lewis: 1980: 98–110). The story of Moses, which is modeled on it, cannot be dated prior to the seventh century BCE. Exodus 2 presupposes no knowledge of Moses, his origins or his name; everything is explained. It is tempting, then, to understand the first written story about Moses (which cannot be reconstructed in detail) to be a reaction to Neo-Assyrian royal ideology, elaborated at Josiah's court. If so, literary production in Judah during the time of Assyrian vassalship could be labeled 'counter-history'. Assyrian royal and military rhetoric would have been taken over and attributed to foundational figures of Judah and Israel like Moses and Joshua.

But the royal image of Moses also makes sense in the context of the Persian period. Since most of the priestly and lay authorities of Persian-period Yehud and Samaria had decided to collaborate with the Achaemenid authorities, they would not have been in favor of movements that wanted to re-establish a 'Davidic monarchy' in Yehud. The acceptance of the loss of political autonomy would explain the transfer of royal functions to the figure of Moses.

After his birth story, royal traits reappear in association with Moses in the episode where Yahweh establishes him as the one who should lead the Israelites out of Egypt. In this account, he is presented as a shepherd, which is a royal title. In the prologue to the Code of Hammurapi, the king presents himself as 'shepherd and the one chosen by Enlil'. Moses is also called Yahweh's servant and is 'entrusted with his house' (Num. 12:8); just as Hammurapi and other ancient Near Eastern kings are called the servants of their patron gods and act as overseers of their earthly realms.

In the plague stories, Moses appears on the same level as the king of Egypt or, perhaps, a higher one. With Aaron as his speaker, he represents Yahweh, just as Pharaoh is representing the Egyptian deities. In Exod. 4:16 Moses is called Aaron's God and in 7:1, Pharaoh's God; both titles are comparable to Hammurapi's designation as 'god of the kings' (see the prologue, ll. 18–19). This underlines Moses' royal depiction, since the king is the representative of the main deity worshipped in his land. The expression in Exod. 7:1 is intended to depict Moses' deity as more powerful than those Pharaoh represents (Exod. 12:12). Moses, who makes the Israelites cross the sea with the help of Yahweh, recalls a royal motif in conquest stories where the river-crossings by kings like Assurbanipal, Croesus and Xerxes are symbolic acts by which they appear victorious (Römer 2005: 134). The mediation of the law is also integral to the king's role. Since this theme is one of the most important in the Torah, it needs to be dealt with separately.

On Sinai, Moses appears not only as the mediator of the law but also as the architect of the mobile sanctuary Yahweh asks him to construct. The building of sanctuaries using a divinely provided blueprint is an important part of ancient Near Eastern royal ideology (Hurowitz 1992). Since the Pentateuch is a collection of diverse Judahite/Judean and Israelite/Samarian origin myths, the temple that Moses builds according to divine order cannot be the temple of Jerusalem, but rather a mobile sanctuary in the desert.

In constructing this story, the Priestly authors of Exodus 25–31 and 35–40 use the old mythological concept of the triumphant creator god having his sanctuary built after he successfully defeats chaos and establishes order. It has often been observed that Moses' construction of Yahweh's sanctuary in the desert in Exodus 40 is parallel to *Elohim's* creation of the world. In Genesis 1, *Elohim* sees that everything was very good, in accordance with what he had said, and in Exod. 39:43, Moses sees that everything the Israelites had built corresponded to that which Yahweh had commanded him. Just as Yahweh achieved his work, so does Moses in Exod. 40:33. These parallels strengthen the royal image of Moses, since he represents Yahweh in supervising the construction of his sanctuary.

The mobile nature of the sanctuary may be explained by the fact that, in the Pentateuch, Yahweh's sanctuary has to accommodate a double identification: for the Judeans, it must be the *typos* of the Jerusalemite temple, whereas for the Samarians, it must be possible to see the sanctuary to foreshadow the temple on Mt Gerizim. It would even be possible to see the idea of the mobile sanctuary as a discrete critique of the ideology of cult centralization being made by the group responsible for editing the Book of Deuteronomy and the Former Prophets. Persian-era Judaism is characterized by diaspora communities, and the idea that Yahweh's holy place is not fixed may well be a concession to this situation. We know from written sources there was a temple of Yahweh in Elephantine and also one in Idumea (Lemaire 2004).

The Priestly account of the portable tent-shrine (*mishkan*) in Exodus may also reflect ideas related to the *qershu* shrine (Fleming

2000) mentioned in some of the Mari texts. The latter houses the deity temporarily for a special sacrificial event and it may be portable. In the Ugaritic texts (KTU I.4, IV.23–24), El apparently dwells in a tent-shrine (*q-r-sh*). In the Book of Kings, Solomon builds the temple of Jerusalem, but in the Pentateuch, the builder of Israel's first sanctuary is Moses.

The fact that Moses is a substitute for the king is also made clear in the only 'law' dealing with a king, Deut. 17:14–19. This text is often dated to the time of Hezekiah or Josiah and understood as an attempt by the Deuteronomistic author to limit the king's power while increasing the power of the court officials. If dated to the Assyrian period, its intention could have been to create a balance between being loyal to Yahweh and being loyal to Assyria: the king should limit his symbols of power and not appear as a threat to Assyria, and he should also show his loyalty to Yahweh by reading the Torah (Dutcher-Walls 2002).

The latter idea, however, makes more sense during the Neo-Babylonian or Persian era, and it seems more plausible to understand the so-called 'law of the king' as the only summary in the Pentateuch of the history of the monarchy narrated in the Former prophets. The opening in Deut. 17:14 ('when you have entered the land and you say: "I will set a king over me, like all the nations that are around me"') foreshadows the first story about the installation of monarchy (1 Sam. 8:5). The divine election of the king in 17:15 alludes to 1 Samuel 8–12 (see 1 Sam. 10:24, but also Yahweh's election of David and Saul's rejection in 1 Samuel 16–2 Samuel 6). The prohibition of placing a foreign king on the throne alludes to the story of Israel and its 'Phoenician' (influenced) kings. The combination of horses and Egypt (17:16) refers to different attempts by Israelite and Judahite kings to ally with Egypt, alluding to the end of the history of the Israelite and Judahite monarchy (see also Solomon's horse trade in 1 Kgs 10:26, which transfers an Assyrian practice to the ruler of the 'united kingdom'). The prohibition against 'many wives' in Deut. 17:16 is a clear allusion to Solomon, whose love of foreign women was the beginning of the end (1 Kgs 11:1–3).

The conclusion in Deut. 17:18–20 is particularly important; it stipulates that the king 'shall write a copy of this torah in presence of the Levitical priests. It shall remain with him and he shall read it all the days of his life'. As we have noted, the king is traditionally the mediator between the deity and the law. Thus, he is, in a sense, the archetype of the scribe; the gods ask him to establish justice and to instruct the people in right behavior (see the prologue to the Hammurapi Code). In Deuteronomy 17, while the king still is a scribe, he no longer is the mediator of the Law; Moses is. He continues copying the Mosaic Law, as Joshua had already done after conquering the land (Josh. 8:32, where he inscribes on stones a copy of Moses' Law).

In the view of Deuteronomy 17, the king is no more the mediator of the law but a mere adherent to it. The story of the rise and fall of the monarchy in the books of Samuel–Kings will be evaluated according to the Deuteronomic law. In Deut. 17:14–20, the king and all political authority depends on the transmitter of the divine law, Moses, who has taken over this royal function. This is the fate of the native king at the hands of the editors of the Pentateuch. This may reflect an attempt to limit the power of the king now that 'Israel' has become an ethno-religious group within an empire, ruled by a foreigner.

ii. Moses, the First of Israel's Prophets

The first figure in the Pentateuch to be called a prophet is Abraham (Gen. 20:7); his prophetic activity consists of interceding with God on behalf of the Philistine king to save his life after he 'takes' Sarah, not knowing she is Abraham's wife. Otherwise, no other prophetic traits or actions are associated with the Patriarch. Rather, it is Moses who receives the first 'call' from Yahweh, which parallels the prophetic calls of Jeremiah and Ezekiel. The divine audition in Genesis 12 is a command for Abram to move from Harran to Canaan; it is not a call to a prophetic mission. It is easy to see that the author of Exodus 3 uses the same pattern that occurs in Jeremiah 1 and Ezekiel 2 to frame Moses' call. It contains the following elements:

— Appeal and sending (*sh-l-k*)
— Refusal (too young, who am I?)
— Divine promise of accompanying ('I will be with you', *h-y-h im*)
— Sign given to the prophet

This pattern appears in Exod. 3:9–12 in a very condensed way, showing that the text presupposes the stories in Jeremiah 1 and Ezekiel 2. It is then developed further in Exod. 4:1–17 via the signs. The same pattern is also used to describe the call of Gideon in Judges 6. For the author of Exodus 3, Moses is Israel's first prophet, but he is also Israel's saviour, functioning in the same way as the so-called 'judges' by delivering the people from their Egyptian and Transjordanian enemies.

The presentation of Moses as Israel's first prophet belongs to the Deuteronomistic redactors and editors of the Pentateuch. It is also expressed in Deut. 18:15–20:

15 Yahweh your God will raise up for you a prophet like me from among your own people, you shall heed such a prophet... 17 Then Yahweh said to me... 18 'I will raise them up a prophet like you from among their brethren, and will put my words in his mouth; and he shall speak unto them all that I shall command him. 19 And it shall come to pass, that whosoever will not hearken unto my words, which he shall speak in my name, I will require it of him. 20 But the prophet who shall presume to speak a word in my name that I have not commanded him to speak, or who shall speak in the name of other gods, that prophet shall die.'

This passage sets out the (Deuteronomistic) idea that Yahweh constantly sends prophets, which is narrated in the books of Joshua to Kings. Since Jer. 1:4–9 clearly takes up Deut. 18:18, and since the book underwent Deuteronomistic editing, it might well be that Jeremiah was considered by the Deuteronomists as the last in the series of Yahweh's prophets and the one who brings prophetic activity to an end. In fact, there is a tradition alluded to in the Talmud that Yahweh stopped sending his prophets after the destruction of Jerusalem or at the beginning of the Persian era. One Talmudic passage states that the divine spirit was taken away from the prophets and given to the 'wise men', which may well allude to the editors of the prophetic (and other?) books (Baba Bathra 12b). The depiction of Moses as the prototype of Israel's prophets in the Pentateuch may then be understood as an attempt to confer Mosaic legitimacy on the 'prophets of judgment'.

The Pentateuch gathers different views about the relation between Moses and the prophets and can be considered an anthology of sorts, exploring the place of the prophets and their link with Moses. In Numbers 11, Yahweh takes a part of Moses' (!) spirit and distributes it on the 70 elders, who represent the people. This angers Joshua, who apparently wants to restrict prophecy to Moses (and himself?). But Moses speaks in favour of such charismatic prophecy.

The ensuing text in Numbers 12, however, insists on a clear hierarchy in which the prophets are to be subordinate to Moses. Here Aaron, representing the priesthood, and Miriam, probably representing prophets, are criticizing Moses because he apparently is being considered to have more privileges than the priests and the prophets. Contrary to Numbers 11, Yahweh's answer to Miriam and Moses in 12:6–8 highlights the fact that no human being compares to Moses (for more details, see the volume on Numbers). The same idea is suggested at the end of the Torah, in Deut. 34:10–12: 'Never since has there arisen a prophet in

Israel like Moses, whom Yahweh knew face to face'. This means that for the redactors of the Pentateuch, Moses was not (only) the prototype of Israel's prophets but also on a higher level than all other prophets, who rarely appear in the Torah.

iii. Moses, Judge and Mediator of the Law

The most important aspect of Moses is doubtless his role as the sole mediator of all the law codes in the Pentateuch. Before the transmission of the first code, the so-called 'Covenant Code', Moses is depicted as exercising the royal prerogative of judging the people (Exodus 18). His acting in this capacity has been foreshadowed in Exodus 2, when one of the Hebrews asks him ironically, 'Who made you a ruler and a judge over us?' (2:14). The exodus story then shows that Yahweh himself has made Moses Israel's judge and ruler.

The story in Exodus 18 (see also Deut. 1:9–18) shows that jurisprudence can be delegated; Moses, following the advice of his Midianite father-in-law, chooses judges who replace him and judge the people on their own. This idea is also expressed in the laws dealing with judges in Deut. 16:18–20 and 17:8–13. In these two texts, the office of judge is presented as an innovation connected with the centralization of the cult (see especially 17:8–13). The origin of these texts is disputed; although they could go back to the seventh century BCE, they certainly applied to the situation in Yehud and Samaria under Persian rule. The Persians permitted local jurisprudence when it was related to problems that did not affect the stability of the province (*medinah*).

The placement of Exodus 18 before Yahweh's revelation at Sinai and Moses' installation as the mediator of the law underlines the idea that there is a difference between 'law', which has uniquely a Mosaic source, and the application and interpretation of the law, which can be delegated. All the pentateuchal law codes are first communicated by Yahweh to Moses, who then is in charge of their communication to Israel. The statement in Exod. 18:26, 'hard cases they brought to Moses, but any minor case they decided on their own', reflects the following principle: any question that refers to a prescription addressed directly in the Torah can be adjudicated by designated authorities; cases that do not seem to be covered by the prescriptions of the Torah must be investigated directly by Moses. This is the situation in Num. 27:1–11. This text is clearly a supplement to the Mosaic Torah: Moses is confronted with a question concerning the inheritance of women for which no answer has been given in the foregoing law codes so he has to consult Yahweh directly.

The answer becomes 'a statute and ordinance as Yahweh commanded to Moses' (27:11).

The covenant code, whose original opening was probably 'These are the ordinances you shall set before them' (Exod. 21:1), has been expanded by the addition of Exod. 20:22–26 immediately before it, to be the new opening. It begins 'Thus Yahweh said to Moses: "Thus you shall say to the Israelites"' (v. 22). The section deals primarily with the building of sacrificial altars, and Yahweh promises to come and bless the people at every place he causes his 'name' to be remembered. In this way, the Covenant Code is made parallel its opening content to the Deuteronomistic Code, which begins with the stipulation by Yahweh that he will select a single place for sacrificial offerings to be made to him (12:4–14).

At the same time, however, Exod. 20:22–26 might be seen to 'correct' the 'single altar' claim of Deuteronomy by allowing the legitimate construction of other sacrificial altars in places of worship wherever followers of Yahweh live, assuming the unit post-dates Deuteronomy 12. This would also require us to assume that the first set of revelations at Sinai are to take precedence over the subsequent ones made in the plains of Moab. Otherwise, it could be argued that Exod. 20:22–26 was placed before the Covenant Code in order to endorse the single-altar law announced in Deuteronomy 12. Since Deuteronomy is presented as subsequent revelation or an 'actualization' of the Sinai revelation that is to apply once the people enter the land, it would supersede the multiple-altar law in Exod. 20:22–26. A third option would be to see the addition of Exod. 20:22–26 as a compromise allowing the existence of sacrificial altars in diaspora communities outside 'the Promised Land' while endorsing a single site within that territory—at Mt Gerizim for the residents of Samara and at Jerusalem for the residents of Jerusalem.

The earliest form of Deuteronomy 12–26 was probably created to replace the Covenant Code, but the editors of the Pentateuch have integrated the two codes into their authoritative writings and attributed both to Mosaic mediation. This decision seems to reflect a view stemming from royal ideology and the king's function as law-maker: a king is never wrong; if a new edict is necessary, it is joined to the older edict. Officially, both laws apply, even if, in fact, the newer one prevails over the older. The story of Esther alludes to this practice: the king allows Esther to write a new edict and to modify the older law, even if 'an edict written in the name of the king and sealed with the king's ring cannot be revoked' (Est. 8:8).

The so-called Holiness Code (Leviticus 17–26) probably never existed as an independent collection but was created to conclude the P material in Leviticus 1–16 and to establish a compromise between, or an interpretation of, the D code and Priestly 'legislation' (Nihan 2004). This explains why there is no clearly marked introduction; it begins simply, 'Yahweh spoke to Moses: "Speak to Aaron and his sons and to the whole people of Israel and say to them..."' (17:1). This introduction continues the format of the preceding priestly instructions (see 15:1; 16:1). Nevertheless, Leviticus 17 also parallels Exod. 20:22–26 and Deuteronomy 12 by presenting the entrance of the 'tent of meeting' as the place where permitted sacrifices were offered.

The law in Deuteronomy 12–26 is presented as a Mosaic discourse in which he reminds the people of Yahweh's law revealed to him on Mt Horeb. In its original form, Deut. 12:1 may, like Exod. 21:1, reflect an older title of a law collection not yet related to Moses. The lengthy introduction in chs 1–11 opens with the suggestion that, in the context of the pentateuchal narratives, Deuteronomy and the Deuteronomic law are to be understood as a recapitulation or an explanation of the former law codes revealed to Moses during his sojourn on Sinai (1:1–5). For the pentateuchal redactors, the entire law was revealed through Moses at Sinai; therefore, Deuteronomy had to be presented as a resumptive speech in which the law was 'remembered'. This means that the redactors of the Pentateuch considered Deuteronomy to have the same degree of authority as the preceding codes in the larger five-book sequence.

All the laws in the Pentateuch are attributed to Moses; it appears that for nascent Judaism, Moses was identical to Law. No new laws are given in the Prophets; Joshua and his followers are expected to follow the 'law of Moses'. The attribution of all laws to Moses reflects the transfer of royal privileges to this figure. In the Pentateuch, he becomes the spokesperson for the major parties (D and P) trying to create a new religion in which ritual and moral 'law' plays a major role. All laws are presented as having been mediated by him except the two Decalogues, which are presented as divine revelation made directly to the entire people gathered at Sinai.

iiia. Moses and the Decalogues. The so-called Ten Commandments occur twice in the Pentateuch, in Exodus 20 and in Deuteronomy 5. The two versions exhibit minor differences for the most part, but one major one concerning the reason given for respecting the Sabbath. As already seen, the inclusion of three different collections of laws (the Covenant Code, the D-Code and the Priestly law) in the Pentateuch necessitated an emphasis on the coherence of the 'multicultural' Torah. The insertion of the Decalogues at two strategic positions in the narrative addressed this need.

The Decalogue in Exodus 20 precedes the Covenant Code, the first expression of Yahweh's law (Exodus 21–23) and the Priestly legislation (Leviticus 1–Numbers 10). Since Exod. 20:11 appeals to the Priestly creation account in Gen. 1:1–2:3 to legitimate the Sabbath, the first Decalogue serves to strengthen the link between Genesis and Exodus; on the literary level this was probably the work of Priestly authors. The Decalogue in Deuteronomy 5, on the other hand, ties the Book of Deuteronomy to the former books of the Moses story, Exodus–Numbers. Deuteronomy 5 presents the motivation for keeping the Sabbath by reminding the addressees of Egyptian oppression. It thus creates a link to the beginning of the Book of Exodus and underlines the coherence of the 'biography' of Moses running from Exodus through Deuteronomy. Like Exodus 20, Deuteronomy 5 introduces an important law collection (Deuteronomy 12–26).

The existence of two Decalogues may then suggest that the Covenant Code, the Priestly legislation and the Deuteronomic Code all have the same authoritative status. The first part of the Decalogue (commandments 1–4) can be understood as a summary of nascent Judaism, a presentation of ideas that became constitutive for the redefinition of the ancient Israelite and Judahite religions in the Persian period. The calls for the exclusive worship of Yahweh, aniconism, the sacralization of the divine name, observance of the Sabbath and the transformation of the cult of the dead ancestors all include explanations or motivations, showing they represent innovations, in contrast to the second half of the Decalogue, where such additional material is visibly absent. Perhaps the redactors of the Torah viewed both Decalogues as a summary of all the law collections in the Pentateuch.

In the introduction to the Decalogue in Deut. 5:4, Moses states, 'Yahweh spoke to you face to face out of the fire' (see also Deut. 4:12–13). The same idea underlies Exod. 20:1 even if the addressees of Yahweh's word are not explicitly mentioned. This direct communication of the divine word to the people distinguishes the Decalogue from the other law codes, all of which depend on Mosaic mediation. However, for the final redactors of the Pentateuch, it apparently contradicted their claim that Moses had been the only person with whom Yahweh had ever communicated 'face to face' (see Num. 12:8 and Deut. 34:10–12, discussed above).

To remedy the situation, they came up with literary strategies to downplay the inherited tradition of the direct communication of the Decalogues. They inserted 19:20–25 to serve as a new introduction to the revelation of the Ten Commandments in Exodus 20. The verses focus on Moses' superiority to the priests and the people, but their ending is enigmatic: 'Moses went down to the people and said to them...' It is often argued that the content of Moses' speech has been lost. However, it appears instead that this phrase is meant to introduce 20:1 as though it were the beginning of a direct speech by Moses in which he relays to the people the contents of the Decalogue that Yahweh had revealed directly to him during his sojourn on the mountain. Thus, it is designed to avoid the impression otherwise given that God spoke words directly to the people.

A similar phenomenon may be detected for the Decalogue in Deuteronomy 5. In the original introduction in v. 4, the statement, 'Yahweh spoke to you face to face out of the fire on the mountain', was directly followed by the phrase *lemor* introducing Yahweh's direct speech that begins currently in v. 6. The final redactors of the Pentateuch interpolated a new statement between v. 4 and its final introductory word that had originally introduced the proclamation of the Decalogue directly to the people by Yahweh: 'At that time I stood between Yahweh and you to declare to you the word of Yahweh because you were afraid of the fire and did not go up to the mountain' (v. 5). In this way, they made the Decalogue in Deuteronomy 5 appear to have been transmitted by Moses, not declared directly by God, just as they had done in Exodus 20. While these additions have not totally disguised the direct revelation of the Decalogue to the people in an earlier form of the text, they demonstrate that for the final redactors of the Torah, Moses had to be the agent responsible for the transmission of the Ten Commandments, just as he was for the rest of the Torah.

iv. Moses, Founder of the Cult

According to the Pentateuch, Moses is not only mediator of the law but also the founder of Israel's cult. Like the king, he is the architect charged by Yahweh to build the tent of meeting, the mobile sanctuary. But Moses is not really a priest; even if the Pentateuch makes him a descendant of Levi (Exod. 2:1–2 and 6:16–25), it is unclear if this genealogy reflects historical memory or is a late literary invention, and not all Levites are priests. In the Priestly and later texts, Moses is related to the priesthood indirectly via his brother Aaron.

Aaron first appears in Exodus 4, where he is described as Moses' 'mouth', his spokesman, while Moses is designated Aaron's god (*elohim*; Exod. 4:14–16). This passage is thought to be a post-Priestly supplement to the story of Moses' call, whose author wants to subordinate Aaron to Moses. The same hierarchical relationship prevails in the so-called plague-stories. In their introduction, Moses is labelled Pharaoh's 'god' while Aaron is Moses' prophet (Exod. 7:1). Elsewhere in the plague stories, however, Aaron acts more like a magician than a prophet or a priest (see on this below).

Aaron's priestly functions are clearly underlined in Exodus 29, in the context of the divine instructions for the mobile sanctuary, where Yahweh tells Moses how to consecrate Aaron and his sons to make them his priests. Their ordination is subsequently narrated in Leviticus 8, where Moses himself offers the sacrifices because Aaron and his sons are not yet priests. Here, Moses is clearly portrayed as the founder of the sacrificial, priestly cult.

In the first part of Leviticus where Yahweh reveals all the rules for sacrifice and other priestly responsibilities, most of the instructions are first communicated to Moses, who then has to transmit them to the Israelites and to Aaron (see, for example, Lev. 1:1; 4:1, 14; 6:1, 8:1). After Aaron has been ordained priest, however, Yahweh occasionally addresses Moses and Aaron together (for example, 11:1; 13:1; 14:34). In one of the latest texts of Leviticus, ch. 10, Aaron seems to have a better understanding of the law than Moses (vv 16–20; Nihan 2007a: 598–607). In this passage, Moses is criticizing Aaron and his sons for not eating the purification offering as commanded in Lev. 6:19. But Aaron, who has just had two sons killed by Yahweh because of an irregular offering (10:1–5), is the better interpreter of the law. His reply to Moses' rebuke implies that the high priest, when profaned by death, is unable to execute the purification offering. The author shows that Aaron has the better arguments and that Moses must accept his superiority here and recognize the authority of priestly exegesis of the Law. This passage demonstrates there were attempts, especially in the last compositional stages of the pentateuchal traditions, to highlight Aaron's authority and to make him Moses' equal or even his superior.

In Numbers, Moses and Aaron sometimes act together or are both victims of the people's rebellion (Num. 14; 16:3; 17:6). Aaron's authority and, by extension, that of the office of high priest, is underlined in the episode where his staff blossoms (17:8–12); it emphasizes the necessity of priestly (Aaronide) cultic mediation. Aaron's authority and independence

from Moses appears elsewhere in Numbers 18, where Yahweh addresses
him exclusively, without Moses (vv 1, 8). Otherwise, however, Moses and
Aaron appear together in Numbers as the addressees of divine speech.

In other texts, Moses and Aaron appear as antagonists. In Numbers 12,
Aaron and Miriam revolt against Moses, whose superiority is confirmed
by Yahweh. When Miriam becomes 'leprous', Aaron can only diagnose
the illness but must then defer to Moses, who, after consulting Yahweh,
gives the (priestly) instructions for a quarantine.

The most negative portrait of Aaron occurs in the story of the golden
calf in Exodus 32 (see also Deut. 9:7–10:11), where he agrees to build
a golden bovine statue to make Israel's god visible. As a result, Moses
accuses him of having brought a 'great sin' upon the people (v. 32). This
story is commonly explained as a critique of Jeroboam's establishing
Bethel and Dan as national sanctuaries where Yahweh was venerated as
a bull. Another option, however, would be to see Exodus 32 as a late story
intended to enforce non-iconic veneration of Yahweh, to which the more
conservative priestly elements may have been opposed. Interestingly, in
this text Aaron is separated from the Levites, who are depicted as loyal
partisans of Moses.

In sum, the various traditions show at least three tendencies. In the
majority of the texts, Moses is the founder of Israel's cult, who legitimates
the Aaronide priesthood. In some texts, Aaron is independent of Moses'
authority, while in a few texts he is depicted in a negative light. This
variety reflects the difficulty of Persian-period Judaism to define who
had the prerogative concerning cultic matters.

v. Moses, Non-ancestor, but Mediator and Intercessor

In the Pentateuch, Moses accumulates almost all the political and religious
functions of the former monarchy. But there is one exception: contrary
to Abraham, Isaac and Jacob, Moses is not an ancestor. Genealogies do
not play a role in the stories about Moses; there is only one in Exodus 6,
which tries to legitimate the ascendancy of Moses and Aaron amongst
Levitical families and provide information about the Aaronide offspring.
In fact, Exod. 6:14–26 is much more interested in Aaron's family than
in Moses'. The Pentateuch shows no interest in Moses' son(s), who do
not succeed him and who disappear from the narrative without further
comment.

The fact that Moses is not an ancestor is also illustrated clearly in
Yahweh's twofold attempt to exterminate the rebellious Israelites and
to create a new people with Moses: 'My wrath may burn hot against

them and I may consume them; and of you I will make a great nation'
(Exod. 32:10); 'I will strike them with pestilence and disinherit them,
and I will make of you a nation greater and mightier than they' (Num.
14:12). However, Moses rejects this divine project to transform him into
a new Jacob. Both narratives reinforce the fact that Mosaic identity is
not genealogical. The treaty Moses mediates between Yahweh and the
people of Israel does not depend on descent but on acceptance of the
'covenant'.

The addition of the Book of Genesis with its patriarchal 'prologue'
to the story of Moses in Exodus–Deuteronomy offered an alternative
construction of identity by genealogy. The editors of the Pentateuch
combined two distinctive ways to construct the identity of the members
of the new religion: by genealogy (Genesis 12–50) and by the Mosaic
Law, which required no pedigree but adhesion. It is quite clear that the
Pentateuch presents two competing origin myths, which both played an
important role in the Persian period; the importance of genealogies is
apparent in Chronicles and in Ezra–Nehemiah, as is also the insistence
that the Law must be respected by all inhabitants of Yehud and
Samaria.

Moses' refusal in Exodus 32 and Numbers 14 to become an ancestor
suggests the priority of his mediation in relation to questions of descent.
In the Pentateuch, Exodus 32 (see also Deuteronomy 9–10) and Numbers
13–14 (see also Deut. 1:19–46) are the stories of Israel's 'worst' rebellions:
the transgression of aniconism, which is certainly a new invention in
the Persian period, and the refusal to enter the Promised Land, which
reflects the opposition of important parts of the Babylonian *golah* to
a return to Yehud in the first half of the Persian period. In both cases,
the people are only saved through Moses' intercession; he appeals to
Yahweh's reputation among the nations. Exodus 32, Numbers 14 and
Deuteronomy 9–10 contain long prayers by Moses, which appear to be
some of the latest insertions in the Pentateuch. Though they are unable
to stay his 'judgment' in Exodus 32 and Numbers 14, they successfully
convince Yahweh to change his mind, showing that only Moses is able
to save 'Israel'. But even he cannot prevent divine punishment, which in
both cases alludes to the events of the fall of Samaria to the Assyrians in
722/721 and the fall of Judah to the Neo-Babylonians in 597/587 BCE.

vi. Moses, Hero and Tragic Figure
In some texts of the Pentateuch, Moses appears as a hero in the Greek
sense of the word; he is portrayed as navigating between the divine and

humans realms. After the miraculous crossing of the Sea, the people believe in Yahweh as well as in Moses, making the two equals (Exod. 14:31). In Deut. 34:10–12, the 'signs and wonders' that designate Yahweh's interventions against Pharaoh and the Egyptians are attributed to Moses. His birth story in Exodus 2 recalls the exposure at birth of several heroes, and, like typical heroes, some texts suggest that Moses has immediate access to the divine world (Num. 12:6–8; Deut. 34:8–10). Of special interest is the episode in Exod. 34:29–35. When coming down from Mt Sinai with the tablets of the covenant, Moses' face has either become shining or horned (in Hebrew there is a word play on the root *q-r-n*). In the ancient Near East, horns are divine attributes expressing strength and power, so the text might suggest that after his long stay with Yahweh, Moses has almost become a divine being.

The heroic portrait of Moses might also underlie the report of his death; according to this story, Yahweh himself buries Moses in a secret place (Deut. 34:6). This curious statement can be understood as a polemic against the idea that Moses did not really die but was taken to heaven, a 'cautious rejection of a myth predicating Moses' assumption' (Loewenstamm 1976: 198). His heavenly ascent is very well attested in Hellenistic Judaism. But even if Deut. 34:6 should not be read in this sense, it still distinguishes Moses from all other humans, since he is the only one who experiences a divine burial.

The Pentateuch ends with Moses' death outside the land, naturally raising the question why this exceptional man could not enter the Promised Land. Here again, the Pentateuch betrays a variety of answers. In Deuteronomy, Moses has to die outside the land because he belongs to the first generation, which will not enter the land. As chief of the people, he is included in the divine punishment (Deut. 1:37; 3:26; 4:21). Against this interpretation of collective responsibility, Numbers 20 explains that Moses and Aaron must die outside the land because of their faults; they had offended Yahweh by placing their confidence in the power of their staff rather than in his law. For this reason, Numbers 20 may be understood as a polemic against the representation of Moses as a miracle-worker inside and outside the Pentateuch (Nihan 2007a: 30). The different answers given in Deuteronomy and Numbers reflect the theological debate about collective or individual responsibility in Persian-era Judaism (see also Gen. 18:22–32; Exod. 20:5–6; Lev. 26:39; Deut. 24:16; Ezekiel 18).

Finally, a third perspective about Moses' death outside the Promised Land appears in Deuteronomy 34. He is said to have died at the age of

120, full of vigour and strength (see, however, the contrary statement in Deut. 31:2). Here, the only reason for Moses' death is he had reached the age limit that, according to Gen. 6:3, Yahweh had established for human life. Despite his exceptional status, in the end, Moses, like all humans, has to submit to this limit, which gives his death an almost tragic note.

His death outside the land is also a message to the Jews of the diaspora, however, who were very concerned about a sepulchre in the land. Perhaps beginning in the Persian period but definitely by the Hellenistic era, wealthy Jews were eager to have their bones interred in Jerusalem or in the 'land of their ancestors'. Against this practice, Deuteronomy 34 claims that one may live and die outside the land as long as one respects the Mosaic Torah.

vii. Moses, Hero of the Diaspora, or Hints of a Censored Moses Tradition in the Pentateuch

Not all traditions about Moses have been fully integrated into the Pentateuch; there is extra-biblical evidence that Moses was a very popular figure among Jews of the diaspora, who had stories about him that were not fully acceptable to the editors of the Pentateuch. Nevertheless, some were integrated discretely.

viia. Moses a magician. In the Priestly account of the plagues that can be reconstructed in Exodus 9–14, Moses and Aaron are depicted as magicians competing with the Egyptian magicians of Pharaoh's court. The latter acknowledge the superiority of Moses and Aaron (and Yahweh) when they declare to Pharaoh, 'This is the finger of God (*elohim*)' (8:15). This expression, attested in Egyptian magic formulas, probably refers to the staff used by Moses and Aaron to conjure. It recognizes the two are able to tap into the power of a god. This story, which perhaps originated in the Egyptian diaspora, takes Egyptian magic seriously but shows Moses and Aaron are the better magicians. The Priestly texts in Exodus 7–12 fit with traditions that existed about Moses as a magician in Jewish circles in Alexandria and the southern Levant as well as in the Greco-Roman world.

viib. Moses, the leper. In Exodus 4, Yahweh provides Moses with many supporting signs that will allow him to accomplish his mission. The first, in which he is able to transform his staff into a snake, and the third, where Yahweh announces that the water of the Nile will become blood, clearly anticipate the plague story that begins in ch. 7. But between these signs there is another, strange sign: Yahweh asks Moses to put his hand inside his cloak, and when he takes it out, it has become leprous. The hand is restored after Moses places it back into the cloak (4:6–8). Unlike the other signs, this one does not anticipate a subsequent story in the narrative in the Book of Exodus. The episode probably alludes to a tradition in which Moses, an Egyptian priest, was the head of a group of lepers who waged war against Egypt. The story is attributed to Manetho, an Egyptian priest living at the end of the fourth century BCE and passed on by Flavius Josephus. This Egyptian priest, named Osarsephos, instituted new laws prohibiting the worship of the sacred animals. At the end of the story, Osarsephos changes his name to Moses (Verbrugge and Wickersham 2000: 160–63). The tradition seems to reflect anti-Jewish sentiments. If diaspora Jews were confronted with such negative stories attacking their founding figure, Exodus 4 could well be an attempt to create a 'counter history'. The charge that Moses was a leper is taken on but put in a positive light, being portrayed as a temporary condition through which Yahweh manifested his power.

viic. Moses and the foreign women. In the Pentateuch, Moses is married to two foreign women: a Midianite, Zipporah (Exod. 2:16–22), and an unnamed Ethiopian. The Midianite connection may be traditional and may even reflect an old link between Moses and the Midianites. Numbers 12:1, however, uniquely informs the reader about a second marriage of Moses with a Kushite woman. She is not to be identified with Zipporah, as is done at times in rabbinic tradition and by some modern commentators. Flavius Josephus and Artapanus both know a Mosaic Ethiopian connection. According to this tradition, while in Egypt, Moses excelled as a military leader in Ethiopia; according to Josephus, he married a princess while there. Josephus probably did not invent the story as a way to explain Numbers 12; rather, the verse may be a discrete allusion to a tradition in the diaspora that legitimated the practice of mixed marriages through Moses. The Ethiopian connection may more precisely reflect the situation of the Jews in Elephantine, located next to the land of Cush.

viid. Moses, a warlord. In the Pentateuch, but especially in the Hexateuch, the conquest of the land is the work of Joshua, Moses' successor. Yet Joshua seems to be an invention of the Deuteronomists; his appearance is limited to the narrative account stretching from Exodus–Kings. 1 Samuel 12:6–8 seems to preserve an alternative tradition that told how

Moses led the people into the land (Ahlström 1980). In Numbers and Deuteronomy, Moses is depicted as a military chief engaged in the conquest of the Transjordanian territories (Numbers 21–33). As just seen above as well, a non-biblical legend can be reconstructed from Artapanus, Josephus and other sources in which Moses led wars against Ethiopia. This story may be the foundation myth of the Jewish military diaspora in Elephantine. The editors of the Pentateuch were probably unhappy with the martial image of Moses and decided to limit passages emphasizing his leadership in wars and conquest.

Summing up, it appears that the Pentateuch is a selected anthology of Moses traditions. Some apparently were considered unfitting for the Moses who became the symbol of the new religion called Judaism. Others might have developed shortly after the publication of the Torah, when additional exploits were attributed to this foundational figure, who already had been portrayed as a royal figure, a prophet, a judge and mediator of the Law, the founder of the cult, an intercessor and a tragic, heroic figure. Additional roles that reflected the interests of various Jewish groups, especially those living in the Egyptian diaspora, Moses' 'home territory' as it were, could expand his 'jack-of-all-trades' image and enhance his prestige in the eyes of the pious.

Notes

1. See Lev. 11:46; 12:7; 13:59; 14:2, 32, 54, 57; 15:32.
2. See Exod. 12:49; Lev. 6:2, 7, 18; 7:1, 7, 11, 37; 11:46; 12:7; 13:59; 14:2, 32, 54, 57; 15:32 (26:46); Num. 5:29, 30; 6:13, 21; 16:16, 29; 19:2, 14; 31:21. On the case of Lev. 26:46, the only 'Priestly' passage to use the plural (*torot*) instead of the singular, see below.
3. See Lev. 6:2, 7, 18; 7:1, 11; 11:46; 12:7; 13:59; 14:32, 57; 15:32; Num. 5:29; 6:13, 21.
4. See Lev. 7:37; 14:54; Num. 19:14.
5. Indefinite forms of the nouns occur together (*torah vemitsvah*) in Prov. 6:23, while the definite compound is used in 2 Kgs 17:34, 37, but is preceded by *huqqot* and *mishpatim* and so is not exactly comparable.
6. Later, 'Mt Gerizim' was changed in the MT text of Deut. 27:4–8 to 'Mt 'Ebal'. According to Deut. 27:14–26, this was where curses, instead of blessings, were to be proclaimed, after the plastered stones upon which the words of Moses' *torah* were written would be erected. With this emendation, the Judean scribes were able to condemn the Samarian sanctuary, which, according to their version, had been built on the wrong hill, failing to fulfil Moses' command, while also condemning any Samarian temple enterprise on Mt Gerizim or Mt Ebal by associating Mt Ebal with cursing.

7. Of the 61 mentions of 'the fathers' in the books of Exodus–Deuteronomy, only eight times are they identified with Abraham, Isaac and Jacob, always as a set phrase (Exod. 3:15, 16; 4:5; Deut. 1:8; 6:10; 9:5; 29:13; 30:20; Van Seters 1972).

8. 1 Kgs 22:19; Pss 29:1–2; 82:1; 89:5–8; 90:10; 102:25 (Eng. 24), 28; Isa. 6:1–8; 14:13; 40:28; 57:15; Jer. 23:18, 22; Ezekiel 1; Job 36:26; Hab. 3:6; Dan. 3:25; 6:26; 7:9–14, 22; Zechariah 3.

9. Gen. 14:19, 22; Deut. 32:6–7 and Isa. 40:28.

10. Exod. 4:22; Deut. 32:6; Isa. 63:16; 64:7; Jer. 3:4, 19; 31:9; Hos. 11:1; Mal. 1:6; 2:10.

11. 1 Sam. 12:18; Psalm 2; 104; Isa. 30:19; Jer. 3:3; 5:24, 10:11–16; 14:4, 22; 51:16; Hosea 2; Amos 4:7; 5:8; 9:6; Joel 4:18 (Eng. 3:18); Zech. 10:1; Mal. 3:10; Job 26:8; 38:25–27, 34–38.

12. Deut. 32:34; 33:2; Judges 4–5; 2 Sam. 22:6–19=Ps. 18:6–19; Pss 50:1–33; 68:7–10; 77:19; 86:9–19; 97:1–6; 98:1–2; 104:1–4; Job 26:11–13; Isa. 40:10; 42:13; Hab. 3:5, 8, 15.

13. Pss 74:13; 89:10 (Eng. 9); Job 7:12; 26:12; 38:8, 10; Jer. 5:22; Prov. 8:29.

14. Isa. 27:1; Job 3:8; 40:25 (Eng. 41:1); Pss 74:14; 104:26.

15. Job 9:13; 26:12; Ps. 89:11 (Eng. 10); Isa. 51:9.

16. Job 7:12; Isa. 51:9; Pss 74:13; 89:11 (Eng. 10).

17. Ps. 104:6–9.

18. Deut. 4:19; 17:3; 2 Kgs 23:5, 11; Jer. 8:2; Ezek. 8:16; Job 31:26–28.

19. Deut. 4:19; 17:3; 2 Kgs 23:5; Jer. 8:2; Mot ('Death'): Job 18:11–14; 28:22; Ps. 49:14; Isa. 28:15; Jer. 9:21; 18:21; Hos. 13:14.

20. Deut. 32:24; Ps. 91:6; Hab. 3:5; Job 5:7.

21. Ps. 91:6; Jer. 29:17–18; Hos. 13:14; Hab. 3:5.

22. Num. 21:6–9; 2 Kgs 18:4.

23. She is only known in a place name in Josh. 19:38 and Judg. 1:33 and as the deity to whom the judge Shamgar ben Anat was dedicated, probably as part of warrior guild (Judg. 3:31; 5:6).

24. Judg. 2:23; 10:6; 1 Sam. 7:3, 4; 12:10; 31:10; 1 Kgs 11:5, 33; 2 Kgs 23:13.

25. The text of Exodus 2 explicitly states that Moses is the first-born, a statement that does not cohere with the reference elsewhere in this story to an elder sister. The introduction of the reference to Moses' elder sister could be the work of a later scribe who wanted to emphasize that Moses had not been entirely abandoned by his family.

Works Cited and Suggested Further Reading

Achenbach, Reinhard. 2005. 'The Story of the Revelation at the Mountain of God and the Redactional Editions of the Hexateuch and the Pentateuch.' In Otto Eckart and J. Le Roux (eds). *A Critical Study of the Pentateuch: An Encounter Between Europe and Africa*. Altes Testament und Moderne, 20; Münster: Lit Verlag: 126–51.

Ahlström, Gösta W. 1980. 'Another Moses Tradition?' *Journal of Near Eastern Studies* 39: 65–69.

Albertz, Rainer. 1994. *A History of Religion in the Old Testament Period, Vol 2: From the Exile to the Maccabees.* Trans. from 1992 German by J. Bowden; London: SCM Press.

Assmann, Jan. 1998. *Moses the Egyptian: The Memory of Egypt in Western Monotheism.* Cambridge, MA: Harvard University Press.

Baltzer, Klaus. 1971. *The Covenant Formulary in Old Testament, Jewish and Early Christian Writings.* Oxford: Blackwell.

Blenkinsopp, Joseph. 1988. *Ezra–Nehemiah: A Commentary.* Old Testament Library; London: SCM Press.

— 2001. 'Was the Pentateuch the Civic and Religious Constitution of the Jewish Ethnos in the Persian Period?' In Watts: 41–62.

Brooke, George. 2002. 'The Rewritten Law, Prophets and Psalms: Issues for Understanding the Text of the Bible.' In E. D. Herbert and E. Tov (eds). *The Bible as Book: The Hebrew Bible and the Judean Desert Discoveries.* London/New Castle, DE: British Library/Oak Knoll: 31–40.

Crüsemann, Frank. 1996. *The Torah: Theology and Social History of Old Testament Law.* Edinburgh: T. & T. Clark.

Davies, Philip R. 2007. *The Origins of Biblical Israel.* Library of Hebrew Bible/Old Testament Studies, 485; London: T. & T. Clark.

Day, John. 1989. *Molech: A God of Human Sacrifice in the Old Testament.* University of Cambridge Oriental Publications, 41; Cambridge: Cambridge University Press.

— 2000. *Yahweh and the Gods and Goddesses of Canaan.* JSOT Supplement Series, 265; Sheffield: Sheffield Academic Press.

De Pury, Albert. 2001. 'Le choix de l'ancêtre.' *Theologisches Zeitschrift* 57: 105–14.

Dietrich, M., O. Loretz and J. Sanmartín. 1995. *The Cuneiform Alphabetic Texts from Ugarit, Ras Ibn Hani and Other Places.* Münster: Ugarit-Verlag, 2nd enlarged edn.

Dutcher-Walls, Patricia. 2002. 'The Circumscription of the King: Deuteronomy 17:16–17 in Its Ancient Social Context.' *Journal of Biblical Literature* 121: 601–16.

Edelman, Diana. 1995a. *The Triumph of Elohim: From Yahwisms to Judaisms.* Contributions to Biblical Exegesis and Theology, 13; Kampen: Kok Pharos.

— 1995b. *You Shall Not Abhor an Edomite for He is Your Brother: Edom and Seir in History and Tradition.* Archaeology and Bible Series, 3; Atlanta: Scholars Press.

— 2007. 'Taking the Torah out of Moses: Moses' Claim to Fame Before He Became the Quintessential Law-Giver.' in Thomas Römer (ed.). *La construction de la figure de Moïse—The Construction of the Figure of Moses.* Paris: Gabalda: 13–42.

— 2008. 'Hezekiah's Alleged Cultic Centralization.' *Journal for the Study of the Old Testament* 32: 395–434.

— 2009. 'God Rhetoric: Reconceptualizing Yahweh Sebaot as Yahweh Elohim in the Hebrew Bible.' In Ehud Ben Zvi, Diana Edelman and Frank Polak (eds). *A Palimpsest: Rhetoric, Ideology, Stylistics and Language Relating to Persian Israel.* Piscataway, NJ: Gorgias Press: 191–219.

Fleming, Daniel E. 2000. 'Mari's Large Public Tent and the Priestly Tent Sanctuary.' *Vetus Testamentum* 50: 484–98.

Frei, Peter. 1996. *Reichsidee und Reichsorganisation im Persereich.* Orbis Biblicus et Orientalis, 55; Freiburg: University Press.

— 2001. 'Persian Imperial Authorization.' In Watts: 5–40.

Gammie, John G. 1971. 'Loci of the Melchizedek Tradition of Gen 14:18–20.' *Journal of Biblical Literature* 90: 385–96.

Grätz, Sebastien. 2004. *Das Edikt des Artaxerxes: Eine Untersuchung zum religionspolitischen und historischen Umfeld von Esra 7,12–26.* Beihefte zur Zeitschrift für die alttestamentliche Wissenschaft, 337; Berlin: de Gruyter.

Grandet, Pierre. 2000. 'L'exécution du chancelier Bay. O. IFAO 1864.' *Bulletin de l'institut français d'archéologie orientale* 100: 339–45.

Handy, Lowell K. 1994. *Among the Host of Heaven: The Syro-Palestinian Pantheon as Bureaucracy.* Winona lake, IN: Eisenbrauns.

Heard, R. Christopher. 2001. *The Dynamics of Diselection: Ambiguity in Genesis 12–36 and Ethnic Boundaries in Post-exilic Judah.* Semeia, 39; Atlanta: Society of Biblical Literature.

Heider, George C. 1985. *The Cult of Molek: A Reassessment.* JSOT Supplement Series, 43; Sheffield: JSOT Press.

Hurowitz, Victor Avigdor. 1992. *I Have Built You an Exalted House: Temple Building in the Bible in Light of Mesopotamian and Northwest Semitic Writings.* JSOT Supplement Series, 115; Sheffield: Sheffield Academic Press.

Kataja, L., and R. Whiting. 1995. *State Archives of Assyria.* XII. *Grants, Decrees and Gifts of the Neo-Assyrian Period.* Helsinki: Helsinki University Press.

Kletter, Raz. 1996. *The Judean Pillar-Figurines and the Archaeology of Asherah.* British Archaelogical Reports International Series, 636; Oxford: Tempus Reparatum.

Knauf, Ernst Axel. 1988. *Midian: Untersuchungen zur Geschichte Palästinas und Nordarabiens am Ende des 2. Jahrtausends v.Chr.* Abhandlungen des Deutschen Palästinavereins; Wiesbaden: O. Harrassowitz.

Knierim, Rolf P. 1985. 'The Composition of the Pentateuch.' *Society of Biblical Literature Seminar Papers* 24: 393–415.

Knoppers, Gary N. 1996. 'Ancient Near Eastern Royal Grants and the Davidic Covenant: A Parallel?' *Journal of the American Oriental Society* 116.4: 670–97.

— 2001. 'An Achaemenid Imperial Authorization of the Torah in Yehud?' In Watts: 115–34.

Knoppers, Gary, and Bernard M. Levinson (eds). 2007. *The Pentateuch as Torah: New Models for Understanding Its Promulgation and Acceptance.* Winona Lake, IN: Eisenbrauns.

Kutsch, E. 1997. '*b^{e}rîth.*' In E. Jenni and C. Westermann (eds). *Theological Lexicon of the Old Testament.* Trans. from German by M. E. Biddle; Peabody, MA: Hendrickson: I, 256–66.

Lange, Armin. 2005. 'Authoritative Literature and Scripture in the Chronistic Corpus: The Use of *bwtk*-Formulas in Ezra–Nehemiah and 1–2 Chronicles.' In Mauro Perani (ed.). *"The Words of a Wise Man's Mouth are Gracious" (Qoh 10,12): Festschrift for Günter Sternberger on the Occasion of his 65th Birthday.* Studia Judaica, 32; Berlin: de Gruyter: 29–52.

Lemaire, André. 2004. 'Nouveau temple de Yahou (IVe s. av. J.-C.).' In Matthias Augustin and Hermann M. Niemann (eds). *'Basel und Bibel': Collected Communications to the XVIIth Congress of the International Organization for the Study of the Old Testament, Basel 2001.* Beiträge zur Erforschung des Alten Testaments und des antiken Judentums, 51; Frankfurt am Main: Peter Lang: 265–73.

Lemche, Niels Peter. 1999. *The Canaanites and Their Land: The Tradition of the Canaanites.* JSOT Supplement Series, 110; Sheffield: Sheffield Academic Press.

Lewis, Brian. 1980. *The Sargon Legend: A Study of the Akkadian Text of the Tale and the Tale of the Hero Who Was Exposed at Birth*. American Schools of Oriental Research Dissertation Series, 4; Cambridge, MA: Cambridge University Press.

Liverani, Mario. 1995. 'The Medes at Esarhaddon's Court'. *Journal of Cuneiform Studies* 47: 57–62.

Loewenstamm, Samuel. 1976. 'The Death of Moses'. In George W. E. Nickelsburg Jr (ed.). *Studies on the Testament of Abraham*. Septuagint and Cognate Studies Series, 6; Missoula, MT: Scholars Press: 185–211.

Loretz, Oswald. 1978. 'Vom kanaanäischen Totenkult zur jüdischen Patriarchen- und Elternehrung. Historische unde tiefenpsychologische Grundprobleme der Enstehung des biblischen Geschichtsbildes und der jüdischen Ethik'. *Jahrbuch für Anthropologie und Religionsgeschichte* 3: 149–204.

Magen, Yitzhaq. 2000. 'Mt. Gerizim—A Temple City'. *Qadmoniot* 33.2: 74–118 (Hebrew).

Magen, Yitzhaq, and Ephraim Stern. 2000. 'The First Phase of the Samaritan Temple on Mt. Gerizim—New Archaeological Evidence'. *Qadmoniot* 33.2: 119–24 (Hebrew).

Moor, Johannes C. de. 1990. *The Rise of Yahwism: The Roots of Israelite Monotheism*. Bibliotheca ephemeridum theologicarum Lovaniensium, 91; Leuven: Peeters.

Mullen, Jr, E. Theodore. 1997. *Ethnic Myths and Pentateuchal Foundations: A New Approach to the Formation of the Pentateuch*. Semeia Studies; Atlanta, GA: Scholars Press.

Nihan, Christophe. 2004. 'The Holiness Code between D and P: Some Comments on the Function and Significance of Leviticus 17–26 in the Composition of the Torah'. In E. Otto and R. Achenbach (eds). *Das Deuteronomium zwischen Pentateuch und Deuteronomistischem Geschichtswerk*. Forschungen zur Religion und Literatur des Alten und Neuen Testaments, 206; Göttingen: Vandenhoeck & Ruprecht: 81–122.

— 2007a. *From Priestly Torah to Pentateuch: A Study in the Composition of the Book of Leviticus*. Forschungen zum Alten Testament, II/25; Tübingen: Mohr Siebeck.

— 2007b. 'The Torah between Samaria and Judah: Shechem and Gerizim in Deuteronomy and Joshua'. In Knoppers and Levinson: 187–223.

Noth, Martin. 1981. *A History of Pentateuchal Traditions*. Atlanta, GA: Scholars Press.

Otto, Eckart. 2006. *Mose: Geschichte und Legende*. C. H. Beck Wissen, 2400; München: C. H. Beck.

Parpola, Simoo, and Kenichi Watanabe. 1988. *State Archives of Assyria*. II. *Neo-Assyrian Treaties and Loyalty Oaths*. Helsinki: Helsinki University Press.

Richter, Sandra. 2002. *The Deuteronomistic History and the Name Theology*. Zeitschrift für die alttestamentliche Wissenschaft, 318; Berlin: de Gruyter.

Römer, Thomas. 1992. 'Les récits patriarcaux contre la veneration des ancêtres: Une hypothèse concernant les "origines" d"Israel'. In Olivier Abel and Françoise Smyth (eds). *Le livre de traverse: de l'exégèse biblique à l'anthropologie*. Patrimoines; Paris: Éditions du cerf: 213–25.

— 2004/2005. 'The Construction of the Figure of Moses according to Biblical and Extrabiblical Sources'. *Annual of the Japanese Biblical Institute* 30/31: 99–116.

— 2007. *The So-Called Deuteronomistic History: A Sociological, Historical and Literary Introduction*. London: T. & T. Clark/Continuum.

Simian-Yofre, Horacio. 1999. "wd, 'ed, 'edut, te'uda.' In G. Johannes Botterweck, Helmer Ringgren and Heinz-Joseph Fabry (eds). *Theological Dictionary of the Old Testament*. Trans. from 1986 German by Douglas W. Stott; Grand Rapids, MI: Eerdmans: X, 495–515.

Ska, Jean-Louis. 2001. '"Persian Imperial Authorization": Some Question Marks.' In Watts 2001: 161–82.

— 2006. *Introduction to Reading the Pentateuch*. Winona Lake: Eisenbrauns.

Smith, Mark S. 1990. *The Early History of God*. London: Harper and Row.

Sparks, Kenton L. 1998. *Ethnicity and Identity in Ancient Israel: Prolegomena to the Study of Ethnic Sentiments and their Expression in the Hebrew Bible*. Winona Lake: Eisenbrauns.

Stavrakopoulou, Francesca. 2004. *King Manasseh and Child Sacrifice: Biblical Distortions of Historical Realities*. Beihefte zur Zeitschrift für die alttestestamentliche Wissenschaft, 338; Berlin: de Gruyter.

— 2010. *Land of Our Fathers: The Roles of Ancestor Veneration in Biblical Land Claims*. Library of Hebrew Bible/Old Testament Series, 473; London/New York: T. & T. Clark International.

Steins, S. 1996. 'Torabindung und Kanonabschluss. Zur Entstehung und kanonischen Funktion der Chronikbücher.' In E. Zenger (ed.). *Die Tora als Kanon für Juden und Christen*. Herders biblische Studien, 10; Freiburg: Herder: 213–56.

Tov, Emmanuel. 2005. 'La nature du texte massorétique à la lumière des découvertes du désert de Juda et de la littérature rabbinique.' In Adrian Schenker and P. Hugo (eds). *L'enfance de la Bible hébraïque. L'histoire du texte de l'Ancien Testament à la lumière des recherches récentes*. Le Monde de la Bible, 52; Genève: Labor et Fides: 105–31.

Uehlinger, Christophe. 2005. 'Was There a Cult Reform under King Josiah? The Case for a Well-Grounded Minimum.' In Lester L. Grabbe (ed.). *Good Kings and Bad Kings: The Kingdom of Judah in the Seventh Century BCE*. Library of Hebrew Bible/Old Testament Studies, 393; London: T. & T. Clark International: 279–316 (German original, 1995).

Van Seters, John. 1972. 'Confessional Reformulation in the Exilic Period.' *Vetus Testamentum* 22: 448–59.

Verbrugge, Gerald P., and John M. Wickersham. 2000. *Berossos and Manetho Introduced and Translated: Native Traditions in Ancient Mesopotamia and Egypt*. Ann Arbor, MI: University of Michigan Press.

Watts, James W. (ed.). 2001. *Persia and Torah: The Theory of Imperial Authorization of the Pentateuch*. Society of Biblical Literature Symposium Series, 17; Atlanta: Society of Biblical Literature.

Weinfeld, Moshe. 1977. 'beríth.' In G. J. Botterweck and Helmer Ringgren (eds). *Theological Dictionary of the Old Testament*. Trans. from 1972 German by John T. Willis; Grand Rapids, MI: Eerdmans: II, 253–79.

White Crawford, Sidnie. 2008. *Rewriting Scripture in Second Temple Times*. Studies in the Dead Sea Scrolls and Related Literature; Grand Rapids, MI: Eerdmans.

Zevit, Ziony. 2001. *The Religions of Ancient Israel: A Synthesis of Parallactic Approaches*. London: Continuum.

GLOSSARY

Achaemenid: of or pertaining to the empire created by Cyrus the Great, who claimed to be the descendant of the legendary Achaemenes. The empire existed from ca. 560–333 BCE.

Akkadian: an East Semitic language spoken in Mesopotamia and used as the official language in the eastern part of the Neo-Assyrian and Neo-Babylonian empires, with Aramaic being used in the western part of the empires. It was written in cuneiform.

Anat: a female goddess worshipped in the ancient southern Levant. In the myths from Ugarit, she is the sister and/or the mistress of the storm-god Ba'al and a warrior goddess. Arrowheads inscribed with her name confirm this idea.

aniconism/aniconic: in religion, the absence or prohibition of the use of images or graphic representations of the divine.

Aramaic: an ancient West Semitic language that became the diplomatic language for the western part of the Assyrian, Babylonian and Persian empires.

Asherah: a female goddess, who was associated during the ninth to the seventh or sixth century with the god Yahweh. Her symbol was a stylized tree representing fertility, and such a tree was apparently placed in the temple of Jerusalem.

ashipu-**priest**: a cultic specialist in Babylonia with magical and medical skills. He was consulted for divination and for driving out demons.

Behistun inscription: an inscription commissioned by Darius I (522–486 BCE) to record his version of how he gained the throne of Persia after Cambyses, after a series of rebellions and the alleged murder of the rightful heir by an imposter. The text is written in Old Persian, Elamite and Babylonian and carved 100 metres up a limestone cliff at modern Behistun, or Bisitun, near an ancient crossroads connecting the capitals of Babylonia (Babylon) and Media (Ecbatanta).

charismatic prophecy: a form of divine relevation in which an individual enters a trance, is possessed by a god's spirit and speaks as that deity.

Code of Hammurapi: a Babylonian law code, dating to ca. 1700 BCE. The code contains 282 laws; however, they do not cover all important areas of social and economical life.

codified: arranged systematically, made into a code or digest.

Deuteronomic: relating to the contents or writing style of the book of Deuteronomy.

Deuteronomistic: passages that are redacted in a way that expresses style and ideology related to the book of Deuteronomy.

Delian League: an association of Greek city-states established in 477 BCE to fight the advance of the Persian empire into Greek lands after the Geek victory at the Battle of Platea in 479 during the second Persian invasion of Greece. It was led by Athens and included between 150 to 173 members. It was dissolved in 404 BCE.

Demotic Chronicle: a papyrus document dating from the early second century BCE in which a series of oracular sayings written on tablets allegedly being interpreted for the founder of the thirtieth Dynasty, Nectanebo I (ruled 378–360 BCE) are given explanatory and prophetic paraphrases that are political in tone, anti-Persian and anti-Greek, looking forward to the ultimate rise of an indigenous ruler who would overthrow the Greeks. It was written in Ptolemaic Egypt, probably under Horunnofri-Harmachi, King of Upper Egypt from 205/204 to 186 BCE.

diaspora: a community living outside its homeland, whether by choice or by force.

didactic: used for teaching.

Documentary Hypothesis: coined at the end of the nineteenth century, this hypothesis held that the Pentateuch resulted from the conflation of four independent and parallel documents: J (Yahwist), E (Elohist), D (the original book of Deuteronomy) and P (Priestly source). This hypothesis has been strongly modified in the last half century.

E/Elohistic source: according to the Documentary Hypothesis, an originally independent document from the eighth century BCE containing major parts of the Pentateuchal narrative and using the divine name name 'Elohim'. The existence of such a document is heavily disputed today.

Eber-Nari: literally, 'Across the River', the name of a large province located west of the Euphrates River, which included the entire southern Levant. It was first used in administrative texts from the Assyrian empire and continued to be used as an administrative unit by the Neo-Babylonian empire and the Persian empire.

Esarhaddon: a king who ruled the Neo-Assyrian empire from 681–669 BCE. He defeated Tarhaqa, pharaoh in the Delta region of Egypt, and was the first to add Egypt temporarily to the Assyrian empire.

eschatological: dealing with final things or with things relating to the end of human history as we know it.

Esdras, Book of: Composed in several stages during the Persian and Hellenistic periods, the non-canonical book tells the story of the first return of exiles and the completion and dedication of the temple in Jerusalem and the promulgation of the Torah by Ezra.

etiology: a theory or assignment of a cause or origin.

etymology: the origin and development of a word.

golah: a term used in the Hebrew Bible to describe people sent into involuntary exile from the kingdom of Judah by Neo-Babylonian kings in 598 and 586 BCE and resettled in various areas of Babylonia. It is also used to describe the descendants of these exiles who returned to Yehud under the Persians or those who stayed in Babylonia.

Hasmonean: name of a Jewish dynasty that ruled semi-autonomously in Palestine from around 140 to 70 BCE.

hatru-**estates**: a system in the Babylonian and Persian periods in which the tenants who cultivated land individually were organized in groups by ethnicity or occupation called *hatru*, which were responsible for the payment and service to the crown.

hegemony: leadership; usually the political dominance of one state or government in a league or confederation.

hypostasis: from a Greek word meaning base or foundation; it designates a personification of an entity or a quality (e.g. Wisdom as a Woman in the Book of Proverbs).

Idumea: Hellenistic name of Edom, which was used to designate a smaller part of the Edomite territory.

J/Yahwistic source: according the classical Documentary Hypothesis, the oldest source, which is characterized by its usage of the divine name Yahweh. The source began in Gen. 2:4 and was supposed to end either in Deuteronomy 34 or Joshua 24. In recent research, 'J' is often used to designate the older pre-priestly texts of the Pentateuch.

Judah: the name of an ancient kingdom located in the southern Levant, south of the kingdom of Israel, from ca. 975–950 BCE to 586 BCE.

lares and *penates*: the deified spirits of ancestors and guardian spirits the ancient Romans believed protected their households.

libation: the pouring out of liquid on the ground or on a victim for sacrifice in honour of a god or a deceased ancestor.

Mishnah: the compilation of traditional oral interpretations of biblical laws and customs made by rabbis ca. 200 CE.

monolatry/monolatrous: an expression referring to the exclusive worship of one deity which, however, does not deny the existence and reality of other deities.

Nabateans: initially a tribe or group of tribes, first mentioned in writing in a battle report in 312 BCE and then a kingdom that occupied the southern part of the Jordanian highlands east of the Dead Sea, the Negev highlands and the northern part of Arabia, with their main city at Petra. They controlled trade between Syria and Arabia, occupying oases and establishing hidden cisterns that collected run-off rainwater through the desert area along the routes they monitored. Trajan (98–117 CE) conquered the kingdom ca. 107 and added it to the Roman empire.

Nabonidus: the last king of the Neo-Babylonian empire, who ruled from 556–539 BCE.

nazir: a person who made a vow to God for either a fixed term or for his entire life, who then, during the period of the vow, did not cut his hair, drink alcohol and avoided contact with corpses, which were sources of pollution. Well-known figures described in this way are Samuel, Samson and also a clan or group called the Rechabites.

Neo-Babylonian: of or relating to various aspects of the culture of the second empire, established in 626 BCE, that controlled the ancient Near East from the capital city of Babylon until 539 BCE, when the Persians conquered the city and became the new empire rulers.

orthopraxis: correct practice or belief; corrective measures to ensure correct practice or belief.

ostracon: a piece of broken pottery used as a surface for writing with pen and ink; the plural form is ostraca.

pardes: the Persian term for 'garden', from which 'paradise' is derived. The word originally referred to large private parks containing exotic plants and animals, enjoyed by royalty and elites.

Pasargadae: one of the capital cities used by the Persians during the time they ruled the ancient Near East, ca. 538–333 BCE. It was established by Cyrus the Great (559–530 BCE), the founder of the

Old Persian empire, as his capital. It lies 43 km from Persepolis in the Fars province of modern Iran.

pehah: Aramaic word for the Persian satrap (governor).

pelak/pelakim: a Hebrew word meaning either an adminstrative sub-district of the Persian province of Yehud or a type of mandatory tax to be fulfilled through the annual performance of physical labour on behalf of the crown. The plural form is *pelakim.*

pesher: 'interpretation'. This word is used frequently in Qumran manuscripts, where the primary texts being interpreted are prophetic books of the Hebrew Bible.

phylacteries: small leather boxes containing copies of certain biblical texts and attached to long leather straps, used by orthodox Jewish males in their morning prayers. One is placed on the forehead and the other on the left arm in fulfilment of the command in Deut. 11:18.

Persepolis: one of the capital cities used by the Persians during the time they ruled the ancient Near East, ca. 538–333 BCE. It was the ceremonial centre, located at modern Takht e-Jamshid, 70 km northeast of the modern city of Shiraz in the Fars province of modern Iran.

Priestly document: inside the Pentateuch there are texts that are considered priestly (P) since they use a distinctive style and reflect topics that are related to priestly interest (Gen. 17: circumcision; Exod. 25–31; 35–40: the construction of the wilderness sanctuary; Lev. 1–16: prescriptions about offerings and purity rules). Some scholars think these texts formed a coherent written source, while others think they were added to existing books by priestly editors.

promulgate: to make known officially; to put into effect by publishing or broadcasting terms or laws.

Punic inscriptions: writings in the ancient Phoenician language, belonging to the Northwest Semitic language family, found at Carthage in northern Africa, which was founded as a Phoenician colony, and elsewhere at Phoenician colonies in the Mediterranean.

Qedarites: an ancient Arab tribe or tribal confederation known from Assyrian inscriptions of the eighth and seventh centuries, which reached its peak in power in the sixth century BCE, when it controlled the region between the Persian Gulf and the Sinai peninsula.

redactor: one who prepares or revises material for publication.

Saite pharaohs: members of the twenty-sixth dynasty of Egypt, who ruled from ca. 672–525 BCE from Sais in the western Delta.

Samaria: the regional seat of the Assyrian, Neo-Babylonian, Persian and Hellenistic province of Samerina and former capital of the kingdom of Israel.

Samerina: the name of the province that succeeded the former independent kingdom of Israel. It was created by the Assyrians in 721 BCE and remained in place under the successive empires ruled by the Neo-Babylonians, the Persians and the Greeks.

satrapy: a Persian administrative unit designating a province. The official in charge of the satrapy was known as a satrap.

sclerosis: hardening of the arteries. It is used metaphorically in order to express a kind of stubbornness or decadence.

Shephelah: the western foothills of Judah that lead down from the Judean highlands or hill-country to the coastal plain bordering the Mediterranean.

Sinuballit/Sanballat: the name of a governor of Samerina who served during the reign of Artaxerxes I (465–425 BCE) and may still have been alive under Darius II (425–405 BCE). He is named as a contemporary of Nehemiah, alive when Jerusalem was being rebuilt, in the book of Nehemiah.

Susa: one of the capital cities used by the Persians from Cambyses (525–522 BCE) onwards during the time they ruled the ancient Near East, until 333 BCE, located in the lower Zagros Mountains ca. 250 km (150 miles) east of the Tigris River, between the Kharkheh and Dez Rivers.

suzerain: an overlord or person of superior political authority.

TAYN texts: a set of texts dug illegally from somewhere near Borsippa that details contracts, some of which were witnessed by people living in 'the town of the Judeans', named after resettled exiles from Judah.

terminus a quo: earliest possible date.

terminus ad quem: latest possible date.

thaumaturge: a conjurer or magician who performs miracles.

theophany: a physical manifestation or appearance of a god to humans.

tithe: a tax, originally one-tenth of a total value or yield of a land's produce, but more general, any tax or levy.

trilingual inscription of Xanthus: an inscription found in the temple of Leto at the site of Xanthus in Lycia, Asia Minor, written in the three languages of Aramaic, Lycian and Greek, dating to the reign of Artaxerxes III Ochus. It records a decree permitting the newly stationed Carian mercenaries to build and maintain a temple to their local deity, the Lord of Caunos.

Wisdom of Ahiqar: a story found on a papyrus at Elephantine dating to ca. 500 BCE about an Assyrian sage renowned for his wisdom. He is conveying sayings and proverbs to his nephew, some of which are similar to what is found in the Books of Proverbs, Ecclesiastes and collections of Babylonian proverbs.

Yahweh Sebaot: a title used to describe god in the Hebrew Bible, usually translated into English as 'Lord of Hosts'.

Yeb/Elephantine: a small island in the Nile River in Egypt, just north of the modern Aswan dam or the first cataract, which housed a military garrison manned by soldiers whose original home was Judah. It was first established by the Neo-Babylonians and continued to function under the Persians.

Yehud: the province created by the Neo-Babylonian king, Nebuchadrezzar, from the former independent kingdom of Judah in 586 BCE. It continues the former name of the area, but uses Aramaic, the international diplomatic language of the western half of the empire, instead of Hebrew.

Zenon papyri: a group of papyri discovered at Philadelphia at the edge of the Feinan oasis in Egypt, which date from the third century BCE. They are named after the secretary who was in charge of them, who worked for an important governmental treasury official in Egypt, and are some of the earliest documents written in Greek known from Ptolemaic Egypt.

INDEX OF ANCIENT CITATIONS

Biblical Texts

Genesis
1 100, 106, 117, 136, 147, 160
1–9 41
1–11 11, 136–7, 144
1:1–2:3 13, 136, 167
2 43
2:4–3:24 137
4 13, 137
4:4 137
4:26 137
6–8 137
6–9 13
6:2–4 133
6:3 173
6:14 115
6:18 150
8 137
9 151
9:4–6 151
9:9–17 150
10 13, 40, 113, 144
10:19 123
10:21 113
11 13
11:4 13
11:28 13, 40
11:30 14
11:31 40, 123
12 13, 114, 162
12–36 11

12–50 171
12:1 123
12:1–13:18 146
12:2–3 13
12:6 146
12:6–7 137
12:7 123
12:8 137
12:10 76
12:10–20 13–14
13 14, 123
13:17 127
13:18 137
14:13 150
14 14, 126
14:14 126
14:18 137
14:18–20 131
14:19 176
14:22 131, 176
15 14, 123, 125, 152
15:7 40
15:8 123, 150
15:13 11
15:17 148
15:19 126
16:13 131
17 14, 145, 151–2
17:1 131, 144
17:2–21 150
17:81 23
17:10–14 151
17:11 117

18:22–32 172
19 14
20 14, 138
20:7 162
20:14–21 114
21 14, 123
21:27 147, 150
21:32 119, 147, 150
21:33 131, 137
22 127, 132, 138, 146
22:5 15
22:19 15
23 15
24 15
24:1–4 80
24:3 40
24:7 40
25 15
25:19–28 16
25:29–34 16
26 15, 123
26:2 123
26:5 96
26:23–25 137
26:28 147, 150
26:34–35 47
27 16, 47
27:1–45 47
27:41–28:9 16
27:46 47
27:46–28:9 70
28:1–9 47
28:4 123

28:10–17 137
28:10–22 146
29–30 16, 114
31 16
31:1–2 16
31:30 134
31:34 147
31:44 150
32 16, 113
33 16
33:18–20 126, 146
34 16, 114, 116, 126
34:30 127
35 16, 113
35:1–5 126, 127
35:1–7 138
35:6–15 146
35:7 131
35:11 144
35:14 146
35:15 123
35:23–26 114
36 16
37 17
37–50 16, 18, 107
38 17
39 17
40–41 17
41–43 76
42–45 17
46 17
46:8–27 32, 115
47 17
48–49 17
49 28, 115
50 17
50:21 48
50:26 32

Exodus
1 18
1–2 154
1–15 12
1:1–5 32
1:1–6 32
1:1–15:21 18
1:6 32
1:6–7 32

1:7 17
2 18, 19, 158–9, 164, 172, 176
2:1–2 168
2:14 164
2:16–22 174
2:23–25 19
2:24 150
3 18, 45, 139, 162
3:9–12 162
3:12 19
3:15 176
3:16 176
3:18 19, 139
4 18, 19, 169, 173
4:1–17 162
4:5 176
4:6–8 174
4:14–16 169
4:16 159
4:18–31 19
4:22 176
4:26 117
5 19, 139
5:1 139
5:3 139
6 19, 170
6:2–3 131
6:3 144
6:14–26 170
6:16–25 168
7 173
7–11 19
7–12 173
7:1 159, 169
7:1–7 19
7:16 139
8:15 173
9–14 173
10:9 139
11 19, 1
12 19, 24, 106, 118, 145
12:1–13:16 139
12:4–14 165
12:12 159
12:38 116
12:40–41 11
12:49 175

13–14 20
13:9 97
13:19 48
14 20
14:31 20, 172
15:1–18 20
15:17 20
15:20–21 103
15:22–27 20
15:22–18:27 20
16–18 20
16:4 97
16:28 96
17 25
17:1–7 20
17:8–16 20
18 20, 27, 164
18:16 96–7
18:20 96–7
18:26 164
19 21, 24
19–24 138, 150
19–40 20, 21
19:3–8 21, 25
19:5 150
19:6 96, 117, 139
19:16–19 21
19:20 21
19:20–25 168
20 27, 97, 152, 166–8
20–23 108
20–24 23
20:1 167–8
20:2–17 21
20:4 22, 139
20:5–6 172
20:8–11 117
20:11 167
20:18–21 21
20:22 165
20:22–26 21, 165–6
20:22–23:33 34
20:23 139
20:24–26 23, 27, 106
20:24–23:19 27
21–23 21, 97, 151, 167
21:1 97, 165–6
23 140

23:14–17 140
23:31 123, 125
24:1–8 21
24:3–6 138
24:8 150
24:9–11 21, 108
24:12 21, 97–8
24:12–14 21
24:15 145
25–31 21–2, 138, 160
25:8 22, 145
25:10–40 21
25:16 152
25:21–22 152
26 21
27 21
27:20–21 24
28 21
28:30 94
29 21, 139, 169
29:45–46 22, 145
30–31 21
31:12–17 21, 151
32 22, 139, 170–1
32–34 27, 139, 150–1
32:1–6 22
32:10 171
32:32 170
33 22
33:7–11 30
34 22, 97, 150
34:10 22
34:11–26 22
34:15–16 132
34:18 21
34:27–28 97
34:29–35 172
35 22
35–40 22, 138, 160
39:43 160
40 24, 160
40:33 160
40:34–35 22, 145
40:35 22
40:36–38 24

Leviticus
1 24

15 138
1–7 23, 95, 138
1–16 23, 166
1–Num 10 167
1:1 23, 31, 96, 169
4 139
4:1 169
4:14 169
5 24
6–7 96, 138
6:1 169
6:1–2a 96
6:2 175
6:7 175
6:17–18a 96
6:18 175
6:19 169
7:1 175
7:7 175
7:11 175
7:37–38 95
8 139
8–9 23, 138
8:1 169
8:8 94
9:23–24 23, 138, 145
10:1–5 169
10:10 23, 108
10:10–11 23, 108
10:11 108
10:16–18 109
10:16–20 108, 169
10:19–20 109
11 120, 147
11–15 23, 95
11–16 116
11:1 169
11:46 175
12 23
12:7 175
13 96, 115
13:1 169
13:59 175
14:2 175
14:32 175
14:34 169
14:54 175
14:57 175

15 23
15:1 166
15:32 175
16 23, 138
16:1 166
17 23, 138, 144, 147, 166
17–26 34, 166
17–27 23 24, 106
17:1 166
17:7 132
18 23, 41
18:21 132
19 23
19:19 117
19:26 135
19:28 134
19:30 21
19:31 135
20 23
20:2–5 132
21–22 23
22:17–30 138
23 24, 26, 139
23–25 23
23:33–36 40
23:33–43 29
23:39–43 40
23:42 99
24:1–9 24
24:10–23 24
25 24, 117, 128
26 24, 39, 120, 152
26:2 21
26:39 172
26:40 122
26:46 24, 175
27 24, 31
27:34 32
7:34 31

Numbers
1 24, 26, 31
1–4 24, 121
1–10 24, 138
1:1 24, 31, 32, 96
1:3 121
2 24
3 24

4 24

5–10 24

5:1–4 24

5:2 134

5:5–10 24

5:11–31 24

5:29 175

5:30 175

6:1–21 24

6:13 95, 175

6:21 95, 175

6:22–24 24

6:24–26 34

7 24

8:1–4 24

8:5–26 24

9 24

9:1–14 24, 41

10 24

11 163

11–15 26

11–20 24

11–21 12

11:1–3 24

11:4–35 25

12 25, 30, 103, 121, 163, 170, 174

12:1 102, 174

12:2 1–2

12:6–8 102, 163, 172

12:8 159, 167

12:9–15 102

13–14 25, 27, 171

14 121, 169, 171

14:12 171

14:23 122

15 25

16 121

16–18 25

16:1–17:5 25

16:3 169

16:16 175

16:29 175

17 121

17:6 169

17:6–27 25

17:8–12 169

18 108, 170

18–19 25

18:1–8 170

18:19 152

19 139

19:2 175

19:14 175

20 25 121, 172

20:1–13 27

20:14–21 25

20:22–26 109

20:22–29 25

20–25 20

20:1–13 25

21 27, 116

21–33 175

21:1–3 25

21:4–9 26

21:6–9 176

21:10–35 26

22–24 26

24:10–24 103

24:15–24 40

24:24 40

25 26

25:10–13 152

25:12–13 150

26 26, 115, 122

27–36 26

27:1–11 164

7:11 165

27:12–23 26, 28

27:21 94

28–29 139

28:1–30:1 26

30:2–17 26

31 26, 114

31:21 175

32 26, 27, 107, 109, 128

32–35 26

33 122

33:1–49 26

33:50–56 26

34 26, 116

34:2–12 123

35 26, 28

35:1–8 26

35:9–34 26

36 26

36:13 31, 32

Deuteronomy

1–3 27, 44

1–11 166

1–30 12

1:1 31, 32

1:1–5 166

1:1–30:20 26

1:5 32

1:8 128, 176

1:9–18 164

1:19–46 171

1:37 172

3 123

3:23–29 27

3:26 172

4 27, 147

4–5 27

4:8 100

4:12–13 167

4:13 22, 97, 150

4:19 176

4:21 172

4:23 150

4:25–31 152

5 166–8

5:2–3 150

5:4 167, 168

5:5 168

5:6 168

5:12–15 117

5:31 98

6 27

6:1 98

6:4 139–40

6:4–5 98, 139–40

6:8–9 7

6:9 143

6:10 128, 176

6:21 155

6:25 98

7 27

7:1 126

7:1–6 143

7:9 150

7:11 98

7:12 150

8:18 150
8 27
8:1 98
9–10 27, 171
9:5 128, 176
9:7–10:11 170
9:9–15 150
10:1–5 152
10:3–5 22, 97
11 27
11:8 98
11:20 7
11:22 98
12 23, 27, 98, 107, 127,
 139–44, 147, 165–6
12–26 23, 27, 34, 139, 150,
 165–7
12:1 166
12:5 142
12:13–14 140
12:13–18 139
12:20–26 147
12:29–30 143
13 27
14 120, 147
14:1–21 27
14:21–23 140
14:22–16:17 27
15:1 117
15:5 98
16 41, 140
16:1–7 140
16:18–18:22 27
16:18–20 164
17 158, 161, 162
17:2–13 140
17:3 176
17:8–13 164
17:11 98
17:14 161
17:14–17 98, 161
17:14–20 120, 162
17:15 161
17:16 161
17:18–19 98
17:18–20 161
18:9–13 135
18:15–20 162

18:18 163
19 28
19–25 28
19:9 98
20 28
21:10–14 28
22:12 118
22:13–29 28
23:3 120
23:6–7 28
23:10–15 28
23:20–21 28
24:1–4 28
24:5 28
24:16 29, 172
25:1–3 28
25:11–16 28
26 28
26:1–15 140
26:5–9 44
26:7–8 155
26:14 135
27 107
27–28 27–8
27:1 98
27:4 107
27:4–8 106, 147, 175
27:14–26 175
28:61 98
29 28, 150
29:9–11 117
29:13 176
29:20 98
30 28, 39
30:4–5 40
30:10 98
30:20 128, 176
31 28
31–34 27
31:2 173
31:9 108
31:9–13 40, 108
31:10–13 108
31:16 132, 150
31:20 150
31:26 98
32 28
32–34 44

32:6 176
32:6–7 76
32:8–9 131
32:24 176
32:34 176
33 12, 17, 122
33:2 176
33:8 94
33:10 96, 108
34 12, 28–9, 100, 106, 109,
 154, 172–3
34:1–4 123
34:6 172
34:8 11
34:8–10 172
34:10 29
34:10–12 29–30, 102, 154,
 163, 167, 172
34:11–12 9

Joshua
1 29, 30
1:7 30
1:7–8 30
1:8 30, 98
8:31 28
8:32 28, 162
8:34 98
9:2 98
13–21 128
13–24 109
13:2 123
14:1 109
17:4 109
19:38 176
19:51 109
21:1 109
22:5 97
23 48
23:6 28
23:16 29
24 43, 48, 125, 127
24:26 99
24:30 48, 134

Judges
1:33 176
2:9 134

2:17 132
2:23 176
3:31 176
4–5 176
5:6 176
6 45, 162
8:33 132
10:6 176

1 Samuel
7:3 176
7:4 176
8–12 161
8:5 161
10:24 161
12:6–8 174
12:10 176
12:18 176
14:41 94
16–2 Sam 6 161
17:8 148
19:11–18 134
20:5–6 135
20:19 135
31:10 176

2 Samuel
2:8 133
2:10 133
2:12 133
3:8 133
3:14–15 133
3:35 148
4:5 133
4:8 133
4:12 133
12:17 148
13:5 148
13:6 148
13:10 148
22:6–19 176

1 Kings
2:3 28, 99
6:1 11
8 41, 142, 145
8:9 152
8:27–30 142

8:44–51 142
10:26 161
11:1–3 161
11:4–22 76
11:5 176
11:33 176
12:28 130
17 36
18 131
22:19 176

2 Kings
2:8 99
14:6 28
17:6 85
17:34 175
17:37 175
18:4 130, 176
21:8 28
22–23 42, 99
22:8 98
22:11 98
23 58, 59, 98
23:4 130
23:5 176
23:6 130
23:7 130
23:10 132
23:11 176
23:13 176
23:25 28–9, 98–9
23:34 76
24–25 44
24:10–17 82
24:29 76
25:1–12 82
25:12 51
25:25–26 76

1 Chronicles
1–9 41
1:1–2:2 41
8:33 133
9:39 33

2 Chronicles
3:1 138, 146
5 41

14:3 97
17:9 99
23:18 28
25:4 28
30 41
30:16 28
31:21 97
34:14 28, 99
36:4 76–7
36:23 40

Ezra
1–2 62
1–6 62–3, 68
1:2 40
1:8 70
2 62, 67
2:4 67
2:7 67
2:12 67
3:2 28
3:12 108
4:4 63
4:24 63
6:8–10 63
6:15 63
7 100–1, 104–5
7:6 28, 74
7:12–26 100
7:25–26 74, 100, 104
7:26 101
8 74
8:3 74
8:7 74
8:13 74
8:15–20 84
8:17 84
9:11 41
9:11–14 79
10 79

Nehemiah
1:1 64
1:4 40
2 36
2:4 40
2:8 64, 66–7
2:20 40

3 70
4 36
4:14 70
6 36
7 62, 67
7:2 64
7:12 67
7:17 67
7:19 67
8 29, 40–1, 100–1
8:1 28, 40, 100
8:13 108
8:13–18 100
8:14 28, 99
8:17 40
8:18 40, 99, 100
9 33
9:3 99
10:31–40 101
10:35 101
11:1–2 64
13:1–3 79
13:15 67
13:23–30 79

Esther
8:8 165

Job
3:8 176
5:7 176
7:12 176
9:13 176
15:7–8 131
18:11–14 176
26:5 134
26:8 176
26:11–13 176
26:12 176
28:22 176
31:26–28 176
36:26 176
38:8 176
38:10 176
38:25–27 176
38:34–38 176
40:25 176
41:1 176

Psalms
1 95
1:1–2 30
2 157, 176
16:3 134
16:3–4 135
16:6 135
18:1 158
18:6–19 176
29:1–2 176
45:7–8 157
49:14 176
50:1–33 176
68:7–10 176
74:13 176
74:14 176
76:2 126
77:19 176
77:21 155
78:70 157
80 155
81 33
82:1 176
83 33
86:9–19 176
88:11 134
89 33
89:4 158
89:5–8 176
89:9 176
89:10 176
89:11 176
90:1 155
90:10 176
91:6 176
95 33
97:1–6 176
98:1–2 176
99:6–7 155
102:24 176
102:28 176
104 176
104:1–4 176
104:6–9 176
104:26 176
105 33
105:6 33
105:25 155

105:42 33
106 33
106:16 155
106:23 155
106:32–33 155
110 126
114 33
135 33
136 33, 155

Proverbs
2:18 134
3:1–2 95
6:23 95, 175
7:2 95
8:29 176
9:18 134
13:14 95
21:16 134

Isaiah
1:10 94
2:1 94
4 147
4:32–40 147
5:13 134
6 130
6:1–8 176
8:16 94–5
8:19 134
8:19–20 135
14:9 134
14:13 176
19:3 134
26:14 134
26:19 134
27:1 176
28:15 176
29:4 134
30:19 176
30:33 132
31:4–5 131–2
32–40 147
34:11–15 133
40:10 176
40:28 176
42:13 176
44:28 62

51:9 176
52:11 62
55:3 152
57:6–7 135
57:9 132
57:15 176
63 9
63:1–9 53
63:11 155
63:11–14 33
63:16 176
64:7 176
65–66 103
65:4 135
66:5 103

Jeremiah
1 45, 162
1:4–9 163
2:20–25 132
3:3 176
3:4 176
3:19 176
5:22 176
5:24 176
6:19 94
7:31 132
8:2 176
9:21 176
10:11–16 176
14:4 176
14:22 176
15:1 155
18:18 93, 108
18:21 176
19:5 132
23:18 176
23:22 176
25:11–12 63
26:4–5 94
29:1–2 82
29:10 63
29:15 82
29:17–18 176
29:20 82
29:28 82
31:9 176
32:35 132

34:18 148
39:9 82
39:10 51
40:1–4 82
40:7 82
41:4 59
41:4–8 59
41:17 77
41:17–18 76
42:14–17 76–7
43:1–7 76–7
44:1 76–7
44:11–14 76
48:13 80
51:16 176
52 82

Lamentations
4:10 148

Ezekiel
1 130, 176
1:1–3 82
2 162
6:9 132
7:26 94, 108
2 45
8:11 108
8:16 176
18 151, 172
10:15 82
20:1–31 33
20:25–26 132
20:37 148
22:26 94, 108
25:12–14 53
35:5 53
35:10 53
35:12 53
39:11 134
39:14 134
39:15 134
40–48 103
44:23 94
44:23–24 94, 108

Daniel
3:25 176

6:26 176
7:9–14 176
7:22 176
9:11 28
9:13 28

Hosea
1:1 94
2 176
4:6 108
11:1 176
12 155
12:4–7 155
12:12–13 155
12:13 155
13:14 176

Joel
3:18 176
4 103
4:18 176

Amos
1:1 94
2:10 155
4:7 176
5:5 127
5:8 176
8:14 127
9:6 176

Micah
6:4–5 33, 155

Habakkuk
3:5 176

Zephaniah
3:4 94, 108
3:6 176
3:8 176
3:15 176

Haggai
1–Zech 8 63
1:1 63, 70
2:1 63
2:10 63

2:10–14 94–5
2:11 94, 108
2:13 134
2:14 94
2:18 63

Zechariah
1:1 63
1:7 63
3 176
7:1 63
7:12 94
10:1 176
14 103
14:1–9 132

Malachi
1:4 53
1:6 176
2:4–9 110
2:7 94, 108
2:8 110
2:10 176
3 103
3:10 176
3:22 28, 155

*Other Ancient
Sources*

Baruch
4:1 110

Behistun
Inscription 61, 79

Ben Sirah
4:16 37
24:23 37
24:23–24 110
44–49 37
44:16 37
45:17 109
49:14 37
49:15 107
49:16 37

Diodorus Siculus,
Bibliotheca Historica
15.41.2 72
19.98.1 54
40.3 38–9

Elephantine
papyri and ostraca
AP7 79
AP14 79
AP17 79
AP21 79
AP30 71, 78, 107
AP31 77
AP32 78
AP37 79
AP38 79
AP39 79
AP40 79
AP 44 79
Ostracon 70 79
Ostracon 271 79

1 Esdras
8:45–46 84

Idumean ostraca 55

Josephus, *Against Apion*
I.3–105 38
I.187–89 70
I.228–52 38

Josephus, *Antiquities
of the Jews*
11.165 64
11.317–19 107
12.8.1 54
12.8.6 54
13.9.1 54
14.4.4 54

Letter of Aristeas 35

1 Maccabees
1:57 36

3:4 36
5:65 54
5:66 54
13:20 54

2 Maccabees
1:8 64
2:13 73
12:35 54

Nepos, *Life of Iphicrates*
2.4 72

Philo of Byblos,
Phoenician History
II.16 80

Qumran
4Q1 35
4Q11 35
4Q17 35
4Q23 35
4Q252 35
4Q364–67 106
4QMMT 35
11QT 106, 109, 111

Damascus
Document 110

Rule of the
Community 110

Temple
Scroll 35

Talmud, *Baba Bathra*
12b 163
14b 42

Ugaritic Texts
KTU I.4 161
KTU IV 23–24 161

Zenon
papyri 55

Index of Authors

Achenbach, R. 48, 176
Aharoni, Y. 52, 54, 69, 88
Ahlström, G.W. 59, 88, 175, 176
Albertz, R. 107, 177
Assmann, J. 156–7, 177
Avigad, N. 58, 88

Baltzer, K. 177
Barkay, G. 34, 48
Barrick, W.B. 59, 88
Ben Zvi, E. 31, 48, 89
Bennett, Jr, W.J. 88
Berquist, J. 89
Blakely, J.A. 88
Blenkinsopp, J. 10, 45–6, 58, 74, 89, 91, 101, 177
Blum, E. 45, 46, 48–9
Boardman, J. 77, 89
Bolin, T. 79, 89
Brettler, M. 48, 50
Briant, P. 61, 63–4, 73, 89
Brooke, G. 111, 177
Brosius, M. 89
Browne, L.E. 84, 89

Cameron, G.G. 61, 89
Carr, D.M. 46, 49
Carter, C. 52, 54, 66, 89
Crüsemann, F. 103, 177

Davies, P.R. 113, 119, 177
Day, J. 132, 177
Demsky, A. 70, 89
DePury, A. 155, 177
DeQueker, L. 63, 89
Dietrich, M. 131, 177
Dozeman, T.B. 46, 49
Dumbrell, W.J. 54, 89

Dutcher-Walls. P. 161, 177

Edelman, D. 52, 54, 56–7, 62–5, 67, 69–72, 89, 124, 141–2, 156, 177
Edgar, C.C. 55, 90
Eph'al, I. 55, 90

Fantalkin, A. 65, 90
Fargo, V.M. 65, 90
Finkelstein, I. 46, 49
Fleming, D. 160, 177
Foerster, G. 67, 90
Frei, P. 104, 177

Gamberone, J. 84, 90
Gammie, J.G. 126, 178
Geer, R.M. 54, 90
Geus, C.H. J. de 57, 90
Grabbe, L.L. 52, 54, 69, 90
Grätz, S. 100, 105, 178
Grandet, P. 156, 178

Hackett, J. 34, 49
Handy, L.K. 135, 178
Hayes, J. 58, 92
Heard, R.C. 113, 178
Heider, G.C. 178
Herzfeld 59, E. 61, 90
Hoglund, K. 90
Holladay, C.A. 37, 49
Huber Vulliet, F. 73, 91
Hulster, I. de 72, 90
Hurowitz, V.A. 160, 178

Kataje, L. 149, 153, 178
Kelso, J.L. 69, 90
Kletter, R. 130, 178
Kloner, A. 56, 90

Knauf, E.A. 156, 178
Knieram, R.P. 154, 178
Knoppers, G.N. 41, 46, 49, 105, 149, 178
Kraabel, A.T. 87, 90
Kraeling, E.G.H. 81, 91
Kuenen, A. 1, 42
Kutsch, E. 148, 178

Lange, A. 101, 178
Lemaire, A. 54–5, 91, 160, 178
Lemche, N.P. 178
Levin, C. 49
Levin, Y. 91
Levinson, B.M. 46, 49, 105, 178
Lewis, B. 158–9, 179
Lipschits, O. 52, 54, 56, 91
Liverani, M. 149, 179
Loewenstamm, S. 172, 179
Loretz, O. 128, 131, 177, 179

McCarthy, D.J. 34, 49
Magen, Y. 107, 179
Mathys, H.-P. 31, 49
Meshorer, Y. 72, 91
Meyers, E.M. 70, 91
Moor, J.C. de 156, 179
Mullen, Jr, E.T. 179

Naveh, J. 55
Nicholson, E. 10, 42, 49
Nihan, C. 49, 107, 166, 169, 172, 179
Nordh, K. 73, 91
Noth, M. 2, 10 42–5, 49, 99, 102, 179

Oded, B. 91
Oehming, M. 91
Otto, E. 48–9, 157, 179

Parpola, S. 149, 179
Pearce, L. 68, 82, 85, 91
Pola, T. 49
Polak, F. 59, 89, 91
Porten, B. 55, 77, 80, 91

Rad, G. von 44, 49
Rainey, A. 52, 91
Rendtorff, R. 45–6, 50
Richter, S. 142, 179
Römer, T. 48, 50, 128, 141, 160, 179

Sallaberger, W. 73, 91
Sanmartín, J. 131, 177
Sapin, J. 57, 91
Schaper, J. 84, 91
Schmid, H.H. 44–5, 50
Schmid, K. 46, 49, 50
Silberman, N.A. 46, 49
Simian-Yofre, H. 148, 180
Ska, J.-L. 105, 180
Smith, M.S. 180
Sparks, K.L. 180
Stavrakopoulou, F. 132, 180
Steins, S. 101, 180
Stern, E. 37, 39, 50, 52–5, 58, 61, 70, 91–2, 107, 179
Stern, I. 55–6, 90, 92
Stolper, M. 59, 61, 70, 92

Tal, O. 65, 90
Tov, E. 112, 180
Tuell, S. 6, 10
Tufnell, O. 65, 92

Uehlinger, C. 180

Vanderhooft, D. 53, 92
VanderKam, J. 35, 50
Van Seters, J. 32, 44–5, 50, 180
Verbrugge, G.P. 174, 180

Wagenaar, J.A. 50
Wallinga, H.T. 72, 92
Watanabe, K. 149, 179
Watts, J.W. 74, 92, 104, 180
Weinfeld, M. 148, 180
Wellhausen, J. 1, 42–4, 50
White Crawford, S. 106, 111, 180
Whiting, R. 149, 153, 178
Whybray, R.N. 45, 50
Wickersham, J.M. 174, 180
Wright, J.W. 52, 54, 92

Yardeni, A. 34, 50, 55
Yellin, J. 58, 92

Zadok, R. 82, 85, 87, 92
Zenger, E. 50
Zevit, Z. 129, 141, 180
Zorn, J.R. 58, 92